HAVE FUN, GET PAID

HOW TO MAKE A LIVING WITH YOUR CREATIVITY

Christopher Duncan

Apress®

Have Fun, Get Paid: How to Make a Living with Your Creativity

Copyright © 2013 by Christopher Duncan

This work is subject to copyright. All rights are reserved by the Publisher, whether the whole or part of the material is concerned, specifically the rights of translation, reprinting, reuse of illustrations, recitation, broadcasting, reproduction on microfilms or in any other physical way, and transmission or information storage and retrieval, electronic adaptation, computer software, or by similar or dissimilar methodology now known or hereafter developed. Exempted from this legal reservation are brief excerpts in connection with reviews or scholarly analysis or material supplied specifically for the purpose of being entered and executed on a computer system, for exclusive use by the purchaser of the work. Duplication of this publication or parts thereof is permitted only under the provisions of the Copyright Law of the Publisher's location, in its current version, and permission for use must always be obtained from Springer. Permissions for use may be obtained through RightsLink at the Copyright Clearance Center. Violations are liable to prosecution under the respective Copyright Law.

ISBN-13 (pbk): 978-1-4302-6100-1

ISBN-13 (electronic): 978-1-4302-6101-8

Trademarked names, logos, and images may appear in this book. Rather than use a trademark symbol with every occurrence of a trademarked name, logo, or image we use the names, logos, and images only in an editorial fashion and to the benefit of the trademark owner, with no intention of infringement of the trademark.

The use in this publication of trade names, trademarks, service marks, and similar terms, even if they are not identified as such, is not to be taken as an expression of opinion as to whether or not they are subject to proprietary rights.

While the advice and information in this book are believed to be true and accurate at the date of publication, neither the authors nor the editors nor the publisher can accept any legal responsibility for any errors or omissions that may be made. The publisher makes no warranty, express or implied, with respect to the material contained herein.

President and Publisher: Paul Manning
Lead Editor: Jeff Olson
Editorial Board: Steve Anglin, Mark Beckner, Ewan Buckingham, Gary Cornell,
    Louise Corrigan, James DeWolf, Jonathan Gennick, Jonathan Hassell,
    Robert Hutchinson, Michelle Lowman, James Markham, Matthew Moodie,
    Jeff Olson, Jeffrey Pepper, Douglas Pundick, Ben Renow-Clarke,
    Dominic Shakeshaft, Gwenan Spearing, Steve Weiss, Tom Welsh
Coordinating Editor: Rita Fernando
Copy Editor: Jana Weinstein
Compositor: SPi Global
Indexer: SPi Global
Cover Designer: Anna Ishchenko

Distributed to the book trade worldwide by Springer Science+Business Media New York, 233 Spring Street, 6th Floor, New York, NY 10013. Phone 1-800-SPRINGER, fax (201) 348-4505, e-mail orders-ny@springer-sbm.com, or visit www.springeronline.com. Apress Media, LLC is a California LLC and the sole member (owner) is Springer Science + Business Media Finance Inc (SSBM Finance Inc). SSBM Finance Inc is a Delaware corporation.

For information on translations, please e-mail rights@apress.com, or visit www.apress.com.

Apress and friends of ED books may be purchased in bulk for academic, corporate, or promotional use. eBook versions and licenses are also available for most titles. For more information, reference our Special Bulk Sales–eBook Licensing web page at www.apress.com/bulk-sales.

Any source code or other supplementary materials referenced by the author in this text is available to readers at www.apress.com. For detailed information about how to locate your book's source code, go to www.apress.com/source-code/.

Apress Business: The Unbiased Source of Business Information

Apress business books provide essential information and practical advice, each written for practitioners by recognized experts. Busy managers and professionals in all areas of the business world—and at all levels of technical sophistication—look to our books for the actionable ideas and tools they need to solve problems, update and enhance their professional skills, make their work lives easier, and capitalize on opportunity.

Whatever the topic on the business spectrum—entrepreneurship, finance, sales, marketing, management, regulation, information technology, among others—Apress has been praised for providing the objective information and unbiased advice you need to excel in your daily work life. Our authors have no axes to grind; they understand they have one job only—to deliver up-to-date, accurate information simply, concisely, and with deep insight that addresses the real needs of our readers.

It is increasingly hard to find information—whether in the news media, on the Internet, and now all too often in books—that is even-handed and has your best interests at heart. We therefore hope that you enjoy this book, which has been carefully crafted to meet our standards of quality and unbiased coverage.

We are always interested in your feedback or ideas for new titles. Perhaps you'd even like to write a book yourself. Whatever the case, reach out to us at editorial@apress.com and an editor will respond swiftly. Incidentally, at the back of this book, you will find a list of useful related titles. Please visit us at www.apress.com to sign up for newsletters and discounts on future purchases.

The Apress Business Team

For my niece, Katy Stites, a creative creature in her own right. I learned these things the hard way. I hope this makes your path smoother.

Contents

About the Author... ix
Acknowledgments xi
Introduction xiii

Chapter 1:   The Creative Mindset ···························1
Chapter 2:   This Is Business ·······························21
Chapter 3:   Becoming Self-Sufficient ·······················41
Chapter 4:   What Do You Want?·····························65
Chapter 5:   Think Like a Start-Up ··························83
Chapter 6:   Image Building ·······························99
Chapter 7:   Spreading the Word···························119
Chapter 8:   Going the Distance ···························135
Chapter 9:   The Power Behind the Throne ·················149
Chapter 10: Paying the Bills·······························163
Chapter 11: Taking Care of Business ························177
Chapter 12: Your Personal Style ····························189

Index 205

About the Author

Christopher Duncan is a creative creature whose work includes writing, speaking, consulting, music, video, and the occasional encounter with technology.

In previous lifetimes, he made a living playing guitar in smoky bars of dubious integrity and also paid the bills as a software developer. A reformed serial entrepreneur, he went on to run a sales and marketing company and bears the battle scars of several dot-com adventures.

He can be reached at ChristopherDuncan.com.

Acknowledgments

Everyone cringes at the awards ceremony when someone walks up to the podium holding a scroll that would have been the envy of ancient Egyptian scribes. Surely there are few things as tedious as listening to an endless stream of names, no matter how heartfelt the gesture. Even so, rarely does a creative project see the light of day without the help and support of others. To leave the stage without at least tipping your hat would be impolite at best.

In this day and age, when it's easy to self-publish and the Internet allows you to speak directly to your audience, there's an ongoing debate about the value of publishers. By the time you've turned the last page, you'll understand the importance that I place on people and relationships. Nowhere is there a better example of this value than in the process of writing a book. It's easy to sit at the computer and write. I'm perfectly comfortable with that. Delivering a quality product is another thing entirely. For that, I need a little help from my friends.

My editor, confidant, and at this point a good friend is Jeff Olson. His were the first set of eyes that saw a new chapter. His perspective and notes helped me see things I'd missed and allowed me to look at the familiar in new ways. The fact that he's as much of a wise guy as I am made the entire process a lot of fun. That's important when you're creating.

Jana Weinstein had an even harder job. As my copy editor, she had the unenviable job of keeping me from looking stupid in public. Don't get me wrong, I was awake for at least half of my high school grammar classes, but without her help you would doubtless suffer from my dubious grasp of the English language.

Behind the scenes, someone has to keep the train on the tracks or it doesn't matter how many talented people I have on my team. Fortunately, my coordinating editor Rita Fernando managed to keep this project running quietly and smoothly even though I happen to know she has a workload that would send most of us scampering for cover.

Without everyone's effort, I would have been hard-pressed to deliver something worth reading. The fact that they work for the business division of Apress and have to play border collie to an author who's about as far from formal as you can get makes my appreciation all the greater.

Acknowledgments

While I'm grateful for the patience of all my friends, who seem to think it's quite normal for me to disappear for months at a time on yet another creative venture, some have been at it far longer than most.

Rarely do I delve into an artistic endeavor without countless hours of cappuccino and conversation with my old friend Deirdre Smathers. Deirdre has endured endless stories of my various escapades and occasionally even succeeded in talking sense into me. More often than not, though, she does what good friends always do, keeping my spirits up and my sanity within bounds throughout all the twists and turns of the creative life.

While I mentioned my niece Katy in the dedication, her mom has the longest history of all when it comes to my somewhat surreal existence. That's because she's my sister, Dana Stites. Before I learned how to have fun and get paid, I was the perpetually broke musician while she, my younger sibling, was the designated adult. As is often the case, my artistic lifestyle hasn't always been looked upon favorably by family and acquaintances. However, from my earliest days of playing guitar to the gypsy life I've lead, no one has ever given me the complete, unconditional, and unfailing support that I get from Dana. Thanks, sis. Next time I'm in town, the tequila's on me.

Perhaps this is a scroll not even worthy of a midsized pyramid, but when the last word is typed, these are the folks who immediately come to mind. No matter what kind of creative creature you may be, you'll never get far without people who are supportive of the work you do. I've been fortunate to have a great many in my life.

Introduction

I've been a creative creature my entire life. It's not something I chose. It's just the way I'm wired, factory defects notwithstanding. I suspect it's the same for you. We don't create because we woke up one morning and thought it would be an interesting way to spend the day. We bring our art to life because we're compelled to do so. I could no more make my creative urges disappear than I could stop my heart from beating.

Self-expression can be great fun, and it gets even better when there's an enthusiastic audience. What it's not so great at is paying the bills. Everyone's familiar with the term *starving artist*, and for good reason. The world is full of incredibly talented people who work at a job they hate because they can't make enough money with their art.

It's a common tale. If you've ever found yourself in that situation, you also know that it's a painful experience. What you may not realize is that most of that pain is self-inflicted. You're not nearly as far from your dreams as you think.

I can't make you rich and famous. Anyone who tells you he can is more interested in lining his own pockets than yours. Besides, I'm not scandalously wealthy myself. I don't travel in my own Learjet and when I come home, it's not to a huge mansion. If I promised that I could show you the path to fame, fortune, and your own fleet of private jets, I'd bloody well better have all that stuff myself. Otherwise, it's nothing but hot air.

On the other hand, most of the creative people I've known in my life don't require millions of dollars to be happy. What they really want is to make a living with their artistic talents. I doubt you'd be opposed to getting rich. However, if you can make ends meet doing what you love and have a little left over for fun and toys, life's pretty good.

Don't get me wrong; I haven't given up on private planes and the occasional Ferrari. By the standards I just outlined, though, I consider my career thus far to be a success. The spoils are modest, but I'm happy and having a great time.

Instead of a mansion, I have a nice little custom-built house in the country, north of Atlanta. The lower level has a high-tech recording studio that I can walk into day or night should the muse strike. I've never driven a Ferrari, but my little red Corvette is perfectly capable of getting me into trouble whenever I like. When the bills are paid each month, there's enough left over to keep me entertained. Life is good.

The most important reason it's good is that every dollar I make comes from one of my creative pursuits. I'm a musician, a writer, a speaker, a software developer, a director, and probably a few other things that don't immediately come to mind. At any given moment, some of these things are helping me pay the bills and live life on my own terms. It's been a long, long time since I worked in factories in order to pay the rent.

This book isn't intended to be a master class. It's a beginning, filled with all the practical, down-to-earth things you need to know in order to build a successful, long-term career with your creativity. Some of what you'll find throughout these pages will be of the nuts-and-bolts variety. However, more than anything else, I want to teach you how to think and act like a professional. That's the heart and soul of any successful career. It's also the missing ingredient whose absence creates starving artists.

You're more than just a talented person. You're actually a small business. Like any start-up, in order to achieve your goals you have to understand the rules of the game so that you can play to win. Most creatives shy away from the world of commerce and marketing, often handing those tasks off to anyone who says they'll take care of them. Just as often, the artist gets screwed sooner or later.

It doesn't have to be that way. You're perfectly capable of managing every aspect of your career, and it's not nearly as scary or distasteful as you might think. In fact, like most things, when you get good at it you'll find it's quite a bit of fun. Success always is.

Since we've already established that I don't have mansions and yachts myself, I can't tell you how to acquire them. What I do have is a very satisfying life paying the bills with my creativity, and that's something I can show you how to achieve. You don't need any special skills beyond your artistic talents, and you don't have to spend money in order to make it work. If you're not afraid of a little hard work and have some commonsense, you'll be surprised at how straightforward career building can be.

There's no magic. Success comes from using your head and putting consistent effort into managing the business side of your art. This stuff doesn't just work for me. I learned it by watching and listening to countless others. These were regular, working-class creative creatures who made a decent living doing what they love.

Maybe you'll win the artistic lottery and become rich and famous one day. I truly hope you do. In the meantime, you still need to pay the bills and eat on a regular basis. That's what we're going to explore. If I've done my job right, when we're through you'll be standing on your own two feet and will be ready and able to take it from there. There's always more to learn, but you'll have a firm foundation in the basics, those things that matter most.

You can absolutely achieve success in the arts, but you're going to have to work for it. Part of that work begins here. The principles I cover are common to all the arts, and of course there are a lot of different art forms. I'll mix it up as we go, using a musician in one example, a painter in the next, and then maybe a software developer followed by a dancer. The concepts will be clear and easy to follow, but it's up to you to translate them into your own world. In so doing, you'll often gain additional insights that you wouldn't have encountered had you merely read a sentence without doing your own thinking.

There are two major divisions in the arts. The performing arts include singers, dancers, actors, and other strange creatures of the night. On the other side of the fence are those who create a lasting product, whether it's a painting, software program, sculpture, drawing, photograph, book, or anything else that lives longer than the act of creating it. I've done my best to touch on as many forms of creativity as possible in my examples.

Even so, they're not distributed with mathematical precision, and that really doesn't matter. There is a common thread that runs through all the arts, and equally common are concepts that apply to making a living with your passion. Not only will it be easy for you to see how the chapters apply to your own field; you'll begin to see how your art form connects to all others. If you think that's a great opportunity to make new friends, you're right on the money.

So, get something nice to drink, prop up your feet, and enjoy the ride. It's far easier than you think to make a good living in the creative arts. You already know how to have fun. It's time to get paid.

Christopher Duncan
September 2013

CHAPTER 1

The Creative Mindset

Creativity is a force as old as humanity itself. From the high-tech marvels of modern society to the humble paintings that adorned the walls of bohemian cave dwellers, many of us are driven to dream, visualize, and express ourselves. The method of that expression varies with the artist and frequently within the art itself, but the urge will not be denied. It is primal.

From the time you were a small child, you probably exhibited such creative tendencies, much like previews of coming attractions at your favorite theater. Maybe you walked around the house singing and dancing. Perhaps you told stories or made clay statues. You might have even been moved to draw big red hearts on the living room wall with red crayons when Valentine's Day rolled around. I wouldn't recommend the last one unless you enjoy having close encounters of a parental kind. Don't ask me how I know.

You are not a creative creature because you chose to be. Much like the color of your hair and the shape of your nose, you're stuck with it. You can no more make it go away than you can force your heart to stop beating by clicking your heels together. That's a good thing, too, for the result in either case would be disastrous. For most of us who feel these urges, they are a core part of our being.

You can, of course, change the color of your hair if you like, but sooner or later the real thing will reassert itself with the tenacity of an underfed bulldog. Many creative people, often referred to simply as creatives in the high-dollar advertising world of Madison Avenue, will try to deny this part of their nature. Sometimes they're frustrated with the difficulties of trying to make a living doing what they love. Other times they just want to fit in and have a normal life. However, try as you might to avoid it, sooner or later your true colors will fly.

You can't hide or ignore your artistic flair. Passion will always find a way out. The sooner you give in, the sooner you can figure out how to make a living doing what you love.

To some extent, creative skills can be learned. You can read a book, watch a video, go to school, or just spend time with someone who's further down the road than you. These mechanics are necessary to express yourself well but they are not the art. They are merely the tools you use to bring forth the desired results.

You can teach a chimpanzee to paint, but that doesn't make it a painter any more than flipping switches in a tin can makes one an astronaut. Neil Armstrong's dramatic last-minute piloting of the *Apollo 11* lunar module saved the day and made a successful moon landing possible. Our small furry friend could have wiggled the same joystick but the result would have been less joyful.

Passion and inspiration distinguish the true creative. They are the source from which all creative endeavors flow. Without a doubt, you must also have the technical skills to bring that dream to life or you're just a passionate primate. Nonetheless, this rocket fuel of the soul is what makes software developers spend days working without sight of a bed in pursuit of their vision. It's the reason musicians are willing to sleep on floors as long as they can make it to the next gig. As a creative, you know what it's like to come to the point where you weigh the benefits of spending that last dollar on food or something that will further your art. Food rarely wins.

The life of a drug addict is nothing compared to that of a creative creature. With the possible exception of love, there is no greater addiction or dependency on the planet than the never-ending pull of artistic urges. In fact, the history of people both great and ordinary is replete with examples of love coming in a distant and winded second to the passion of someone's creative pursuits. To say that our artistic compulsion can be disruptive to a normal and healthy personal life is an exercise in understatement.

And yet, we persist. We spend time and money we don't have to enable our addiction. I was going to call it a "hobby," but that simply doesn't do it justice. If you asked the average creative if he'd rather have a long and healthy life or create a brilliant masterpiece, he'd have to think about it. We're not always the most logical of beings.

All Roads Lead to Home

If home is where the heart is, then it's no secret where we live. There are, however, a great many ways to get there. In each generation, there will be a lively discussion surrounding what does and does not qualify as art. For the most part, these conversations serve no purpose beyond entertaining or infuriating a roomful of artistic types. The one thing that doesn't change is the fact that throughout the human race, creativity has been expressed in wondrous variety.

That's not to say that the limit is one form of expression per customer. On the contrary, it's not at all uncommon to find someone who expresses herself in many different ways. An actor may also be a screenwriter. A sculptor might find gratification in painting. Software developers are often musicians. These are, of course, just a few examples.

In my own life, the creative urge that started out as a passion for music has spread to a number of disciplines. In addition to writing songs, I found that I also enjoyed writing stories, columns, and books. Jumping up and down on stage led me to explore, for a very brief period, modern jazz dance. The combination of books and my stage experience led to public speaking. When personal computers became common, I stumbled into software development. In a similar fashion, I began to expand my recording studio to include video production, writing, and directing a comedy Web series. Movies aren't far behind.

In the game of life, I've barely reached the halfway point, so as time goes on I'll probably find even more ways to express myself. This doesn't mean that I'm particularly gifted or special. As my friends would be quick to point out, it more likely indicates that I have the attention span of an overcaffeinated squirrel. Be that as it may, it does serve to illustrate the diversity pursued by a great many of us in the creative arts. It may not make us rich and famous, but it certainly keeps boredom at bay.

All of which begs the question, What is a creative creature? Even if I hadn't experienced such a delightful variety of opportunities in my own life, it's not hard to realize that any definition must be broad and expansive. Since my purpose is to help kindred spirits make a better living pursuing the things they love, it might be worth taking a moment to touch on some of the arts that we'll be visiting in our travels together.

One of the first things that comes to mind when we think of creativity is the performing arts. Live performance in theaters had been with us since long before the days of the ancient Greeks, although the venues may not have been as grand. We tend to think of just the actors on stage as being involved in a performance, but of course there are countless related disciplines required to bring it all together. A stage would be a dreary place indeed without a good set designer, and appropriate wardrobe is recommended for all but the most risqué of productions.

Plays are often performed on the same stages used by dance companies, another art that was doubtless with us even in our caveman days. Of course, what's a good dance without music? Singers and instrumentalists abound throughout the history of the arts. The performance of poetry is another time-honored craft, a heritage to which modern rap owes allegiance.

When you take any or all of these elements and point a camera at it, you have yet another method of expression, from the great cinematic masterpieces of movies to the modest entertainment of cat videos. Of course, if you have a video of a kitten that can perform a rap version of Shakespeare while dancing to a lively tune, you've probably pushed the boundaries of cross-disciplinary expression or, at the very least, good taste.

While implicit in many of the disciplines discussed thus far, writing is also a world unto its own. From theater and poetry to short stories and books, as long as there's a way to embed words in a permanent medium, there will be someone who has something to say. Fortunately, rumors about large quantities of chimpanzees and Shakespeare notwithstanding, there are no documented instances of the feline community encroaching on this territory.

Although the term "starving artist" has been appropriated by pretty much anyone who attempts to make a living with their musings, in some cases that starving creative is, in fact, an artist. Whether it's in the form of drawing, painting, or computer graphics, the visual arts have been one of the most enduring accomplishments of humanity. Perhaps they danced by firelight outside of their ancient caves, but what we remember is the decorations on their walls.

Technology also affords us with variations on the theme. Once limited to a single image, visual artists can now string them together to present animated movies, from the blockbuster CGI creations of today's box-office hits to the delightful hand-drawn adventures of Bugs Bunny and his friends in the 1930s and 40s. Cameras, of course, also started life by producing a single-frame experience, giving rise to the art of photography.

Our high-tech computerized tools give us a number of other ways to express ourselves as well. Software development and Web design, while often funded by boring business types, are nonetheless highly creative endeavors. Along with animation and graphic design, many creatives also work in three dimensions when they use CAD software capable of designing anything from pepper shakers to robots capable of looking for salt on the surface of Mars.

This list does not encompass all of the creative arts by any stretch of the imagination. It does, however, offer a setting in which we can consider the many things we have in common, chief among them a desire to pay the bills by doing what we love.

It's not practical to discuss concepts and then offer specific examples for each and every art form known to man unless you happen to be writing an encyclopedia with an unlimited amount of pages at your disposal. What we'll be doing instead is looking at the challenges we face in our careers and presenting solutions in a manner that will allow us to map them to our own reality.

This is not nearly as difficult as you might think. Regardless of the manner in which you create, you are a part of a larger community of kindred spirits who share a great many things in common.

Common Ground

As we've already considered to a degree, the one thing I think we can all relate to is the desire to express what we feel inside or see in our mind's eye. (I was going to say the voices in our heads, but as that tends to end badly we'll just skip it for the moment.)

To do this, we need an audience. This compulsion we feel to share with others that which we bring into being is not only at the very heart of the creative community; it's our bond with the rest of the human race. Without someone to enjoy what we've done, there's little joy or purpose in the endeavor.

While it's true that the best art is often created for the artist herself, it's of little value if others can't share in the experience. The adrenaline we feel when the crowd delights in our presentation is equal only to the depths of despair that we experience when it goes over like a lead zeppelin. Without people we are nothing.

While you may want to create art for no other reason than to satisfy your soul, it's a lot more fun if you share the experience. It also pays better.

I'm not an art critic by any definition and neither do I consider myself an authority on the matter. I have, however, observed that there are two fundamental approaches to what we would call art. They are distinguished not so much by what is created but rather by the mindset of the person doing the creating.

Emotional art is something that touches a wide range of people, as everyone has feelings. This can be something as simple as a country song about how bad it feels to lose your wife, your pickup truck, and your dog all on the same day. Most of us have experienced heartbreak, so it's easy for an emotional song to resonate with us. We may not own pickup trucks, but the feeling is the same even if what we lost was just a four-door Chevy.

Personal experiences, however, are not the only way an art form can be emotional in nature. A painter may work from a place of deep melancholy and with canvas and oils produce a scene that makes us want to cry just by looking at it. When a creative starts with emotion and pours that into her work with the primary motivation being to express what she feels, it's what I would consider emotional art regardless of the techniques used to convey it.

This is not the only way that people approach the creative arts, of course. There is another school of thought, typically employed by those who are well educated in their craft, that prizes analysis.

While it can be argued that there are no rules in art other than that you should be true to your inner artist, there are without a doubt a great many rules in most of the disciplines. Many of them are subject to lively debate. Even so, they exist because, at least in some cases, they've been demonstrated to have value. For example, there are colors that tend to go well together just as some notes produce better harmony when placed next to each other than others. In many disciplines, these rules can be both deep and complex as, for instance, in the writing of a science fiction novel.

People who are passionate about a particular art form, or perhaps a genre of the art, such as a science fiction novel, may study that specific subject at universities or many other venues. In their education, they may be walked through the history of the art and the different directions it's taken as the result of various movements. The nuts and bolts of technical execution may also be addressed. In a purely intellectual approach to art, it's common to dismiss how it makes the audience feel, focusing instead on how well it was crafted based on the set of rules and precedents at hand.

As you might imagine, these approaches can produce very different sets of opinions about what's good and what's bad. I've seen some heated arguments that I thought would come to blows when a work was discussed by those of the differing philosophies. And yet, in the arts, there is no right or wrong. An intellectual approach to creation is just as valid as an emotional one. You can even mix the two in whatever proportions you like. All that matters is that you create what you're compelled to express.

For most artists, getting the acceptance of their respective audience is a critical matter. An intellectual may care about the pronouncements of highly respected critics. To an emotional performer, the response of the crowd may be the only validation that is needed. Either way, we stand on the widest patch of common ground. We create, and how our creation is received affects us deeply.

However, all of that pales in comparison to our greatest common bond. For those who dream of doing nothing but pursuing their passions and being able to eat on a regular basis, the challenge of actually pulling it off is something we can all relate to.

As we explore the perils and pitfalls of paying the bills in notoriously fickle creative industries, we'll find that while our methods of creation may differ greatly, the roadblocks look very much the same. In an ever more connected world, that's actually a good thing. We can now learn not only from our own domain but also through the experiences of those in related fields. Though it's unlikely that we'll ever unite all creative creatures in a single harmonious community, our goals, dreams, and desires bring us ever closer together to the benefit of all.

We Are Legion

As we've seen, defining creativity is a tricky proposition even on a good day. It gets even more complicated when you factor in all the new opportunities that our high-tech society provides.

Once upon a time, if you wanted an orchestra, you had to hire a roomful of musicians, each playing a different instrument. Today, a composer in the recording studio can fire up software and write an entire symphony, assign the instruments to some very realistic-sounding libraries, and hit play. Poof. Instant orchestra.

The composer of this symphony didn't actually play the French horn, the clarinet, or any of the other parts. So, did she really create the performance of the symphonic recording you're listening to? Some instrumentalists might call it fake or otherwise invalid. However, the music sounds real enough to me, so she gets my vote for being the creator.

It gets fuzzier still when you listen to contemporary music. In the rap and hip-hop genre, it's common for people to take a sample of someone else's recording and use it as an instrument in its own right. Hit the drum here, play the piano there, kick off the selected sample next, and then back to the piano. You can stretch that further and have a song consisting entirely of samples from the work of others. Who did the creating? It's a question that doesn't lend itself to a simple answer.

If you're a dancer, you may think you're immune to this until you see that videos of several of your performances have been spliced together, placed over some music with graphics added, and presented as a creative work of their own. If the video tells a story in its own way, using your dance as an artist might use a paintbrush, who did the creating? You did the dancing but someone else wrote the music and composed the graphics, not to mention coming up with the concept of the video itself.

These are all very simplistic examples of what will, I suspect, become an ever more complex environment for the creative arts. Computers and a global information network have empowered us as never before, not just in terms of reaching an audience but in how we're able to combine sometimes-disparate elements into something new and notable in its own right. While there are certainly moral implications in terms of respecting the intellectual property rights of others, it is also a very exciting time to be a creative creature.

An additional consequence of our environment is the rise of the common man as a creative force. If it can be expressed digitally—and much of our creativity can—the barriers to entry are dropping so fast that it's hard to keep up with it all.

Once upon a time, if you wanted to write a book, produce a movie, or record an album, you had to go through the gatekeepers of that industry. There was little choice in the matter due to the economics of creating the work. Creating an album required a recording studio with very expensive equipment costing hundreds of thousands of dollars or more. Some mixing consoles cost almost a million dollars alone.

Imagine the plight of some guitar player barely making enough to eat by playing bars. Such a studio would typically charge more per hour than he made the entire weekend. It was simply out of reach. Publishing books required a similar infrastructure for printing. Both of these endeavors were trivial in cost compared to making a movie.

Even if you happened to have a printing press in your backyard, there were still barriers. Merchants only dealt with certain distributors, who only dealt with the major publishing companies. It matters little what you could create if no one would ever see it.

Fast forward to five minutes ago and you'll see a very different world for those of us who seek to transform dreams into something more tangible. The cost of physical tools for digital content creation has plummeted while their quality has increased to professional grade. Million-dollar recording consoles are no longer required to make high-quality recordings, and the same is true for video. Additionally, with the advent of eBooks and print on demand (POD) technology, authors no longer need to own a printing press.

On the distribution side of things, Amazon, YouTube, and many other such sites have given us the power to get our product directly to our audience without the need for a middleman. All of this has significant implications for the working-class creative, both good and bad.

Having this affordable and accessible power at our fingertips means that there are more creative people vying for attention than ever before. So much so that it's a greater challenge cutting through the noise and reaching an audience than it is creating the work in the first place. That's a lot of competition for ears, eyeballs, and money.

With this lower barrier also comes a loss of quality control. There are some absolutely brilliant people out there who have, for one reason or another, never landed a traditional contract. Unfortunately, they're lost in a massive sea of very unprofessional, amateur-grade content that is in no way comparable to the work people would pay for.

It's not my intent to belittle those who aren't yet creating at a professional level. For some, it's just a hobby and they don't want to spend a lot of time on perfecting the art. Others may shake the world in a few years and are just at the beginning of their careers for the moment. We all start at the bottom. And of course, there are chimpanzees that bang on the keyboard whether they understand the Bard or not.

None of these considerations matter when you're trying to reach your audience. In the democratized world of the Internet, there is no quality control. Anyone can share whatever they like. A potential fan has to wade through it all, including the good, the bad, and the artistically challenged, in order to find you. Often, they'll never complete that journey.

Modern technology makes creativity easier than ever, but it also generates millions of competitors. You can work with a gatekeeper, find partners, or do the marketing yourself. Have a plan, or be ignored.

Gatekeepers are the institutions that we love to hate. Big media companies are evil, greedy, and heartless. Power to the people! That's all well and good when you're having a spirited discussion with your fellow out-of-work creatives, and sometimes it's even true. However, many people overlook the value that gatekeepers bring to the party. They are quality-control specialists. That doesn't mean everything that gets past them is good. It does, however, increase the odds of that being the case.

I've been on both sides of the street. The book you're reading was produced through a traditional publisher. I've worked with them before and always had a great experience. I also like the people I work with, which is far more important than you may realize. This particular subject was a good fit for them and we had a preexisting relationship, so I went through a gatekeeper.

I've also spent many nights playing guitar in rock and roll bars of dubious reputation. Like many such musicians in the days before the Internet laid waste to the recording industry, I dreamt of getting a record contract and becoming a rich rock star. While I did have the opportunity to sign a record deal when living in New York, it wasn't a particularly good one (we'll touch on the importance of being able to read a contract later on), and thus I declined.

My lack of stardom probably has more to do with the fact that I'm an average musician than the narrow filter employed by gatekeepers. Nonetheless, if I wanted to pay the bills by playing music, it was either lots of gigs in sometimes-dicey establishments or nothing at all. No gold records. No limousines. We'll leave conversations about groupies for another day.

In today's world, this limitation no longer applies. Were I still in the mood to get a record contract, it would be a fool's errand for a different reason. The industry is in meltdown. Why on earth would I run into a burning building? When I had my current house built, I designed a recording studio on the lower level that now handles audio and video. If I wanted to sell recordings, I'd go directly to the people. No more lopsided record contracts. No more fine print.

As you can see, we have a wealth of options available to us today but with them come a new set of challenges. I personally enjoy the fact that it's not an exclusive choice. I can work with a traditional media company in the morning, go directly to the people at lunch, and at dinner work with a different media company. Having options is great.

What most people tend to gloss over is the fact that with power comes responsibility. Yes, I can go directly to the people and in some cases I'll do exactly that. When I do, the responsibility for moving the merchandise is all on me. No one is going to cut through the noise for me, use preexisting relationships to better position my work, or provide me their years of expertise in marketing and promotion.

In my case, I spent a decade teaching sales in a previous lifetime, so I'm comfortable with doing it on my own. Many creatives don't have such a background and that means a learning curve along with the additional effort. You can do it, and it's great to be empowered. Nonetheless, it's always wise to know your environment. You have tremendous opportunity at your feet, but you're standing in a very crowded room.

Creatives Just Wanna Have Fun

Problems of quality and building an audience can be solved. All it takes is effort and education, and you're certainly capable of that. Regardless of what you wish to learn, there are countless tutorials on the Web. Of course, as we just considered, some of it is very high quality, some not so much. Nonetheless, you have all the tools you need to figure this stuff out and make a good living as an artistic individual.

In fact, since I happen to know that you read books on the topic to improve your skills, I can safely tell you that you have several distinct advantages over your less motivated brethren. The first and foremost is that you're actually thinking beyond your art.

The problem with most creative creatures is that all we want to do is play. If you're a graphic artist, you want to spend all day drawing. If you're an actor, you just want to stand in front of the camera. Musicians just want to make music. Okay, there may also be some drinking and chasing of the opposite sex involved, but you get the picture. We just wanna have fun.

Lack of motivation is the single most debilitating affliction that you can have if you truly want to pay the bills with your art and not work a day job. It is also the most prevalent thing we have in common across all artistic disciplines. If you think because I've written a book about this sort of thing that I'm immune, I'll be happy to have a serious conversion on the topic. But you know, right now I think I just want to go work on my next film, and then maybe grab my guitar for a while. Maybe later, okay?

There are moments in the creative process when most of us want to find the tallest building we can leap from. Having a vision and bringing it to life in the way we want is often frustrating. This is especially true if your art form is group oriented and you have to deal with all those pesky humans who tend to have their own way of looking at things and are willing to argue with you about it. Even so, that's the fun stuff. We're following the muse, even if she leads us off a cliff.

The moment you mention business or marketing to the average creative person, you'll be lucky to finish the last syllable before they've exited the building. The dust will settle before your words have the chance to echo off the nearest wall.

This is a problem of two parts. The first is sheer terror. We tend to fear anything that we don't understand. If you went to school for your art, chances are good they didn't teach you a lot of business. If they did, there's an equally good chance you cut that class to party with your friends. The second difficulty is that it's boring. Actually, once you're immersed in the noncreative aspects of your career, you'll find that the business end is anything but dull. However, to most artists, if it's not directly related to the creation of their art, their eyes glaze over. Right before they bolt for the door.

The business side of creativity can actually be a lot of fun once you get the hang of it. The first and most important step is accepting the fact that you and you alone are responsible for promoting your work. No one else will care about it as much as you do.

Being a creative is not just an activity. It's a lifestyle, and that's all the life that most creatives want. There's also an attitude of entitlement that you'll find in most of the business adverse. The general thinking is that we should create. That's our part of the deal. Selling this stuff and bringing in the money? That's someone else's responsibility. Any time you point out that the real world doesn't work that way, you'll get a long lecture on how unfair it is. Of course, the last time I checked, the real world wasn't fair.

Among the many problems with this attitude is the fact that it renders the creative completely powerless. Any time you hand over responsibilities to someone else, you also give up control. The end result is not only that you don't have to do any of that scary business and marketing work, you also don't make any money.

It's easy to spot the artistic person at the local bar. He's the one who will bend your ear for hours on end about how unfair his particular creative industry is and how he's tired of always being broke. Of course, he'll also ask you to pay for the drinks.

It's sheer foolishness to tilt at windmills, insisting that the world be other than it is. If you have the power to change the world, that's another matter. Creative people do have the ability to change their world. However, expecting most of them to do so will result in nothing but broken lances and smug windmills.

When I was talking to my editor about the market for this book, I told him it would apply to a wide range of creative arts. I immediately followed that with a caution that this was not nearly as big a market as one might think. I would be surprised if even 10 percent of creatives were willing to pull themselves up by the bootstraps, educate themselves, and do the work required to take control of their careers. Nonetheless, it's that small sliver of motivated people whom I greatly admire, and it is therefore to people like you that I dedicate my efforts.

What does all of this mean to you? In the parlance of military strategy, it represents a massive tactical advantage. No matter what art form you work in, you're going to have competition. As we've discovered, with the lower barrier to entry today, that competition is greater than ever. And yet, most of your competition will simply sit there doing nothing and waiting for the world to be delivered to them on a silver platter. This reduces the number of people with whom you have to compete to a fairly small and manageable amount.

Yes, I really just want to immerse myself in creative endeavors and enjoy myself. However, what I want more than that is to be successful in reaching an audience. Without readers for my books, listeners for my music, and viewers for my films, I'm nothing but a guy with some gear in his house. So, I embraced the business side of things. As a result, I discovered that I actually enjoyed a lot of it. More importantly, I've been making a living doing the creative things I love for many, many years. When I was first getting started, I worked in factories, dug ditches, and even cleaned toilets. Let me assure you, doing creative work is much more fun, even if also involves the business side of things.

Artistic Idealism

Another problem that many people struggle with is their sense of artistic idealism. It's great to be passionate about your art and admirable to want to hold yourself to the highest standards. Personally, I also think it's great to eat on a regular basis, but perhaps I'm just shallow. Nonetheless, to many in our line of work, art should be completely pure and untainted by such corrupting influences as money.

You'll hear a lot of talk about selling out in these conversations, usually defined as getting paid for your work. Those who are particularly snobby about their craft may hold the opinion that anything commercial must by definition appeal to the masses and thus be unworthy of consideration as true art.

Personally, I don't subscribe to the belief that art is only pure if no one is willing to pay for it. I think that appealing to the masses is not only acceptable but also provides a much needed service to society.

Appealing to the masses is not only acceptable but also serves society. You can remain true to your art no matter how large your audience. Having a lot of fans also makes it easier to eat on a regular basis.

Maybe I only see it that way because I've never traveled in the lofty circles of the elite. I'm one of the common people. I know what it's like to sweat the bills, to work jobs I hate, to lose in love, and to experience all the dilemmas we can encounter in life. If your creativity can lift my spirits, give me hope, or just let me escape my troubles for a few hours, I think they should erect a statue in your honor. At the very least, they should pay you.

Another thing that makes people uncomfortable when merging creativity and commerce is the fact that they're the product that's being marketed. I've experienced this one myself and, even though I'm a battle-scarred veteran of many sales and marketing adventures, I had a really tough time with it.

My Web site naturally has information on the various projects I'm involved in as well as any products or services that I might offer at the moment. I've been running my current company for twelve years. It's a small business by conscious intent—just me and my work—due to my desire to keep it simple. I do speaking gigs, commercial copywriting, consulting and coaching, a little audio/video work, promote my books, and offer other things of that nature.

I'm perfectly comfortable with all of that. I give my best effort to my clients, am honest about what I do and don't cover, and turn away work when I don't feel qualified in a given area. That's not the problem. The difficulty arises when it's time to do the marketing.

All of the offerings I just listed have one thing in common. They're all about me. I write books. I speak at conferences. I do copywriting. Me, me, me. Writing in the first person, as I prefer to do, can be very relaxed and personable. For books and articles, this point of view is fine. Once you start hawking your wares, it's just plain weird. As I wrote promotional materials, I felt like a huge, obnoxious egomaniac who was telling the world how great he was. That doesn't make me feel special. It makes me want to turn off the computer, go take a hot shower, and wash all the marketing sleaze off of me.

Meanwhile, back in the real world, products and services don't get sold unless you promote them. You don't have to be a snake oil salesman and it actually works against you in the long run if you're dishonest, but you have to sell them. It's your job to tell people how your offerings solve their problems and why they should, therefore, give you their money. It's the nature of commerce and it hasn't changed in thousands of years, no matter how many hot showers I want to take.

A hard-nosed businessperson might laugh at such discomfort, but creative people tend to be sensitive about these things. I had a dilemma. I needed to effectively promote my work, but I had to do it in a way that didn't make me feel embarrassed. In truth, I'm not sure there really is a solution that completely answers both concerns. Sometimes, you just have to suck it up and do what needs to be done. I did, however, find a compromise that allowed me to accomplish my objectives without therapy. I wrote in the third person, and I used my full name.

Everyone knows me as Chris. Nobody ever calls me Christopher unless I've been bad. In fact, I once asked my mother why she bothered giving me this long name since no one used it. She just smiled, patted me on the head as mothers tend to do and said, "In case you ever need to be important, dear."

Needless to say, I don't really relate to Christopher. As it turned out, that was perfect. On my Web site and anywhere else I needed to talk up my work, I spoke as the unseen announcer would on a radio commercial.

"Christopher speaks on a variety of career and leadership topics, always ensuring that your audience has a good time in the process." Okay, still pretty weird but I can live with it and not completely kill the payments for my hot water heater. I don't know who this Christopher guy is but he seems to know what he's talking about, and the services he's selling are straightforward enough. Yeah, I guess I can write about this guy.

Does that seem silly to you? Perhaps it is, but it worked for me and got me past a debilitating problem regarding my marketing. This may or may not be a worthwhile approach for you but that's not really the point. What's important is the realization that as idealistic creatures, we're going to run into problems like this that more traditional businesses would never encounter.

Recently, I revamped my Web site and finally shifted it back to first person. It's more down to earth and personable, and it's also just the way I write. I was only able to do so because I've been around long enough that I no longer twitch about such things. Besides, I was probably the only one who thought it was weird in the first place. We're always our own worst critic.

Nonetheless, whether it's the notion that art should be pure, the twitch factor that comes from having to sell yourself like a can of green beans, or any number of other such things, you have to face it head on. Understand yourself for who you really are, take another moment to see the world as it truly is, and find the path that allows you to live in the real world, not the fantasy creation of the idealistic mind. You'll eat much better.

Patron Saints

The creative world was not always this commercial. In times past, the role of the artistic class served different functions and often different audiences. While there was probably always someone who would grab an instrument and sing a song at the local tavern, music was often just a method of passing along information. Traveling minstrels went from town to town playing ballads that were written about the events of the times. Songs were also used as a way of teaching and retaining the history of a people.

Hundreds or thousands of years ago, we didn't have anywhere near the amount of luxury time that modern society offers. Whether you were a farmer or tradesman, you put in long, hard days, working until the task was done. The idea of a nine-to-five job with its after hours and weekend leisure would have been as alien a concept as an electric guitar. Both would probably get you burned at the stake.

In such an environment, people had little time for lofty and frivolous pursuits like dance, poetry, or the fine arts in general. There would be the occasional festival or two, but making weekend plans to catch dinner and a show simply wasn't a reality of the day. Well, for the working class, anyway. The ruling elite, on the other hand, lived by an entirely different set of considerations.

If you're smart about it, you can have your cake and eat it too: You can create art for the masses and enjoy the benefits of commissioned works for your patron. The two aren't mutually exclusive.

To begin with, rulers tended to have a lot more money than the common man. It's why they got into the business of being a ruler in the first place. Among the many things that money could buy, leisure time and the diversions to fill it were high on the list. This led to the practice of offering patronage to the notable creatives of the day. The arrangement was simple and straightforward. The artist did his thing; the rich patron paid the bills. It was a great gig and everyone was happy with the benefits.

Obviously, only a small amount of artists were able to be supported in such a manner. Fortunately for the creative communities of the day, there were a lot less of them to go around, so the relative percentage of those who found patronage was much higher than it would be in today's flooded environment.

Of course, the other thing that's different today is that patronage now appears in other forms. Particularly in America, there aren't a lot of kings to go around. My history teacher would be quick to point out that we planned it that way, but that's of little consolation to the out-of-work artists with no palace to lounge in. This doesn't mean that patrons no longer exist. You just have to know where to look for them and understand how the rules have changed.

Nowhere is patronage more alive or better disguised than in the real-life world of *Mad Men*, slang for the high-earning Madison Avenue advertising executives. To those who have never worked in advertising, it's easy to assume that a display ad or TV commercial exists to sell a product. In theory it does, but it's often not carried out in the way you would expect.

If I wanted to sell you a Whack-o-Matic for $19.95 so that you could rid yourself of all those pesky moles in the backyard, I might give you a hard-sell list of benefits, add a little urgency so that you felt pressure to buy right now, and then ask for the purchase. In fact, if you've ever watched late-night TV, a great many commercials do exactly that. Were you to spend a lot of time throughout the day paying attention to other advertisements, however, you might be surprised to find that this is the minority of cases.

There is another concept in advertising that's known as brand awareness. The thinking is that if you're continually exposed to a product's logo and packaging, then the next time you're out shopping, you're going to gravitate toward that brand out of instinctive familiarity.

These guys spend a lot of money on this research, and they wouldn't take this approach were there not proven results. The data, however, tends to be statistical in nature. This is in distinct contrast to the direct cause-and-effect relationship you can see in a late-night commercial and the number of calls the center gets.

A company might know that they ran an ad one thousand times in August and that sales increased by 11 percent. The problem is, businesses rarely do just one thing. There will be a number of other ways that the product has gotten mentioned as well. It's more difficult to tie cause to effect. The old joke in the ad business is, "Half of my advertising doesn't work. I just don't know which half."

If you're wondering how we went from tales of kings and patrons to the world of slick automobile ads and animated product mascots, let's connect the dots. Simply put, most of the ads you see use way more creative horsepower than is needed to sell a product. You'll see clever skits, sexy actors, cutting-edge graphics, and more special effects than a Hollywood blockbuster movie. What does all this have to do with moving the merchandise? I'll let you in on a little industry secret: nothing at all.

Advertising agencies put out the most polished, creative, and sensational ads that they can convince their clients to pay for. The most notable ads win advertising-industry awards. And, of course, award-winning firms can charge higher rates. The glitzy ads the agency produces for this purpose are sold to the client under the banner of brand awareness. After all, it would be a much more difficult sale to tell you that they want to do some really cool stuff so that they can win an award and charge you more money.

So, the agency will create a really cool cutting-edge commercial. Viewers will be impressed with how creative and entertaining it is and might even talk about it in its own right. The Super Bowl commercials are the reason for parties as often as the game itself. And even if all people are talking about is the animated sheep bouncing up and down on a CGI pogo stick, they'll see your brand on the sheep's posterior; thus increasing your brand awareness. Or so the sales pitch goes.

Rather than draw up a simple and straightforward campaign to sell your company's widgets, these companies put together a project that is a smaller-scale version of a Hollywood big-budget movie. In fact, they often use the same graphics and animation vendors as their motion picture counterparts do.

Now, think like a graphic artist, if you don't happen to be one yourself. You want to play with all the latest tools, do cool new things, and get paid for it. Problem is, there aren't always practical applications for that sort of thing. It's difficult finding someone to pay you to just play around. Where do you go? Madison Avenue or its equivalent, wherever you can find it. In many ways, these are the modern-day patrons of the arts. Not what you'd expect, is it?

Of course, this isn't the only place where patronage can be found. In many ways, the large media companies also serve in this capacity. Returning to our musician friends, let's say you want to make a few records. Studio time is expensive. You can easily spend from $500,000 to $1,000,000 producing a record. Then, there's the obligatory music video, which can be just as large and expense. Of course, you need to make a living while recording your timeless classic, so the record company gives you an advance (the industry term for an interest-free loan).

Add it all up and there's a lot of money being invested in your record. Clearly, you will need to sell a heck of a lot of units just to recoup the expenses. The musician's attitude? That's someone else's problem. The band gets paid and goes on tour. Maybe the record company makes a profit. Maybe they lose a ton of money. Either way, the creative people got what they wanted—a patron to pay them so they could play.

Most of us are familiar with stories of how media companies screw performing artists, and much of that is true. As you can see, there's also another side to the story. If the record sells and there's lots of money coming in, maybe the label and the band will both make out. Maybe the band gets screwed. However, if the record doesn't sell, the band got the patronage and the label got the shaft. The modern-day patron system is complicated and full of risk on both sides. Maybe those kings weren't such a bad lot after all.

Charting a Course

Another type of opportunity that our modern society has enabled can be thought of as a form of micropatronage. Thanks to the power of the Internet and digital technologies, we can now make our case directly by asking our audience for their financial support.

Let's say you've written a delightful play about a boy and his cybernetic dog and want to take it on the road. Instead of dealing with the larger apparatus of promoters and industry infrastructure, you can arrange the venues and dates yourself. To make money, you can promote your show directly to potential fans using the Web, e-mail, and the occasional freelance owl.

It's not the same as getting a big recording contract and a gazillion-dollar advance from a record label with deep pockets. Instead, you have to make lots of little sales in the hopes that they add up to the larger number that you need in order to keep you, your cast, and crew on a high-quality peanut butter and jelly diet. This can be exciting and may also be just what you need to provide creative freedom and financial stability.

In fact, there are many other business models that will allow you to make a living doing what you love. Some involve steady but less glamorous gigs. Others allow you to build a business. There are also ways to generate multiple streams of income from different sources. We live in a time of incredible opportunity for those who wish to live the creative life.

This is a time of incredible opportunity for creative people. Put in the effort to take care of business, and you can make a living doing what you love.

There's only one problem. Creative creatures, by and large, don't want to do anything but play with their toys and be the artist. As we've seen, this doesn't apply to just one artistic discipline. It's a mindset that is common to the entire artistic community, and probably always has been.

Fortunately, the problem is one of attitude and effort, and these are difficulties that can be overcome by those with sufficient motivation. If there were simply no way for us to pay the bills beyond working for the local factory, life would be bleak indeed. Instead, opportunity abounds for the aspiring artist who isn't afraid to stretch beyond her comfort zone and put in a little extra effort.

If you want to make a living doing what you love, success is within your reach. This is only possible, however, if you're willing to embrace a new phase of your career, one in which you take responsibility for your own needs and chart your own course. It won't always be easy, but the view is infinitely better when you're the captain of your own ship.

CHAPTER 2

This Is Business

There's nothing like the thrill of getting paid for doing what you love. While most with artistic talent care first and foremost about what they're creating, for many the ability to make a living or at least supplement their income by doing the work they love runs a close second. And why shouldn't you be paid? If your creations bring beauty and entertainment into someone's life, you've provided value. In fact, that's one of the most fundamental principles of business. One person provides something worthwhile; the other person pays for it. When you look at it that way, the creative community is no less deserving of compensation than any other trade is.

You can't create great art without understanding the basics of your discipline. If you tried to put on a concert before learning to play your instrument, you'd only succeed in looking foolish. The same rules apply to making a living. In order to turn your creative passion into a reliable source of income, it's important to become acquainted with the world of business. With that in mind, let's turn our thoughts for a moment to marketing, partnerships, people skills, and yes, even taxes. We'll leave death for another day. The Grim Reaper can find his own gigs.

With the exception of the purists, those altruistic and occasionally arrogant souls who believe that commerce somehow cheapens the art, most of us would agree that we have a right to be paid for our work. However, lest we slip into a sense of entitlement, believing that the world owes us something, let's look a little more closely at the mechanics of making money.

No matter what your views on the relationship between artist and merchant, the reality of the matter is quite simple. If money changes hands, it's business. Therefore, if you want to get paid, you are by definition entering the business world. That doesn't mean you have to rush right out and buy a three-piece suit. You just need to pull your head out of the sand, look beyond the borders of the bohemian lifestyle, and embrace the real world. If you stand on the railroad tracks and close your eyes, the train will flatten you just the same.

If you want to get paid for your ponderings, you are by definition going into business. Embrace that fact and you can build a larger audience than you ever imagined possible.

One of the first harsh truths with which you must become comfortable is the fact that in the business world, no one gives a rat's rear end about your art. Those who can help you make money don't care whether it's innovative and cutting edge or populist and accessible. Even more shocking, they don't care if it's critically acclaimed or absolute rubbish. What they do care about is how these and other aspects of your work translate into a paying audience. The critics can flame you and your peers may disown you, but as long as someone is able to move the merchandise, you'll have a friend in the world of commerce.

Fortunately, unless you're doing really bizarre and obscure things in the name of art, you'll find that, as with any other industry, quality sells. When dozens of your friends tell you that a movie sucks, chances are good you'll give it a miss. In the same spirit, when everyone you know is raving about the performance of a dance troupe that's in town this week, you'll beg, borrow, or bribe your way into that show if it's the last thing you do. In other words, no matter what the elitist snobs may say to the contrary, you don't have to crank out garbage to make a buck. Do great work. That's step one.

No matter how much blood, sweat, and tears you pour into your creativity, step one is by far the easy part. This makes your work no less important, but we all know that talent and quality do not guarantee revenue. Step two is understanding enough about the business of your art form to translate that quality into cold, hard cash. That sort of thing tends to come in handy when the rent is due.

There is no magical secret that will guarantee you wealth and fame. On the other hand, if you're willing to bypass magic and live with high probabilities rather than guarantees, I can offer you the next best thing. It's not exactly a closely guarded secret, but that doesn't diminish its effectiveness. If you want a core concept around which you can build many streams of income, all you have to do is help other people make money. I know that sounds terribly simplistic, but you'll find that many of the world's great truths are equally as plain once you've stripped them of their glamour.

Of course, you can't just walk randomly into the streets helping every stranger you meet. Actually, you can and they'll love you for it, but it won't necessarily improve your own chances of making money. For it to be profitable, you need to connect with the right people. They're not hard to spot. In every corner of the creative world, there are promoters, merchants, agents, media companies, tech start-ups, and a host of others who make their living off of creative people like you and me.

The people who need to be helped that I just described often have a bad name among artists. There are countless tales of actors, dancers, painters, and every other species in our little universe being taken advantage of by the shrewd, manipulative, and unethical. In fact, this reputation for companies and individuals who take advantage of the talent is often enough to discourage people like you from even thinking about the business side of things. After all, what's the point of doing something new if you're just going to get screwed anyway, right?

With that in mind, allow me to digress for just a moment. Everyone's familiar with how the animal kingdom revolves around survival of the fittest. This principle tells us that in the world of bunnies, only the very best should live long enough to make future bunnies, thus ensuring a strong and vibrant community of fluffy, long-eared mammals. However, when a hungry tiger happens by and spots one, he couldn't possibly care less about who should survive and who shouldn't. He's only interested in dinner. Perpetuation of the bunny clan is not his problem, nor should it be. He has his own species to think about.

In such a scenario, there are only two kinds of bunnies—the aware and the dearly departed. The responsibility for choosing a category falls to the individual. If you're preoccupied with a particularly interesting little flower or you don't consider tigers to be all that dangerous, there's not much mystery about your fate. The bunnies that live to nibble another day are the ones who see danger coming and are out of town before it gets there.

The moral to this story—and of course any tale including bunnies and tigers should have a moral—is that there's nothing wrong with being a tiger, only a stupid bunny. If you're about to chastise me for overlooking the behavior of the unethical, I can assure you it will be a waste of time. I'm not in the business of passing judgment or seeking vengeance on those who do bad things, and neither are you. The world is neither safe nor fair and all the protests in the world will not change that. Let tigers be tigers and tend to your own little patch of clover.

It falls to you and you alone to determine who is a predator and who is not. If you avoid every class of creature who could make money with you because one of them might be a tiger, you won't have to worry about being someone else's dinner. You'll starve to death first.

With that in mind, go back and read that last paragraph again and this time make note of the fact that I didn't speak of someone making money off of you. I referred instead to those who could make money with you. To the self-aware bunny, this is a crucial consideration. When you find the businesspeople who populate your little slice of the arts and weed out the ones who seem overly predatory, what you're left with is a collection of potential business partners. This is a very valuable group of people.

Don't think of promoters, agents, distributors, and others who will help you sell your art as people who make money off you. Think of them as people who make money *for* you.

Because it's one of the easiest situations to understand, let's use a booking agent as an example. These people work on commission. When they book a gig for you, they get a cut. If they don't bring you any jobs, they make nothing. Percentages vary according to industry as well as how successful an agency is, but let's ballpark their commission at 20 percent. The math on this is pretty simple. Every time they bring you a job, you only get 80 percent of what the client paid. By the same token, each time you have no work because you chose not to do business with an agency, you get 100 percent of nothing.

The agent needs to pay her bills just like you do. If she brings you no work, she doesn't eat. Among the many things that we have in common with agents is our love of dining on a regular basis. This is someone who is motivated. She's also someone who sees you as a potential source of revenue.

That doesn't make her a tigress. It makes her a potential ally. When you approach such a person with a value-based suggestion, you'll get her immediate attention. The proposition is very simple. You need work, and you'll be delighted to pay her every time she provides it. In other words, you've just introduced yourself as someone who can help her make money. That's usually the beginning of a good conversation.

You also have to demonstrate that you're a product that can be sold. If she wastes her time on the talentless, she'll go hungry. You want her to invest her time and energy to find you work, and you don't have to pay her anything up front for her efforts. With that in mind, it's not at all unfair that she would want to see some tangible assurances that you're a good investment of her time. Demonstrate that, and you'll become fast friends and both of you will make money in the process.

Of course, self-preservation is always important. How do you know if she's a predator or not? The easiest way is to look at how she's treated people in the past. For better or worse, whatever she did to others, she'll do to you. As we all know, tigers rarely change their stripes.

With that in mind, you should be on the lookout for the types of businesses and individuals who can profit by helping you make money. For each of these types, the next step is to perform due diligence to assure yourself as much as is possible that you're not dealing with someone who's going to leave you twisting in the breeze.

Having narrowed down your candidates to the most promising, you then have to look at things from the agent's point of view and be prepared to demonstrate how a relationship with you will make him money. Following these steps won't guarantee that you'll become a wealthy and widely celebrated entertainer. It will, however, put you on the path to making a decent and steady living with your art.

You'll find more on agents and other representatives in chapter 10, "Paying the Bills."

Death and Taxes

As we've already seen, if money changes hands, you're doing business. I live in America and can't speak to the details of other nations, but I can, without a doubt, guarantee you that where there's a government, there's taxation. If you're engaged in commerce, then sooner or later, the tax man cometh.

I can assure you that in matters of taxes more than any other, aversion will not be an effective strategy. If you think it's a hassle having less money because you had to give up a percentage of it to the authorities, that discomfort pales in comparison to the joys you'll experience if you try to avoid, through negligence or outright deceit, the filing or payment of what's due.

You have two, and only two, choices. Encounter a little discomfort today by taking care of business or experience a great deal of unpleasantness later when the long arm of the law wraps its bony little fingers around your bank account, with interest and penalties far exceeding the original amount.

I'm hoping this entire conversation makes you twitch. I truly want to press home the importance of being responsible in this area. If the road to fame and fortune is littered with broken dreams, many of those wounds are self-inflected. That's both unfortunate and avoidable. If you're smart enough to read, you're smart enough to avoid such unnecessary complications in your otherwise idyllic life.

When you work for someone as an employee, at least in my country, the taxes are withheld from your paycheck. If that's the way you make your living, life is pretty easy. Do the paperwork at the end of the year and you might even get a refund. Making a living in the creative arts, however, is often an entrepreneurial adventure. Whether you're running a company such as a graphic design firm or simply doing freelance work on a gig-to-gig basis as an actor might, you have no such luxury. You get paid the entire amount, and it's up to you to stash money away for paying taxes at the end of the year.

If you're a self-employed artist of any kind, no one is withholding taxes from your paychecks (except in certain rare circumstances). Plan to put aside money every month to ensure you have enough to pay estimated taxes quarterly or the full amount at the end of the year.

In terms of financial disasters, not putting away money is probably the most common trap that you can fall into. Life in the arts is often a hand-to-mouth existence. Your focus, therefore, tends to be on paying the rent each month, not what you'll do about your taxes eleven months from now. If things are tight, it will be very tempting to spend everything you receive. From a perfectly logical point of view, if you're that tight for the money to pay one month's rent today, what do you think the chances are that money will fall from the heavens to pay an entire year's worth of taxes when they come due?

While it's not technically correct and varies based on your income, dependents, legitimate business expenses, and so forth, one easy way to keep track of things is to memorize the following phrase: "Every dollar is fifty cents." That's all you get to spend today and not a penny more. The other half goes into a savings account wired to ten thousand volts of electrical current that will fry you in a heartbeat if you try to access it before tax time.

When the end of the year rolls around and you do the required paperwork, you'll probably find that the money you saved exceeds the taxes you owe. At this point, you can open a second savings account for the excess. That's your emergency fund. You're going to need one in this line of work, so this provides you with a method of building one and covering your posterior with the government at the same time.

Most of us have to look at our expenses and the realistic potential for income and decide whether or not our pursuits will be a full-time or part-time venture. When you make this assessment and are calculating how much money you can bring in this year, remember, every dollar is fifty cents. Plan based on that and you'll be on solid footing both for the monthly bills and the annual governmental gala.

All of this requires discipline, a personality trait not commonly associated with people such as ourselves. However, no matter what type of talent you possess, you had to put in a lot of hours to get good enough at it for others to enjoy. This means you actually do possess a fair degree of self-discipline when it's important enough to you.

If you're just starting out in your field, you're going to have to trust me on this or talk to others who have been down the road before you. Money management and taking care of your financial obligations is something that is very, very important to you. Should you not be willing to take anyone's word on this I can assure you that you'll learn it the hard way. Given that I learned most of what I know from the school of hard knocks, I have a row of battle scars that attest to this fact.

Marketing Mischief

One of the cornerstones of any business, and a term sure to strike fear in the hearts of creative creatures everywhere, is marketing. This practice has a reputation for being sleazy, scary, difficult, or all of the above. It is without a doubt the single most dreaded task that any artistic person has to face. In fact, many will go to great lengths to avoid coming nose to nose with it. Of course, these are the very same people who wonder why they're having a difficult time paying the bills with their art.

No matter what your product or service, and regardless how great you think it is, when you're trying to make a living, nothing happens until a sale is made. That sale can be someone telling you that you passed the audition or a fan of your show buying a t-shirt online. Either way, before money can change hands, your customer has to be sold.

When most people think of sales, what comes to mind is those terribly obnoxious late-night TV commercials that scream at you and seem to be permanently bonded to the price of $19.95. Running a very close second is the local used-car salesman, with his cheesy dialogue, plaid jacket, and all. If that's what it took to make a sale, I'd hide under a rock and never go near the entrepreneurial realm again. Fortunately, that's not the case.

Sales happen all the time in much more benevolent climates. Think about your favorite restaurant, the one you go to when you have a few extra bucks and really want to treat yourself. The food isn't free. When it's all said and done and the last crumpled napkin is laid on the table, your server walks over and hands you the check. Not only do you pay, you may well hum a happy, contented little tune while doing so. And yet, a sale was made.

As another example. Let's say that a new book comes out by your favorite author. Perhaps it's a light-hearted romp through the woods with a herd of vampires, two zombies, and the occasional chainsaw. It's unlikely that the writer paid for a late-night commercial to beat you into submission. Far more likely are the chances that you read a previous book, enjoyed it, and have been following that author on the Web waiting for the announcement of a new title. No one pressured you to buy the book. Chainsaws were indeed involved, but none of them were aimed at you. You were probably not only happy to spend the money, but you'd also been anxiously awaiting the opportunity to part with your hard-earned cash. And yet, a sale was made.

Zombies, napkins, and the occasional gas-powered hedge trimmer aside, these two examples share a very important common thread. Before the sale could be made in either of these enterprises, you had to know about what was being offered. That's the short definition of marketing. Doesn't sound nearly so scary now, does it?

If you're going to get paid for your work, someone, somehow, has to make the sale. If you're a sculptor, you may sell a piece directly to a customer. If you're a fashion designer, there may be a chain of purchases and sales that happen between the time of your idea, the manufacturer, the wholesale distributor, the retailer, and the ultimate consumer. However it works, somewhere down the line, a person coughs up some money and some or all of it makes its way into your pocket.

Either you make the sale or someone makes it for you. The choice of scenarios may be dictated in part by how your particular art works. As often as not, it also has a great deal to do with how comfortable you are taking the reins and handling the process personally. As with everything else in business, there is no one right answer. In the end, it's all about trade-offs and which are best for you.

Let's say you don't want to have anything to do with sales and marketing. You just want to do your thing and have someone hand you a check. Nice work if you can get it. However, while you've relieved yourself of the burden that is marketing, you've paid for that luxury by giving up control. When you trust someone else, particularly where money is involved, you're vulnerable.

Is the person to whom you've entrusted your marketing honest and ethical in their dealings? Even if she is, how dependable is she? If you put someone in charge of booking your band but she never gets around to visiting the local bars, you don't eat. It's also common knowledge that money can alter someone's behavior. A person whom you once trusted with a key to your house now suddenly avoids your phone calls when you're trying to get paid for that last gig she collected on.

The world is full of good, hard-working, dependable people. All rumors to the contrary, a great many of them work in marketing. You may very well find someone you can trust who will be diligent in bringing home the bacon and putting it in your pocket. Nonetheless, if this is the path you choose, it's important to be aware of your vulnerabilities so that you can keep an eye on things and pull the plug early if it all goes south on you.

When you hand over the marketing of your art to another person, you give up control. This leaves you completely dependent on the integrity, work ethic, and goodwill of somebody else, who will, even under the best of circumstances, focus on her own self-interest. Know the risk before taking the leap.

The other option is to handle the marketing yourself. This can be as simple as reading the trade publications and going out to auditions for any dance company you think you have a shot at. It will be up to you to keep tabs on the appropriate notices, ask around and network with friends, and do everything else necessary to keep your ear to the ground. When you see an opportunity, you will need to make the contact and arrange the audition. That's marketing.

You can also be more proactive about it. In addition to waiting for the right kind of company to post auditions, let's say that you've been a dancer for quite some time and have even done a bit of teaching. Having expertise to share in your particular style, you can start writing a regular blog and even do some video tutorials. You'll need to be active on social media and when contacted by people with questions, you should always take time to help them as best you can.

Over time, your reputation will grow and a great many people will know of you. When the day comes that your favorite company has an opening, rather than hold auditions, they'll first pick up the phone and call you to see if you're interested because they've heard so much about you. After a pleasant conversation and dropping by to spend some time with them, you will ultimately get the gig. You didn't cold call people or make an annoyance of yourself in any way. Quite the contrary, you established yourself as someone who possesses not only talent but a pleasing disposition. That's marketing.

We'll be delving into the world of sales and marketing in greater detail a little later on, but these illustrations give you an idea of your options. No matter which approach you choose, you'll get results. All that's left is to consider the benefits and trade-offs and determine what works best for you.

People Skills

I intentionally covered sales and marketing first to get the uncomfortable stuff out of the way. People expect to see those words in a business book. They also tend to have preconceived notions about how good or evil these areas are. To a very large degree, though, there is a common umbrella that they fall under that is much more comfortable for the artistic mindset. When you get right down to it, getting noticed and turning that attention into a transaction isn't about sales or marketing. Your ability to make money and further your career is all about people.

One group of people you encounter is the collection of kindred spirits you collaborate with when creating your art. A novelist may work in solitude while cranking out the first draft, but ultimately she'll interact with editors, copy editors, illustrators, indexers, compositors, and perhaps a few others. Together, they'll transform the author's words into a polished, finished product that can be sold, sometimes known as a book.

If you play in a band, this collection of coconspirators is a familiar sight, including not just the other singers and instrumentalists but also the crew who set up the stage, mix the sound, and run the lights. Whether it's separate people for each job or a few people wearing multiple hats, before the show can go on, these are people you need.

No matter what kind of work you create, you want to get people talking about you, preferably with nice things to say. This can start from your fans and general word of mouth and go all the way up to hosts of network TV shows and other such celebrities. Whether it's the Web, major media outlets, or just word on the street, before anyone will show up to see what you do, you need such a group behind you.

If all goes well and you've managed to get your act together without throwing the drummer out the back of a moving van, word will spread and people will come to your show. This is an extremely important group of people to establish, as one might imagine. Even if you sell pottery at flea markets, the people who come by your table are the reason you went to all the effort of creating something in the first place. They are the consumers of your craft, those people you hope to turn into devoted fans.

That might seem like the end of the story, and in some cases, such as that of our master of clay, it could very well be. There is, however, one more group without whom you will not be able to pay the light bill. These are the people who can actually make you money.

In the case of an artisan selling his wares at festivals and outdoor markets, the consumers of the work are also the people who can make you money. In this case, we'll allow them to wear two hats, mostly because it looks really cool in the group photo. They are not the only kinds of people you will need in order to prosper, however, even in the case of the potter.

There are lots of open-air markets that take place anytime the sun is willing to peek out from behind the clouds. If you exhibit at one and have quality art, you'll probably make some money. Because of that, the supply of artists often far exceeds the space available. Even you live in some transdimensional galaxy where the normal laws of physics don't apply, you still typically need someone's permission to attend. That person is also one who can make you money.

In some arts, the money comes from more abstract places, such as a concert promoter who pays the band a fixed fee, sells the tickets, and then prays that he brings in more than he spent. The famous Woodstock festival of the 1960s was actually supposed to be a paid concert. However, when half a million stoned hippies crashed the gates in an ever so peaceful manner, eventually they had to just bow to the inevitable and call it a cultural event. What you might also call it is a promoter losing his shorts on the deal.

Regardless of how it works out for the promoter, he's a person who can make you money. An agent also fits this description. Even though she only booked you at the bar and the club owner is the one who will pay you, it's the agent who made that payment possible. Independent filmmakers also deal with such abstractions and typically work with producers, financiers, and other sources of revenue, hopefully with enough left over to get paid once the cost of the film has finished depleting the bank account. Should that payday actually arrive, all of these people were necessary since they were the ones who brought in the money.

You now have a roomful of people, each performing a vital function to your career and none of whom you can safely do without. Previously, we were considering the topic of sales and marketing. To many, those are skill sets that seem alien or at the very least uncomfortable. After reviewing our four critical groups, however, you may be seeing how this all comes together. Hopefully, you're also beginning to realize that you don't have to have a mercenary mindset to make a buck. In fact, over the long haul, that sort of attitude hurts you. People remember, and people talk.

The book I wrote before this one, *Unite the Tribes*, explores the principles necessary for building a successful organization. One of the chapters speaks directly to promoting your personal agenda, whether that involves getting the lead role in a play or selling out a fifty thousand seat stadium. It's simply titled "Persuasion," but it's the subtitle that's particularly relevant to our current discussion: "Never Forget That You're Dealing with People."

This brings us to a central point when it comes to making a living with your art. As you can see, your success depends on people. It's not a matter of which group you need. You need them all. But then, so does everyone else, including your competitors. Of course, if you're a singer in a Broadway production, you might not think about the other shows as competition, but that's exactly what they are. Your audience has only so much disposable income. Who they choose to spend it with is up for grabs.

In all aspects of your career and business, never forget you are dealing with people who need to be educated, persuaded, influenced, and cajoled in varying degrees. Good people skills can turn others into your biggest boosters and take your business to new heights.

As I detailed in the chapter on persuasion in *Unite the Tribes*, the key to success is understanding human nature and possessing good people skills. If you want to abuse people and beat them over the head until you get what you want, you'll succeed in a tiny percentage of cases, only to guarantee that the vast majority will want nothing to do with you. I didn't call the chapter "Manipulation" or even "How to Lie, Cheat, and Steal." Both of these accurately describe the sales tactics of the ethically challenged, but morality aside, that's simply not good long-term thinking. You'll be creative for the rest of your life, so it's good to think about the future.

When you want people to do something for you, you ask. If they're not inclined to say yes and you feel you've made a reasonable request, you make your case as eloquently as possible. That's persuasion. They may still say no in the end. A certain percentage always will. What's important is how you go about it. If you understand people, believe in treating them well, and can articulate both what you want and why it would be in their interest to do so, people will respond. You'll gain the support of the four groups you need and you'll generate no ill will in the process. In fact, you'll end up making friends. Doesn't that sound a lot more pleasant than sales and marketing?

Opportunities

The topics of marketing and finding the work are both pivotal to your ability to make a living as a creative creature, so I've devoted an entire chapter to each a little further on. However, as a preview of coming attractions, and more importantly to round out our overview of the business aspects of your art, let's take a brief tour of the types of opportunities that are most common. As with everything we cover, some of these will relate directly to your art and others may serve as examples that you can map to your own world.

Being Discovered

If you've ever seen a movie about someone who dreamed of being a star, chances are good that much of the hopes and dreams of our hero rested on being discovered. While the specifics of that phrase vary a bit from industry to industry, what it generally implies is good fortune falling in your lap by way of someone seeing your talent and hooking you up with someone else who can give you a lucrative contract.

If that sounds like a fantasy worthy of a good movie, you're not far from the truth. Yes, there is such a thing as a talent scout. In the music business, they're known as A&R people (artist & repertoire). Regardless of your art, you have about as good a chance of being hit by a piece of space debris that reentered Earth's atmosphere and managed to avoid being burnt to a crisp as you have of being plucked out of that dive bar you're playing and swept away in a limousine.

The chances of this magic happening are further diminished by the ever-contracting fortunes of those industries most likely to be searching for talent in this way. The Internet has wreaked havoc with the recording, movie, and publishing industries. There may be talent scouts roaming the country, but they're probably spending most of their time scavenging for fire extinguishers to douse the ashes of a once-thriving industry.

Discouraging? Sorry. I realize it's unpopular to dash someone's hopes and dreams, but I'd much rather see you take a path that has a realistic chance of keeping you fed.

Venues

While the digital media industry is busy searching antique bookstores for any ancient reference on how a firebird actually rose from the ashes, another form has survived admirably. If you're a member of the performing arts, physical venues could be your bread and butter.

Your audience can hold up a cell phone and record your entire performance, and there's really not much you can do about it. Nor can you keep them from posting it on every Web site on the planet. Even so, it just doesn't matter.

There is simply no substitute for being there in person, in the moment, part of the crowd who experiences a once-in-a-lifetime event. No two performances are ever identical, and the group energy, for lack of a more scientific term, cannot be replicated by a computer.

Across the world, there are countless theaters, bars, symphony halls, festivals, conferences, and coffeehouses. That doesn't even scratch the surface of the venues available and the creative promoter can probably come up with a few more on the fly.

This is obviously a solid opportunity for the performing artist, but it is in no way limited to that art form. As an author, I do my work through a word processor. However, I also speak at conferences and other venues, including modest meeting rooms and the auditoriums of major corporations. Programmers, graphic artists, and Web designers do the same thing. Poets do readings at coffeehouses. Novelists sign books at stores. Sculptors give seminars and filmmakers speak at universities. The versatility of the physical venue is impressive indeed.

Merchants and Merchandising

When we think of merchants, it brings to mind colorful local markets in Third World countries or massive supermarkets selling everything from ant farms to zebra pillows. For the physical artisan, selling their wares may very well take place in such a context. As with venues, however, it only scratches the surface of the potential.

Similar to stores, galleries and exhibits also provide opportunities for painters, sculptors, and other such creative professions. They can range from the glamorous to the humble, but at either end of the spectrum you're exposing your work to an appreciative audience. They may purchase one of your pieces or even commission you to do something just for them. As a networking opportunity, this could extend even further, such as a chance to handle all interior design and art for a national chain of upscale restaurants.

If you happen to be in a more digital world, you'll be looking for additional streams of revenue. More and more, people seem resistant to the idea of paying for intellectual property. As an example, filmmakers have depended a great deal on the sale of DVDs since the chances of getting shown in a large number of cinemas is only slightly better than a singer being discovered in a biker bar somewhere south of Peoria, Illinois. With piracy rampant and paying consumers moving toward digital streaming, those who make movies need to find other ways to bring in revenue.

The sale of licensed merchandise is one such way to generate more money, which works not just for movies but also for bands, dance troupes, and pretty much any creative who can build a following. T-shirts, ball caps, directors' chairs, beer coolers, you name it. If it can be branded with your group or creation, you can make money selling it.

It's typically difficult to get your product on the shelves of the large retail outlets. On the other hand, flea markets, festivals, software user groups, and many other such places provide a lower barrier to entry. There's also the time-honored tradition of selling your merchandise at your performing venue.

Of course, the same digital technology that's caused so much financial heartache to the entertainment industry is also exceptionally empowering to the common man. In an age when people are accustomed to buying things online, you can get by with something as simple as a Web site and a credit-card processing account. There are also large online retailers as well as another breed of useful creatures who will allow you to design products and then print them up one at a time, as the order comes in.

The world of merchandise is another of the great hopes for the average artist. It's also a growth area, so the opportunities we see today will only improve over time.

Selling branded items, from hats to coolers, is a great way to bring in extra dollars. It also increases awareness for your band, theater group, or other creative ventures. Businesses pay advertising agencies millions of dollars annually to create branding campaigns because it works.

Advertising

As mentioned earlier, the advertising community offers artists, animators, musicians, and many other audio/visual creatives a way to make a regular paycheck and receive such unheard of benefits as health coverage and paid time off. For some, this stability will be very appealing, but it's certainly not the only way to use advertising for fun and profit.

A variation on the theme is to work as a freelance creative who does contract work for agencies. Alternatively, you can set up shop, find clients, and do the work and billing yourself. It's higher risk than a nine-to-five job, but it offers more creative freedom as well as the chance to make better money.

You can also reverse the equation and put advertising to work for you. For producers of movies, TV shows, and Web series, it's becoming more common for the content to be posted online with embedded ads as a means of support. The advertising rates on the Web are a tiny fraction of what the cable and TV industry pays, but money is money.

For software developers, mobile apps are another area where advertising support is commonplace. Many apps offer two versions, one that's ad supported but free to download, and the other a paid version that, at minimum, offers an ad-free experience. So, even in their absence, ads are trying hard to help you make a buck.

The merchandise we previously discussed can also benefit from advertising. This can range from traditional display or video ads to something as simple as an ad-words campaign on an Internet search engine.

For movie and television series producers, product placement is another form of advertising revenue. Imagine a scene where people are drinking beer, eating potato chips, and watching a ball game. If you wrapped the beer and chips in plain-white wrappers to avoid trademark infringement, you'd miss out on all that legal fun, but you'd also have a very unrealistic looking TV show.

Many manufacturers will pay a fee and give you permission to use their wares on your show. It gets the product in front of the audience in a subtle and real-world manner and as such is appealing to many with an advertising budget.

You can also get backing for a performance, gallery showing, or other such affair by having a corporation sponsor your event. This is commonplace and typically involves hanging the company's banners and doing other things to make them visible. It's a way for companies to support the arts, generate some goodwill, and do a little advertising all at the same time. Everybody wins.

Corporate Gigs

Speaking of corporations, ad agencies aren't the only ones who offer you a shot at a normal life while allowing you to pursue your art. Corporate gigs are also a major source of work for the tech industry. Software developers who don't want to take the risk of developing and marketing their own products can get steady, good paying gigs working for companies as a regular employee. In fact, this is probably the most common source of employment for programmers.

An alternative approach is working through recruiting companies. These organizations scout out the gigs by sending reps out to potential clients and then filling those positions at an hourly rate, much like an employment agency. The client pays the recruiting company and the recruiters pay the developers, taking a cut off the top for their efforts in the same way that a booking agent works on commission.

A third option is straight-up freelance work, similar to what we've covered already. This involves doing your own marketing and billing, offers less security but of course more freedom, and allows you to earn 100 percent of the revenue. Well, you know, after giving a cut to your favorite tax man.

A popular source of revenue for programmers, corporate gigs also exist for many of the other arts. Graphic designers, animators, special-effects gurus, video producers, and many other such talents are needed on a regular basis in the corporate world. While a company may farm out its advertising creative work to an agency, there are still a great deal of sales and marketing materials to be produced. There's also a demand for internal-training materials and a host of other multimedia needs for the modern-day company.

Writers can get in on the action as well. In a programming shop, there's often a need for technical documentation. Tech writers work both as employees and on a freelance basis, either individually or through the same recruiters that programmers enjoy.

If the structure and detail of tech writing isn't gratifying to you, you can also pursue a gig within the corporate communications department. This can entail everything from writing mind-numbing HR statements to engaging newsletters, marketing materials, press releases, and other such propaganda.

Teaching

An opportunity that applies to every single art form, teaching is a well-established way to generate primary or secondary income. The joke among working-class musicians who frequent smoky bars and tend to turn equipment up to eleven is that you don't go to college to learn how to play guitar. You go so that you can get a teaching gig when the work is slow.

Academia has the most stringent entry requirements, whether you're teaching grade school or at a university. The pay is less than other options, but the benefits are excellent, and with universities, the chance to get a tenured position and its implied job security are of great value to many.

On the other end of the spectrum is the individual instructor or tutor. A good example of this type of work is the person who gives your daughter piano lessons or teaches your son how to improve his trumpet playing. Sometimes you'll go to the student's home. Other times you'll partner with a local music store, typically the kind who sells band instruments, and hold lessons on the premises.

Private lessons are not limited to the musically inclined, of course. Dance instructors join the ranks of painters, potters, sculptors, drama coaches, and a host of other disciplines. If you're an artist, there's always room to improve. One of the best ways is by getting one-on-one instruction from someone who's been down the road before you.

Sometimes teaching blossoms into a business enterprise all its own. There are probably very few cities in America that don't have at least one dance school. There are also small businesses that teach drawing and painting and pretty much every other art. It takes someone with both creative and entrepreneurial skills, and the risk is much higher. So, too, of course, is the potential for reward.

You want to make a living doing what you love? Consider teaching. It pays the bills, and gives you the freedom to pursue your art on your own terms. It also offers its own special joys. There's nothing quite so rewarding as passing along your love of an art form to another person.

Somewhere in between the private tutor and the small businessperson lies the arena of seminars. If you can put together a high-value learning experience that you can deliver in a day or two, people will pay you for the privilege of sitting in. It is another high-risk, high-reward scenario. One of the ongoing challenges of this type of teaching is finding an appropriate venue to conduct them in. Hotel ballrooms are common but expensive choices.

Alternatively, you can partner with a dance school or its equivalent in your discipline. It provides the venue, and often is an excellent source of attendees. You deliver the seminar and split the revenue between you. The risk is slightly lower in this type of arrangement because the school has the venue whether it's filled or not, whereas the hotel requires payment whether one or a hundred people show up.

Speaking

A variation on this theme is public speaking. If you can deliver a talk that educates your audience, you can land gigs at conferences and corporate events.

You can also find work as a straight-up entertainer doing the after-dinner circuit. In this case, your audience need not be artists at all, let alone in the same discipline as you. If you can tell entertaining, uplifting, or motivating stories that keep the audience engaged, your particular expertise serves only as a launching point for your stories.

Of course, if you're able to offer the best of both worlds, it naturally delivers the highest value to your audience and makes you more in demand as a speaker. I've seen plenty of people recite facts and figures that were completely accurate but, well, less than inspiring. On the other hand, if entertainment is all you do, you'll find that it's very hard to be funny on demand, as those who do stand-up comedy can readily attest to.

Like many others, I've spent years on stage entertaining the crowd, in my case singing in bands and dodging the occasional airborne tequila bottle. Consequently, I like to combine information and entertainment, so my personal approach is to deliver down-to-earth ideas that the audience can use coupled with a degree of lighthearted fun.

In either case, the most important thing when choosing a path for speaking is to go with what comes naturally to you. As with any other performing art, a forced presentation is always apparent while the person who's at ease in her environment will naturally connect with the crowd.

Perspective

For all the ground we've covered, perhaps the single most important consideration is how you look at your career. If you want to get paid for doing the things you enjoy in life, you have to rise above the mindset of the artist. To make money, you have to understand that this is business and embrace that concept with unbridled enthusiasm.

It would be great if you could just sit in the corner and do your thing. That's an option you may in fact choose to pursue, but it usually involves marrying someone willing to support you and let you play. While such relationships certainly exist, when the kids arrive life gets more complicated and the carefree days of the patronized artist dwindle. More importantly, if you're just using someone to get a free ride, society has some rather unflattering words for you.

Short of finding a convenient king or half-drunk millionaire to serve as your patron and provide you a lavish and carefree existence, if you want to make a career of your art instead of slinging burgers during the day and searching for gigs on the weekends, you're going to have to work for it. The good news is that regardless of the artistic discipline, there is a wealth of opportunity available to all who are willing to put forth the effort. And that's a really good thing when dinnertime rolls around. A person can take only so many cheeseburgers.

CHAPTER 3

Becoming Self-Sufficient

For those who immerse themselves in the creative arts with hopes of doing it for a living, life can be full of twists and turns. If you happened to notice that signpost up ahead, you also know that the real world can often be surreal. It's certainly not always fair. Even so, we dream, we create, and we look for ways to keep the wolves at bay without losing sight of the muse. It is not a journey for the faint of heart.

Then, there's that moment in the spotlight. After hours on the road, bad diners, worse motels, and hangovers the size of Texas, you stumble onto the stage, blink twice and suddenly come alive. Everything else falls away as you remember why you chose this path. Whether your stage is real or figurative, it makes the journey worthwhile.

Eventually, however, you step out of the limelight and back into your everyday life, already in progress. There's food to buy, bills to pay, and the knowledge that even if you work on the road, you're eventually going to want a roof over your head when you get home. All of this requires money.

In a perfect world, you would present your work, the people who enjoy such things would show up, and adequate funds would magically appear in your checking account. It doesn't take an MBA to see the holes in this scenario. There are many levers to pull between the creation of your art and a check clearing the bank. That means countless opportunities for things to go wrong, leaving nothing but insufficient funds and unpopular excuses when the rent comes due.

One of the most fundamental issues you will face throughout your career revolves around who pulls those levers. There are certainly plenty of people in your particular industry who are less than competent in that regard. Some of them might even come through on a regular basis. That doesn't change the fact that more than any other business, the performing arts suffers from a high degree of flakiness and deceit. You can either see this coming ahead of time and be prepared for it or learn it the hard way. Because I have a fairly large collection of battle scars just below the waterline, I heartily suggest the former.

Although it's rarely possible to do every single thing yourself, you can to a very large degree become self-sufficient if you're willing to face some hard truths and put forth the effort. The reward is a career path that you can count on rather than trusting your fate to the winds. And trust me, in this line of work you're going to meet a lot of blowhards.

Choose Your Discomfort

Since a perfect world doesn't appear to be forthcoming anytime soon, what it really comes down to is which particular batch of uncomfortable experiences you're most willing to tolerate. I read a quote attributed to Napoleon once saying that the first quality of a soldier was not to fight but to endure. That's certainly something that those of us in the world of creativity can relate to. Suffering for one's art is a concept as old as art itself. Consequently, we're perfectly capable of choosing a direction and dealing with the difficulties that may arise.

There's a myth that circulates among the more conservative types suggesting that those of the artistic persuasion are lazy. I can see how they might acquire that misconception since most of us bolt for the exits when someone wants us to work a day job. However, that doesn't mean we're unwilling to put forth concerted effort. It's more about what causes we feel are worth our time and toil. Slogging through the days of a nine-to-five factory job isn't going to bring out our best. On the other hand, how many times have you gone one or two days without sleep because you were immersed in one of your projects?

Earlier, I mentioned hard truths. Chief among these is the fact that the most successful artists are those who are willing and able to take care of business, whether they enjoy it or not. In fact, in a world that often rewards mediocre talent over creative brilliance, it's often the deciding factor. If you have both talent and tenacity, you're extremely well positioned in your field. Learning what to do is easy. Making yourself do it is the hard part, and that's where a great many otherwise gifted people fail. So, you have to ask yourself a very blunt question and expect an equally unvarnished reply: how badly do you want to achieve your goals?

The truly successful artists know how to take care of business, even if they're not wild about that aspect of the career. Do you want to achieve your goals? Then become involved, intimately, with the nuts and bolts of creating and sustaining a business.

With that in mind, let's take a look at the two major paths of career management, acknowledging the good and the bad of each. From there, you can make your own choice based on the relative merits.

Our first contestant is the road most travelled. This type really just wants to sit back and do fun stuff and would prefer not to have to deal with any of that yucky business stuff. This is a perfectly acceptable choice as long as you know what you're getting into. On the plus side, you can dedicate your entire being to the pursuits that you so love. You can be nothing but an artist and will never have to work outside your comfort zone.

The most effective way to employ this path is to have a regular job that pays your bills and allows you not to depend on your art for money. When you work and get paid, it's a bonus and you can use it for fun since your daily needs are already met. That's another plus, because having a day gig removes the stress and financial pressure from your creative endeavors. You'll enjoy creating more, the income will be purely recreational, and you won't have to do anything you don't want to do.

The trade-offs for this choice begin with having to work a traditional job in order to pay your bills. If you seek to work full time as an artist, that would be a nonstarter. However, you don't have to have a day gig. You can trust your income to others, such as agents and promoters, and build up to full-time income in that manner. Handing off the responsibility of finding work to someone else can be appealing, but you also relinquish control over your career and introduce a greater degree of financial instability into your life.

That last bit might seem counterintuitive and thus deserves an explanation. After all, if you don't feel comfortable booking gigs and instead give the task over to an agent, why would doing so add up to more instability instead of less? The problem lies in motivation.

An agent, no matter how smooth talking he may be, has one and only one loyalty—his bank account. If you look like a good opportunity for income, you'll get a lot of attention. If others in the stable look more promising, you could get pushed to the back of the room and receive little to no attention at all.

Furthermore—and this is something that many new people don't think about when dealing with them—agencies usually want an exclusive contract. That means that for the duration of the contract, however many years that may be, you're stuck. If your agent books no gigs for you at all, you don't work because you're not allowed to hire someone else to find them for you either. You do have the option of booking them yourself, but you'll have to pay him a commission on every job you acquire even though the agent did nothing. It's just the nature of the business. The irony in this scenario is the fact that you chose this route because you didn't want to do the booking in the first place.

If you're not in the performing arts, you may not need an agent, but this serves to illustrate the first and most important problem. No one cares as much about getting you work as you do. Therefore, it's difficult to find people that you can truly count on. You make an arrangement and duties are assigned, but frequently the person you hired just doesn't follow through. This is true of humanity in general, but in the "I'd rather party than work" atmosphere of the arts, it's even more pronounced.

The other problem that you have with this path is trust. The only way you can be guaranteed that you'll be paid for work is if you collect the money yourself. Those who have had the pleasure know that even then it's not assured, as the promoter may give you excuses instead of cash at the end of the evening. When there is a chain of people between the client who pays for the service and the artist who should be paid, the potential for dishonesty and fraud is extremely high.

If you've ever read about people in the arts, probably one of the most common stories you've encountered is that a talented person gets a manager who sees great potential and the manager goes out to book lots of gigs and makes the artist a star. Fast forward a few years and the artist is living in a cardboard box eating leftover cat food from discarded tins in the dumpster because the manager embezzled all the funds and left the country. Usually with the artist's significant other. And the cat.

This is another of the hard truths you must face. No matter how much you wish it were otherwise, there are a great many people you simply can't trust. When money is involved, the odds of meeting them skyrockets.

I do appreciate the fact that this sounds jaded and cynical. I can assure you it's not my preferred perspective. It's one that I've learned both from personal experience and from being close enough to the train wreck of someone else's career to get my jeans singed. I like people and I believe there are a lot of truly wonderful, trustworthy folks out there. I also believe in giving people a chance. That said, I always sleep with one eye open. If you want me to trust you, you're going to have to demonstrate that trustworthiness through consistent behavior over a respectable period of time.

As an aside, it's worth mentioning that I hold myself to that standard as well. In all of my dealings, be they business, creative, or personal, I don't expect people to take me on faith. That even applies to the books I write. If what I say is true, you should be able to go out into the streets and see it demonstrated in a fairly consistent manner (nothing in life works 100 percent of the time). If it doesn't turn out to be the case, I'm not worthy of your trust.

I apply that attitude to all of my dealings with people and it has an added value beyond just living true to what I personally believe. By working to earn people's trust, I tend to have a lot of positive interactions. That's not terribly surprising since this attitude demonstrates respect for the other party. When you treat people well, that tends to create good relationships.

I'm not a perfect person by any stretch of the imagination and I may very well screw up more than the next guy. Nonetheless, I sincerely try to be a good guy and do the right thing. The problem with blindly trusting people to manage your affairs is that there are just too many people out there who don't care about such things, and that makes you terribly vulnerable. You can relinquish power over your career to someone else, and the benefit is being free of uncomfortable tasks. The risk is getting screwed, over and over again.

The other path isn't a walk in the park, either. You simply have a different set of problems to consider. If you decide to become actively involved in the business details of your career, you gain much more control and greatly reduce your vulnerabilities. Note that I didn't say eliminate. Even when you're the person collecting the money, you can still get stiffed, and there are countless other ways that things can go wrong for you. That's just life in the big city. Still, better odds mean less chances of encountering such unpleasantness.

You'll also be more exposed to the highs and lows of everyday transactions. When you have a manager handling your affairs, you're buffered from the rejection inherent in running your business.

Consider this. In many sales jobs, if you get two sales after pitching ten people, you're a rock star. That means you have a rejection rate of 80 percent. That's a lot of people saying no to you, and even if you can develop the thicker skin required of such work, it still gets old after a while. A manager typically tells you just the success stories. Should you fail to get a particular job and the bad news has to be delivered to you, she'll soften the blow in conversation. You have no such luxury when you're doing it yourself.

As with any respectable coin, there are of course two sides. There's a feeling of empowerment that goes along with charting your own course. In a previous lifetime, before I ran my own sales-consulting company, I started out as a salesman. When you're moving the merchandise for a living, compensation varies from job to job and it's usually a trade-off. More guaranteed income with a lower percentage of the sale or higher points coupled with less financial security. I always chose the latter. Risky? Yes. However, it also meant that rather than depending on someone else, I could write my own paycheck. Got some extra bills this month? Need more money? No problem. Work harder, make more money.

When you're captain of your own ship, this feeling of power courses through your veins. Every success is an excuse for cartwheels. When times are tough, you don't have to sit by the phone wondering if your agent is even trying. You just get out there, pound the pavement, and make it happen. Just don't bring the ship along. It's a little rough on the asphalt.

I'm obviously an advocate of handling your own affairs wherever possible. Honestly, I'd rather just sit back, do my thing, and let others take care of all the noncreative stuff. In fact, early in my creative career I did exactly that. The aforementioned row of battle scars and the insights I've shared are a direct result of those experiences.

Still, I realize that we're all individuals, so you have to go with what works for you. If you choose to let others manage your affairs, I will at the very least recommend that you stay in the loop as much as possible, be educated about the work they're doing, learn to read contracts, and understand where every penny goes. In other words, if you're asking yourself if having a manager gets you off the hook in terms of your workload, the answer is no, not if you want to minimize your vulnerability to the greatest extent possible.

As you can see, no matter which path you choose, there's going to be some work and discomfort involved. That said, there is a third path that's a variation on the first. You can ask others to do the work for you, offer blind trust, and hope that it all works out for the best.

Do I really need to connect the dots for you on this one?

Hire an Expert

No matter which path you choose as an overall strategy, wouldn't it be great if you could retain the services of a consultant to advise you on the many choices you'll face along the way? Someone who was an established expert in the very things that are important to you? While I rarely take on career-coaching clients these days (most people expect magic answers and are shocked to discover that I give them homework), I actually have a much more qualified person to recommend than myself. You.

You're going to be doing this for a long time. You're going to grow in your art, and your interests and goals will change along the way. Your industry will also undergo change, and you'll see different opportunities and other interests that weren't previously possible. There will never be another person on this planet who will know what you want to accomplish better than you. When it comes to your personal career, you are the undisputed expert in your field. I recommend that you take full advantage of this valuable resource.

A good consultant will work with you and help you review and understand all of your options for a given scenario. Even our rocket-piloting chimpanzee friend can spread those options out on the table for you. It doesn't take much expertise to look around at what's possible, make a list, and scribble it on your whiteboard. Okay, perhaps you have to be tall enough to reach the markers, but that's a modest constraint.

What requires true expertise is looking at those options and weighing the pros and cons of each against your personal desires, discomforts, work ethic, and the degree of risk you're willing to accept. That's a lot of calculations that have to take place. Of course, anyone with a pocket calculator, otherwise known as a cell phone, can do the math on the positives and negatives, but only if they have the X factor. The only person who understands this magic variable, the intimate knowledge of how you feel and what you're willing to do, is you.

Eventually, you will discover that you are your own best advisor, consultant, and guardian. Once you do, you'll gain the confidence you need to knock on doors, make inroads, persist, take chances, and all the other ingredients of a stellar career in the arts.

You'll also never find another soul who is more dedicated to the cause than you. Our art is a highly personal affair and no one truly appreciates the connection we have with it. It's a part of our very being. Additionally, no one really cares about your financial situation or what color of cardboard box you live in more than you. Sure, your friends love you, so naturally they're concerned about your health and well-being, but not as much as you. They're also who you turn to when you need someone to talk to about your dreams and desires. Maybe they get it, maybe they don't, but regardless of how close the two of you are, they'll never feel it as intensely as you.

In addition to having a career consultant you can count on to consistently provide a reliable perspective, you could use another person on your team. Think of the position as that of a career bodyguard. As we've already seen, there are countless opportunities for you to get screwed, and not just for money. Petty politics among the circle of people you work with could leave you holding the least desirable opportunity. People who promise favors or introductions suddenly give their loyalty to another. Some employ character assassination to eliminate you as competition for creative positions or paying gigs. The list is a long one. It's a rough universe out there. Who's going to watch your back?

Once again, the fiercest and most loyal defender you will find is you. When you get jerked around, no one else feels the pain. When you get stories instead of payment, no one else is eating yesterday's pet food. When opportunities arise, the only person you can count on to tell you about them is you.

I've played lots of rock-and-roll gigs where the crowd shows up on a Harley and blood on the floor isn't entirely out of the question. When you mix alcohol, loud music, and the opposite sex, you're standing in a room full of gas just praying nobody wants to light a cigarette. In the real world, things can go wrong. No matter how big, bad, and scary looking you might be (and I'm not), there's always someone scarier. Having a bodyguard is not a guarantee of safety. On the other hand, when pool cues and skulls collide, they're darned handy to have around.

If you accept such a position in defense of your own career, you will without a doubt have to duck the proverbial cue ball flying through the air. That's part of the gig. You'll see things going wrong, or about to go wrong, and as your own personal career bodyguard, it falls to you to get your client out of harm's way. Having personal experience in a wide variety of rather exciting situations, proverbial and otherwise, I have one very encouraging thing to offer. In almost all cases, the highest form of self-defense, be it personal safety or career security, is the ability to see trouble coming and be somewhere else before it arrives.

I was playing a gig once on the wrong side of the tracks and during a break was sitting at the far end of the bar away from the door. Suddenly, I heard six distinct pops outside. Naturally, everyone rushed to the door, and as one of them passed he asked if I was interested in what was going on. I told him I knew exactly what was going on. The sounds coming my way told me that it was a snub-nosed 38, six shots had been fired, the shooter was currently reloading, and judging by the crowd gathered at the door, he already had sufficient targets. I was perfectly content to stay seated on my stool behind a very big chunk of wood. The trouble was outside. I chose to be elsewhere.

Knowing what's going on is important. As your own private secret service agent, you find yourself constantly gathering intelligence, checking the horizon, verifying information, and in general checking to make sure your perimeter is secure. When it looks like there's a chance for someone to screw you out of money, you see it coming and alter the arrangement to prevent the possibility from even existing. If there's a hint of malicious rumor, you're able to nip it in the bud. When others are after your gig, you're aware enough to reduce your vulnerabilities either through better performance, a stronger relationship with the person providing the gig, or other such preemptive measures. In other words, unlike so many others, you avoid being a professional target.

With just a personal coach and your very own career bodyguard, you've made a huge difference in your chances of long-term, consistent success. You sleep better at night because you know without a shadow of a doubt that you can trust the people who are on watch. And none of this cost you a dime. If you're going to invest in your career, this is without a doubt the best value on the planet.

Reality Check

I've been a creative creature all my life and in that time the most enduring, if not endearing, advice I've heard is to be realistic. This is usually offered by noncreatives who are trying to convince me that I should give up my evil ways and get a real job. In other words, go to school and become a doctor, a lawyer, or perhaps embrace other such respectable occupations. My responses and level of patience with this line of reasoning have generally been moderated by how much I cared about the relationship, meaning I would at best nod and politely smile. At worst, it was unlikely that I'd be invited back to that particular party. Probably best for all concerned.

In fairness, I do see such advice for what it is. If you live in a small world, anything beyond the known borders represents the edge of the earth, where dragons lie. Seen through their eyes, this is advice meant to save me from certain doom. How can you not appreciate such an effort? I also know that there is another translation, which is the part I really object to: Dreams are dangerous. Be safe. Don't dream. Many of these people had their own fantasies but gave them up without even trying, or perhaps after the first cold, hard bump into reality.

The world is full of people who are quick to tell you what can't be done, either because they failed at the attempt or were discouraged by the mere thought of dragons and thus never even tried. I don't need naysayers in my life. It's hard enough to leap the hurdles I encounter without the weight of all that negativity dragging me down. I'm a typical creative creature, meaning I have enough nagging insecurities, self-doubt, and bad experiences to overcome as it is. I need people to encourage me, to lift my spirits when I'm down, to kick me in the pants when I'm being lazy.

Somewhere down the line, though, I realized I needed something else. Rather than the self-defeating futility of those who fear the open sea, I needed the seasoned sailor who had seen the edge of the earth, had a drink with the dragon, and lived to tell the tale. Someone who understood what the sky looked like right before the weather lost its mind and the ocean turned upside down. A guide who could have warned me that walking into that particular tavern was a very bad idea.

Bulletproof idealism is the birthright of the young and the treasured possession of the young at heart. It's also the equivalent of painting three red concentric circles on your posterior so that life has a convenient target to shoot at. I was making far too many mistakes. I don't mind that so much, as it's nature's little way of helping me learn. What I do mind is making stupid, avoidable mistakes that a more practical perspective would have never allowed. I needed to start seeing the world as it truly was, not as I wished that it could be.

I can't put my finger on exactly when or where it happened, but I found myself using such phrases as "practical" and yes, heaven help me, "realistic." However, in my own defense, I have a completely different use for that word than my dragon-fearing friends of old. It has nothing to do with clinging to security or giving up dreams. It's all about commonsense, which I realize is not exactly a frequent flyer in the world of the artistically enabled.

Include words like "practical" and "realistic" in your vocabulary. Doing so will train you to think and act in a results-oriented manner.

If you're playing a gig with a hundred Harleys parked outside, you don't walk in wearing a Honda T-shirt. You may like Hondas, and I'm sure they're very nice motorcycles. I'm equally sure that this is going to end badly, as such bikers take a rather dim view of brands not made here in the good old US of A. You don't have to agree with that perspective. You should, however, know what you're getting into before you walk through the doors. Like knowing where the safest place to be is when someone's testing out his brand new snub-nosed 38 in the parking lot, that's just commonsense.

On matters closer to home, many of us hold views on our art that are at odds with reality. One example of this is the conviction I've seen in many different art forms that if your work is good enough you'll succeed because people appreciate quality. I agree that the cornerstone of your career should be top-notch talent. However, if you think that's all there is to it, you're in for a bit of a letdown.

I encountered a similar attitude in my years teaching sales. I had numerous applicants tell me in interviews that if the product was good, it would sell itself. In my own defense, in the many times I heard that, I only laughed out loud once. If good products sell themselves, would someone please tell me why I'm paying a commission to salespeople? I love cars and for years have driven Corvettes. You might have different preferences and I'll be happy to arm wrestle over which is best, but at the very least, most people will agree that a 'Vette is a quality product. Ever see a Chevy dealership without salespeople?

Another deeply cherished belief is that artistic people shouldn't have to know about all that business and marketing stuff. That's not their job. It's for someone else to do. That's not only cocky and arrogant (at least that's how it came out back when I used to say it), it's simply not realistic. There's nothing wrong with having someone with a proven track record book your jobs or sell your products, but you better understand every stitch of what she's doing or you have no way of knowing if you're getting the shaft or not.

My personal favorite of all the dumb beliefs I used to cling to is that if you have a good act, you'll be discovered. In very rare instances this does happen, but putting every penny you possess on "17 Red" and spinning the roulette wheel is not an effective way to plan your long-term career. For the record, it's not that bright of an idea in Vegas either. Make sure you keep cab fare tucked into your wallet for the ride back to the airport.

A better approach would be to map out a series of incremental successes you'd like to see happen, one step after another. They should be based on actual gigs and opportunities that ultimately conclude at the top of the heap. If you happen to hit 17 Red before then, you've lost nothing. If your fortunes are no different than the average Vegas attendee, you're still well on your way to the top.

It's also a good idea to see the world as it really is, by taking some chances when you see an opportunity but having a contingency plan should things go awry. Ask any combat veteran and he'll tell you that no battle plan ever survives first contact with the enemy. Being bold and daring can be an excellent way of improving your station in life. Maybe it works this time, maybe it doesn't, but if you don't have an exit strategy, you don't live to fight another day. And who knows, that next time around could be the one that puts you over the top.

Being realistic isn't about giving up dreams. It's about taking a cold, hard practical look at the world around you and seeing it for what it is, warts and all. This gives you power. By understanding that the laws of physics do in fact apply and knowing how to pull the levers, you can accomplish some amazing things. If, instead, you base your plans on wishful thinking, you're just going to ding up the paint job. Be bold. Be brilliant. And be smart about it.

Managing Expectations

We can extend this concept to expectations, both yours and that of others. Part of being realistic is seeing people for who they really are. Some are able to understand the nature of others through natural-born instinct, but even if that's not on your resume, it's a skill that can be learned. It's also a very important one to have.

The ultimate in self-sufficiency is being able to do everything yourself. Naturally, that's not something that everyone can accomplish, nor is it always practical. When you need to bring someone else into your circle to perform a particular task, there are a number of different ways it can work out. You can get lucky and find that she's everything she said she was. Things get done, no problem. At the opposite extreme is someone who wasn't as capable, motivated, or trustworthy as advertised. You usually find that out the hard way at the end of the exercise when it all comes crashing down on you. In the latter case, you then have to dust yourself off, clear away the debris of the disaster, and start over with another person, at which point you either get lucky or you don't.

If that doesn't sound like a particularly efficient approach, you do have alternatives. If you can hone your ability to see people for who they really are, you're in a position to size them up before ever agreeing to work with them. If they have catastrophe written all over them, it's hugs and kisses all around, but you move on to the next candidate. Few of us are infallible in our judgment even when we work very hard at our assessment skills, but if the dial goes from zero to one hundred, I want the needle as high as I can get it.

Perceiving a person's character and capabilities intuitively is something that many can do, but it's not easily taught. A method that's easier to reproduce involves research rather than using the Force, even if the latter does give you an excuse to buy that nifty looking light saber you've always wanted. The concept is easy enough to grasp. How a person treats others is good indication of how he'll treat you. The trick to this is to observe a large enough sample size.

Let's take the owner of a dance company who is a tightfisted and miserly guy and cheats his dancers whenever possible. Enter a new ballerina who is highly attractive and willing to entertain his advances. Since he has romantic desires and wants to win her over, he might give her gifts, preferential treatment, better pay, bonuses, and the like. Everyone else still gets treated like dirt.

If the only time you see him is when he's out and about, doting on the object of his affection and treating her like gold, you might come to the conclusion that this is a great guy and you really want to work for him. Should you choose to work for him, however, your life would be as miserable as everyone else's. And yet, you judged him based on his actions. The problem is, you had a sample size of one. Had you done enough research to see how he treated, say, twenty people, you would have quickly come to the conclusion that his treatment of the new prima ballerina was out of character and drawn a more realistic conclusion.

You'll rarely have all possible information, but in general if you perform due diligence, you're going to have a pretty good idea of who you're dealing with. It's also important to consider the source when doing your research. Let's reverse the previous example and use a guy who treats his dancers like family. A new face comes into the crowd, and after a time he does his best to completely ignore her whenever possible. You talk to people who turn out to be close friends of hers and hear story after story of how terrible he is. You then talk to various industry people who know him professionally but aren't among his circle of friends. They say just the opposite.

It turns out that he hired her because she's a big box-office draw. He then discovered that she's also a drunk, a thief, a liar, and has a violent temper. Beyond the bounds of getting the job done, he wants nothing to do with her and can't wait for her contract to expire. You have received equal amounts of opposing information. In one case, you spoke with those who were loyal to the troublemaker and had an axe to grind. The other group were people who were informed but didn't have a stake in the matter one way or the other. Suddenly, you don't have two equally weighted sets of data and are able to come to a realistic conclusion about what he'd be like to work with.

Having insight into the ethics and skills of another person requires some effort. It is easy to get the wrong impression when you listen to one or two people who may have axes to grind or debts to pay. Before you enter into an important business relationship with someone—be it a gallery owner, troupe leader, agent, or what have you—talk to as many people as you can about their experiences so that biases can be averaged out.

In addition to knowing how capable, dependable, and trustworthy people are along with the nature of their ethics, it's also important to understand a bit about their own dreams and ambitions. All other things being equal, this can be a very good indicator of how they'll behave in a given situation.

If they're morally ambiguous and an opportunity comes along that would require dishonesty on their part, maybe they go for it, maybe they don't. Having a good sense of just how far they'll go has a lot to do with knowing how appealing that particular carrot is. You're never going to have a roomful of people who are all as pure as the driven snow. Everyone has their weaknesses. Those of us in the arts have even more.

A fundamental part of crime prevention has less to do with punishing people than it does with helping them to avoid temptation. Don't put people in an unsupervised room with huge stacks of money in unmarked bills. They may be perfectly reliable in 99 percent of situations. Why set them up for failure when you could instead arrange for success?

Another benefit of knowing people's dreams is the ability it gives you to motivate them. This is not only very effective, done properly it's a positive experience for all involved. Let's say you need someone to book your band. Two of your candidates are agents and do this very thing. They're qualified and have a good reputation, but ultimately you'd be just another commission to them.

The third person has an equally impressive track record but is also a longtime fan and supporter of your band. She only works part time as an agent and has no desire to do it full time. What she really wants is to manage your band and be a part of the family, helping you grow and succeed. All three are capable of booking you and if you looked at nothing but their track record, it might be a tough call. However, by knowing that the two agencies desire to grow their companies by bringing on more bands and the part-time agent dreams of seeing you succeed, the decision gets easier. Who do you think will work the hardest for you?

Another consideration when dealing with people is understanding how easily they're influenced and who does the influencing. Sometimes the person you're talking to isn't the person you think. Using the same band, let's say that you're locked, loaded, and on your way to the big time. The music is good, the gigs are improving, the players get along, and everything's going your way. Everyone also seems equally committed to the effort. In any collaborative art, dedication to the cause is a critical consideration. Success takes time, and that means you need people who are going to stick around and occasionally sacrifice for the good of the group objectives.

With the information at hand, it looks like you're ready to make the jump from part time to full time. This involves everyone quitting their day job and going on the road. In meetings, your people are highly enthusiastic about this, so you give your new manager the go-ahead and she books six months of work for you, scheduled to begin a few weeks from now. A week before you're ready to hit the road, the bass player is suddenly skittish and balks at the idea of quitting his job. With only a few days before your first gig, you don't have enough time to bring in a new player. You're suddenly in a very bad spot.

As it happens, the bassist in question is a good player, a great guy but a weak personality. He also has a girlfriend who has a very specific vision including marriage, kids, and a house in the suburbs. Of course, this also includes a husband who is home and has a steady source of income. She is a quiet person and not conspicuously manipulative, but she is clearly the power behind the throne. All the time that you were talking to the bass player, you thought you were talking to the decision maker. To your dismay, you discover at the last moment that he's not the one who had to sign off on the road trip. She was.

In this particular situation, understanding who the influencer was would have allowed you to give your bass player a hug and a beer and begin auditions for a replacement before you started booking jobs. Regardless of the art you're involved in, if it's a group effort such relationship difficulties are common and familiar, but the concept is the same whether you're dealing with bass players, actors, club owners, distributors, or any other human being.

It's also important to set appropriate expectations for anyone you interact with. No matter what their contribution to your effort, people have varying degrees of talent and skill. Some will be masters of their craft while others will just be average producers, always consistent but never setting the world on fire. There's a place for all of them. The trick is matching the right person to the right task so that it's an opportunity for them to succeed rather than fail.

In my years of training salespeople and managing client organizations, I saw an endless parade of people. It's a transient workforce by nature, and there are also many who want to give sales a try but end up having no capacity for it. In every company, there were always a couple of superstars. What they did in a day was sometimes as much as the rest of the group combined.

You would think that the goal would be to fill your sales force with such people, but that's actually not where the money is. Top producers are finicky, high maintenance, and difficult to manage. They're also somewhat unstable. For a month or two, they're setting the world on fire. Then, inexplicably, they go into a slump and can't give stuff away, let alone make any money. Meanwhile, the steady, consistent, average producers keep delivering the same predictable business they always do.

There is an honored place in the world for the average and dependable. If you have expectations that they will grow and eventually do what your rock stars do, you're setting both of you up for failure. If, on the other hand, you leave them room to improve but plan your growth on realistic expectations, they'll serve you well until the end of time and you'll all be happy with the experience.

As with people, you put yourself in the best position when you understand the reality of a situation, knowing what the possible outcomes are and the probability of each happening. This allows you to plan effectively and be happy with the way things work out.

Let's say that you're a painter. There's a gallery down the road that caters to famous, high-end artists, and there's much glory associated with having a show there. You're good at what you do and your work is of high-enough quality to be appropriate for the venue. As you might expect, there's also an unruly horde of very talented artists vying for the few open slots.

There's a smaller gallery downtown. It has a good reputation and working with it would be a profitable experience. Showing your work there wouldn't make you rich and famous, but it would keep you eating on a regular basis for a while and continue to further your career. Because of your talent and experience, your work is a couple of notches above what they usually show. You'd be real catch for the manager of the gallery and you know he'd love to work with you.

There's no reason you can't do both. The trick is understanding the profit and percentages for each scenario and planning your life accordingly. The rock star gig is a long shot. If you were to get it, you could live for a year off of what you would make and could therefore concentrate on painting instead of trying to scare up work on a regular basis. The downtown gig would only keep you fed for two months, so you couldn't really slack off on looking for new opportunities even if you did get it. Knowing that it's unlikely you'll land the major job any time soon and that the smaller one seems more realistic, you work toward both but assume you'll have to keep chasing opportunities.

Most situations aren't "either/or." Instead, think in terms of "both/and." Surprisingly often in life, you can have your cake and eat it too.

If you only get the lower-paying gig, you haven't stopped looking for other things so you'll be in a good position. The show will probably go well, you'll make some money, people will make a fuss over you, and your career will have moved forward a notch without you missing any meals. If you happen to get the other gig as well, you can both enjoy your success and count yourself among the fortunate. Either way, because your plans were based on realistic expectations, you had opportunity combined with minimal risk. That's the best of both worlds.

The Long Game

In order to gain control over your career, and by extension your personal life, you're going to need to apply consistent effort over an extended period of time. Whether it's improving your craft, marketing, or even that New Year's resolution to lose a few pounds, the most common mistake people make would look like a very sharp spike if you saw it on a graph.

When you're excited about making something happen, it's easy to generate that initial burst of activity. Your mind is full of ideas, the possibilities seem endless, and you dive right in. For a week, maybe even a month, you live on cheap pasta, bad coffee, and no sleep while you slave away to accomplish your goals. And then, nothing.

Month two finds you doing very little in comparison to the previous period. Maybe you spend a few hours here and there, but it feels more and more like drudgery. Gone is the excitement and the adrenaline that accompanied it. With little effort, there are likely few results, so you don't have that to keep you fired up, either. By month three, the goal's pushed to the back burner, that time-honored place on the stove for projects that we're hoping the cat will make off with in the dead of the night so that we no longer have to look at them.

Not only is this approach less than productive, it can also be a drain on morale, a critical consideration. When you try and don't succeed, it takes some of the wind out of your sails. The next time you have a bright idea, part of you will be excited but in the back of your mind you'll remember all that work you did for nothing and it will dampen your enthusiasm. Fortunately, there is a better way.

The definition of hard work isn't a Herculean burst of effort over a short period of time that almost kills you. Hard work is chipping away at the stone just a little each day, and repeating that process with consistency. Let's say you're a sculptor who wants to carve an elephant out of a huge block of granite. As any good artist knows, the proper procedure is to start with your stone and then simply remove everything that doesn't look like an elephant.

You're creating a life-sized replica, so there's going to be a whole lot of chipping going on. Granite is also known for its resistance to change. Since you're intimately familiar with stubborn stones and the sweat required, you dive right into it and work seven days straight around the clock, pausing only for an hour's nap here and there when you're ready to collapse.

At the end of a week's time, there's still a lot about your project that doesn't look like an elephant. Unfortunately, you've neglected your body and get sick. After another week in bed, and low energy for days afterward, you just don't feel much like romancing the stone and give up on the project. The elephant you left stranded inside a huge block of granite is not amused.

Seeing that you're not going to do anything with this big chunk of rock in your backyard and wanting to get a little extra practice in, your apprentice decides to spend her spare time seeing if she can free the pachyderm from its predicament. She can only spend a couple of hours after work on Tuesdays and Thursdays, but she figures every little bit helps. You don't give it another thought, as you've moved on to other projects and don't spend much time outdoors anyway.

The following year, you happen to walk into your backyard. and glancing up, you see a magnificent, polished elephant glaring down on you in mock disapproval. An elephant never forgets. People, however, do and having long since forgotten about this project, you're stunned by the sight. Furthermore, it's actually a very nice piece of work, exhibiting tremendous attention to detail.

You call some of your sculptor friends over for a party. Everyone admires the elephant. A review gets published in an important magazine and before you know it, your backyard is the talk of the town. Of course, your apprentice is getting the much deserved attention for her work and soon finds herself considering a number of lucrative opportunities. The elephant couldn't be more pleased.

You worked a hundred times more intensely in that week than she was capable of, and you also possess a high degree of skill that exceeds that of an apprentice. You also only put in seven days of work. Your apprentice, on the other hand, just kept patiently chipping away at the stone, week after week, month after month. The chunk of granite became an elephant-shaped lump, and then a crude rendition of a large, leathery mammal. From there it progressed into a decent statue but with continual effort, tweaking, and attention, it eventually became a magnificent, highly refined work of art, even though it was just at the hands of an apprentice.

When you have goals in mind, it's usually because you need or want something. Because we humans can be an impatient lot, we often want it right away, because our need is now. If, for instance, what you're trying to generate is money, having more of it today would be really nice. What we tend to forget, however, is that this time next year we're still going to need it.

Building a career requires long-term strategy, not short-term thinking. You're going to want better opportunities, more money, and greater prestige this year to be sure. The same can be said a year from now, and though it's so far away it might seem like another planet, you're even going to want it twenty years from now. Take care of business to address today's demands, but play the long-term game. That's what really gets you down the road, and that's where time management can be incredibly valuable.

Know Thyself

The first rule of effective time management is actually a pretty good starting point for any venture. Know thyself. If you plan with your enthusiasm rather than your brain, you're just going to end up with an unsightly chunk of stone in your backyard, and the neighbors will talk. The first step, then, is to look in the mirror and see your strengths and weaknesses as they truly are. No good, no bad, no judgment; just an honest and realistic assessment of what you have to work with.

Are you hyperorganized in your life with a penchant for control and a phobia of anything being three millimeters out of place? Should you follow the advice of one of your friends who suggests that you be more spontaneous and just make it up as you go along, your life would probably become a complete disaster. If you've ever waded out into the ocean and tried to swim against a very strong current, you know that fighting with more powerful forces makes you very tired. Sure, it can be done. The question you should ask is whether or not that's the most efficient use of your resources.

Many artistic types are more abstract in nature. Structure, schedules, and timetables etched in stone make them break out in a cold sweat. If you try to force yourself to perform a specific task at 6:35 each evening, your initiative won't even last a week. You're swimming against the current and you're going to look very foolish when the lifeguard has to come fish you out.

What we're looking for is consistent effort over an extended period of time. This might be applied to booking gigs, improving your skills, expanding your audience, or any number of objectives. Whatever the goal, if it's something that's going to take a large number of hours or is repetitive by nature, like getting jobs, you need a plan to ensure that you actually spend the time it takes.

The first part of the plan involves looking at your life on a typical week. You probably spend a certain amount of time working jobs, a chunk of hours honing your craft, and a very necessary block of time just goofing off and enjoying life. If you look at your life over a longer stretch of time, say a few months, and you're honest with yourself, patterns will emerge. You'll be able to see that on any given week, you could come up with five hours without making unrealistic demands on the time required by other needs.

If you're highly ambitious and a real go-getter, that may not seem like much time. Resist the temptation to declare a larger amount of hours because you think you can beat yourself into submission through sheer force of will. You'll burn out in a week and be left with an unsightly chunk of granite on your back lawn. If five hours is comfortable and consistently realistic, go with it. As our long-nosed friend would be quick to point out, it all adds up.

Next, apply that time to what you've discovered about your tendencies. If you're structured by nature, you can simply plot out which day or days you'll perform the tasks each week, and off you go.

Should you be more of the abstract variety of human, that's not going to work, but you still need to apply consistent effort over an extended period of time. The way you do that is by using larger blocks of time instead of the fine granularity a structured person would employ. Some people will be able to commit to five hours on a weekly basis and specify the days and times this will happen. A more relaxed approach might be to say that at the end of the week, by the time you go to bed each Sunday night, you will have found your five hours.

Five hours a week: that's all the time you need to move a mountain over the course of a year.

Others might twitch at even that harsh of a schedule, so perhaps it would be better for them do ten hours every two weeks. Just don't get too far into extremes or you have no plan. Telling yourself that your plan will come out to 260 hours by the end of December may be technically correct but it's functionally useless. Make the chunk as small as you're capable of by nature, but no smaller.

For all personality types, the critical consideration is keeping the promises you make to yourself. That's something that no one can teach you to do. You just have to reach down, find some inner strength to draw on, and show a little backbone. That said, the easiest way to find that power is by focusing on what it is you wanted in the first place. If you find you're having trouble keeping your own promises, there's a very good chance that you don't care about the goal as much as you thought you did. Find a goal that motivates you. You'll find the conviction to stick to your plan.

You might have noticed in passing that five hours a week is 260 hours a year. That's the equivalent of six and a half forty-hour weeks of working full time, nonstop toward your goal. If you could spare a month and a half to do nothing but work on a specific goal, imagine how much you could accomplish.

You might say in January of this year that it's hard to get excited about something you won't achieve until Christmas. What you have to remember is that this time next January, you're still going to be alive and kicking, sitting in the same chair, and having the same desire to move your career forward. However, what you'll have sitting in the chair next to you are the fruits of your labors, those benefits you earned by finding five hours a week the year before. It can be very rewarding indeed and you can get there putting forth very little effort each week.

When you first start working on long-term goals, time management, and self-discipline, chances are good you're going to fall flat on your face—and more than once. You'll have false starts, encounter distractions, get frustrated, deal with unexpected life situations, and in general screw up in an impressive variety of ways. If you're like most people, you'll be tempted to come down hard on yourself for failing. It doesn't take much imagination to realize that this doesn't help you. Furthermore, you don't deserve to be criticized. You're trying something new. What, you thought you'd be perfect on the first try?

It's going to take you a few tries to get the kinks out of the system and find the groove that works for you personally. It doesn't matter if your best friend does it one way with great results. You have to find the approach that's comfortable for you. No one else's style matters.

You also need to become good at rebooting. You're going to get knocked off track over and over again. Life is an unpredictable adventure and there's not a thing you can do about it. Your only recourse, then, is to gradually get better and better at starting over. There are a couple of things that will help with this.

First, leave your self-recrimination at the door. It may feel like you're doing something constructive by criticizing yourself, but all you're really doing is letting the air out of your tires. That tends to be a little hard on the rims. You won't even realize you've fallen out of your routine for quite some time. Then, one day, it will hit you. The correct response at that point is to find your notebook, get something nice to drink, and review whatever step one was. No big deal.

The second portion is related to the first. You not only need to avoid getting angry with yourself; you need to acquire the ability to let go of the entire thing. A month has gone by and you did nothing? No worries. That was last month. This is now. Shake it off, think about this week instead of last month, take another sip of whatever it is you're drinking, and be happy. Life knocked you for a loop, but you just put yourself back on track. That's something to feel good about, which is precisely what you should do. Happy people do the best work and have the greatest endurance. They also make some pretty cool looking statues.

The end result is that eventually, and it may be a year or two, you'll get good at this. You'll know what your personal flow is and how to get in harmony with it so that you can be your most productive. You'll employ long-term thinking and become practiced at creating and executing plans, and one step at a time you'll be moving yourself down the road. That's a pretty good feeling.

Get Smart

Another thing that feels good is continually educating yourself. As with planning and time management, we each have our own style of things that work for us. Today, more than ever, there's something out there for everyone.

If you have a little money to spend on classes, books, seminars, or other such learning tools, that's great. If you don't, the Internet is a huge free resource for those with the patience and commonsense to use it properly. Whatever your passion, there will be others who share it and many of them enjoy passing along what they've learned.

Rather than paying with money, you'll pay for this type of education with time and effort. First, you have to use such things as search engines, referrals from friends, and Web links on one site connecting you to another to find relevant sources of knowledge.

Next, you have to validate that knowledge. My neighbor's cat can put up a Web site in about ten minutes, and that's if she's not busy making videos of herself. There will be a lot of good stuff out there, but it will often be buried amid a bunch of content that's either inaccurate, unprofessional, or just plain hard to follow. This is research. If you take your time and put in consistent effort, you'll be rewarded.

You'll also find that you're drawn more to some methods of learning than others. A friend might prefer video tutorials while you like to read a good book. Someone else might really need a classroom environment with an instructor who can answer questions. There is no right or wrong. Once again, it's all about finding what works for you personally. If you do, you'll be rewarded.

It's also worth noting that the way you like to learn may be different depending on the time of day or circumstances. When I get up in the morning, I read the news feeds I'm subscribed to for current events, artistic interests, entertainment, and anything else of interest. I'm bleary-eyed, clutching desperately to a hot cup of coffee, and am in no mood for sudden moves or jarring noises. If I see a link to a video, I bookmark it and run fast in the direction of the nearest article.

Later in the day, when I need a break from intense concentration, a video may be just the thing I'm in the mood for. It helps me relax and there are some things that lend themselves better to that type of presentation. Watching it at the right time of day or when my mood best suits it, a video can bring me much value. You may find that your preferences are a bit fluid as well. If they are, just go with it.

You might also maintain a list of areas where you'd like to improve. Personally, I never seem to run out of such possibilities, but that doesn't mean I'm always at the right place in my day or in my life to work on them. Keeping them stashed away somewhere allows me to come back to them when the moment is right, find the one I feel comfortable working on, and continue to move myself forward.

Your list can also be a good springboard for learning resources. As you're looking for a good resource for one area of your career or life, you may bump into something for another. Using computers, notepads, or even cocktail napkins (I kid you not), in line with what works for you personally, you can keep your goals and your methods organized so that they're handy when you need them. Just don't use the napkin to support an actual drink. Ink tends to get rather snippy about that sort of thing.

Becoming self-sufficient is a lifetime adventure. Don't try to get there overnight and don't let the effort become a source of stress for you. As you've doubtless discovered in many other areas of your life, getting better at something feels pretty good. So relax and allow yourself to have a little fun with it. Celebrate the successes, don't sweat the mistakes, and before you know it, you'll have a very impressive looking elephant in your backyard.

CHAPTER 4

What Do You Want?

Before you can get what you want, you have to know what it is that you want. If that sounds redundant and obvious, it is. That doesn't make it any less of a potential roadblock on the path to creative success.

You might think that everyone on the planet has a clear picture of their desires. It may therefore surprise you to learn that it's very common to find that we often have at best a fuzzy picture of our dreams. To further complicate matters, our ambitions change as the years go by. Sometimes this is due to shifting circumstances or exposure to new ideas. Other times it's a sign of success. Having climbed that rather impressive looking mountain, we eventually become bored with the view and seek out new conquests.

We take for granted that we know what we want. Perhaps some people do. Even so, it's well worth the exercise to take a moment and examine your passions. Before you can reach the summit, it helps to know which mountain to climb. If you don't, the Sherpas you hired as guides will just laugh at you.

What Is Success?

If you whip out your cell phone to get directions to a particular destination, it will immediately ask you where you want to go. Sure, you can say you'd like to go to New York City and the app will be happy to oblige you. Once you hit the city limits, however, you're going to be stopping strangers on the street to ask where that famous pizza joint is that you wanted to visit. That always goes over well in New York.

Perhaps you're a bit more familiar with the area and consequently tell your phone that you'd like directions to Ray's Pizza, a legendary source of all things cheesy. To your utter dismay, your phone will promptly ask you which one. There are a lot of Ray's pizzerias in the city. Which one is the original location or the most authentic has been a topic of lively debate since long before your cell phone was born.

My personal favorite was The Famous Ray's Pizza at the corner of Sixth and Eleventh in Greenwich Village. If you're on foot, or are foolish enough to drive a car and dodge the psychotic yellow cabs in the area, that information's going to be enough to get you to your destination. Your cell phone, however, could not possibly be less impressed. It will patiently ask you for a street address. It is a very stupid device. It probably doesn't even know that you have to sit on the sidewalk outside and lean against the building to eat your slices.

We tend to think of technology and all things computerized as being smart. The truth of the matter is that a computer isn't blessed with an abundance of commonsense. In fact, it's a very simple-minded creature. You program it to do extremely specific things and it will do exactly that. Nothing more.

The fact that a modern processor can do this with extreme speed, switching back and forth among a large set of specific instructions, makes it seem more intelligent than it really is. I spent a lot of years as a software developer, and I can say with authority that the light switch on your wall is smarter than the fundamental components that do the work in an integrated circuit. At least it has a dimmer as opposed to the simple true-or-false mentality of computer logic.

With that in mind, unless you tell your cell phone the exact street address or GPS coordinates you have in mind, it will give you vague results at best. What most people don't realize is that our lives behave in very much the same manner.

If you say that you'd like to make a living as a professional dancer, you may think that you have a very clear and specific goal. You do not. With no-more information than this, you could end up working the midnight shift as a pole dancer at the Pink Pussycat. Not what you had in mind? Your career trajectory, being no smarter than a cell phone, doesn't know the difference between that and the Bolshoi Ballet. You told it you wanted to be a dancer. Both are dance. There's just no convenient place for the audience at the Bolshoi to put your tips.

Additionally, in your illustrious career as a stripper, you may find yourself living in a rat-infested fleabag of an apartment with barely enough money to eat. Once again, your simplistic career path would suggest that it's met your requirements: You're not working a day job and the only thing you're doing for money is dancing. You may not be eating prime rib, but you're eating. You're also still alive. Therefore, you're making a living as a dancer.

If you develop software for a living, you'll often find yourself talking to your creations using less than family friendly language when an unwanted result appears on your screen. The response from the app is always the same. It will just roll its eyes and say, "Hey man, I did exactly what you asked me to do. The complaint department is down the hall." You'll find that your career will often speak to you in the exact same manner. Unless you know precisely, and I do mean in mind-numbing detail, what you want, you're not going to like the results.

It's worth noting that clear and unambiguous goals do not guarantee success. They are, however, one of the requirements. With that in mind, take some time to spend in reflection and self-evaluation on a regular basis. Ask yourself what you really want and record the answer in as much detail as you can.

I use the rather low-tech method of scribbling my answers down on a legal pad. That's what works for me. You might want to talk into your Web cam, record audio on your cell phone, write out documents on your pad, or utilize any other such method. Only two things matter about your chosen medium. First, it has to be something capable of capturing very specific and fine-grained detail. Second, it has to be something that feels natural and comfortable to you, or you simply won't do it at all.

Once you've made it through your list of goals, go back to the top and challenge each one. This is a great time to get in touch with your inner six year old. All you have to do is ask simple questions such as, "Why?" Another phrase you might employ is, "What, specifically, does this mean?" As you work your way through the list, looking for any hint of vagueness and forcing yourself to dig deeper, you'll quickly discover that knowing exactly what you want is a lot harder than you thought. It may give you newfound respect for your cell phone.

Repeat this cycle of writing down your goals, challenging them, and then refining the answers until you simply can't think of anything else to add. Then go through your responses and reword them into clear, concise, and detailed statements that leave no ambiguity about your desires.

It's worth noting that less supportive people, and even friends or family with good intentions, might look at your results and tell you that you're being very unrealistic. If you truly dream of working full time as a prima ballerina with the Bolshoi Ballet, don't water down your dreams because those of less ambition think it's too hard. The most important part of this entire process is honesty. You, and only you, know your heart's desire. If you merely parrot what other people think you should want, you're never going to be happy.

There is one last aspect to this practice. In addition to spelling out what you want, you should also be specific about the timeline. If you just graduated high school and want to dance with the Bolshoi Ballet by Christmas, a lot of things are going to have to come together before you can succeed, but at least you'll know what you're shooting for. On the other hand, if you want to achieve this goal by the time you're twenty-three years old, the extra time will allow for a different set of interim steps.

Either way, you have to know how much time it's going to take to transition from where you are to where you want to be in order to plot an effective course. Without a hard-and-fast date of completion, there's a very good chance that you'll spend your entire life drifting. Dreams are vague. Goals have deadlines.

Dreams are vague. Goals have deadlines.

Understanding Your Need for Validation

There's actually another deeper level of introspection required if you're to find true happiness with your art. We are creative creatures because we're driven to bring our vision to life. We also seek validation for what we do. Many talented people would immediately become defensive were we to discuss this last point.

I've had numerous songwriters tell me that they wrote what they felt and didn't need anyone's approval. These same minstrels will move heaven and earth to get a gig at the local bar so that they have an audience for their musings. I don't bother to point out the obvious to them. If they really didn't need validation, they would just sit in their living room.

Whether we're designing that hot new Web site or a fall line of clothing, we need an audience. Their attention, their applause, and their patronage fill one of our fundamental needs. Of course, for all but the most narcissistic among us, that's not the only motivation. To deny that those things exist, however, is to build little more than castles made of sand. Success can only be built on the foundation of honesty.

With that in mind, it's important to understand exactly what validation you require. This may not be the most comfortable of exercises. It requires you to look deep into your soul and express your innermost wants and needs. To do so is to enter a moment of great vulnerability. We tend to put up thick and insurmountable walls between our true desires and the interaction we have with others. When you remove these defenses, it's very easy to be hurt. When you're wide open, even the most casual remark from someone else can be devastating.

Guys will often have an even harder time with this than girls. They're equally as vulnerable, but in many environments male culture requires a sense of machismo to maintain respect. It's socially acceptable for a woman to get in touch with her feelings. If a man does it, he's a sissy. Anyone with a brain knows that this is complete nonsense, but it doesn't matter. If you open up and people make fun of you, it's going to hurt whether the attack was right, wrong, or completely unintentional.

The good news is that regardless of gender, there is no risk involved with evaluating your need for validation. It's a conversation that takes place only in your own mind. It's not important that you write it down or in any way share it with the world. All that matters is that you're truthful with yourself and come out the other end of this exercise with an accurate understanding of your emotional needs.

The difficulty comes when your inner dialogue is not a product of your personal convictions but rather what's been pounded into your brain by friends, family, and society. As you open up to yourself, you may flinch, expecting to hear someone making fun of you for a particular need. It's a conditioned reflex, and it may take some effort to work past it, but in time you can do exactly that. It may take you weeks or months to do so but that doesn't matter. You're going to be alive for a very long time, and the insights you gain will serve you for all of those years.

It's critical to understand the type of validation you seek as a result of your creative endeavors. Without this knowledge, you may never feel satisfied, no matter how large your audience or bank account. What we're considering at the moment is actually a two-part exercise. The first part is deeply personal and emotional, involving the need for love, acceptance, status, and a great many other such things. That creates the setting. From there, we move to the specific. By knowing what little corners of our soul we need filled, we can then look at our creative future and ask relevant, practical questions that will help us chart a course.

We each create for different reasons and thus require different results in order to be gratified. There is, of course, an almost endless supply of considerations. Some want to make a living at what they do while others just need an audience. Regardless of money, it's also worth noting that audiences come in different shapes and sizes. If you're a performer of some sort, you can stand in a roomful of people or reach your following through TV, movies, the Internet, magazines, books, or other such venues that are more virtual than physical.

Recognition is also a frequent flier in the skies of career ambition. To some, it doesn't matter that they have millions of screaming fans if they don't have the respect of their peers. Another form of recognition is obtained through what we call gatekeepers. The Internet allows us to take our art directly to the people without anyone's permission. You'd think that would be a good thing, but there's a flip side to the coin.

For example, this book you're reading was released through a traditional publisher. To some, that's a means of validation. A publishing company can put out only so many books per year. There are a great many authors in the world, but they picked me. The status that comes with being selected by a gatekeeper is based in part on a sense of exclusivity. They chose me. They didn't choose someone else. Therefore, in the minds of some, I must be special. Of course, my friends will be quick to tell you that there's nothing even remotely special about me, but that's a conversation for another day.

Be that as it may, the sense of validation that comes through gatekeepers is important to a great many people on both sides of the printed page, or any other such medium. To the creator, making it through the gate fills that internal need for validation by saying that she's good enough to be chosen. That may sound dumb to you, but there are some incredibly gifted people in the world don't believe they have any talent whatsoever. Being selected is important to them, even if it's not to the rest of us.

Many in the audience care about the status of being selected as well. You can find a wealth of blindingly brilliant people on the Internet, but in the eyes of many, if you weren't chosen by a gatekeeper in your particular industry, you're just an amateur. That's not true, of course, but in many areas of life perception becomes a truth of its own. Over the years, I've discovered that ignoring that reality tends to leave some rather interesting scars just below the waterline.

As an example of how this effect works, I enjoy public speaking. I'm an entertainer by nature, I love the feedback that I get from a live audience, and helping people is something that I get excited about. Because my books are released through a traditional publishing house, I'm assumed to have a degree of credibility. That makes it easier to get speaking gigs. Had I self-published this book, which was certainly among my options, would I still be credible? Personally, I don't think it should matter. However, when you're considering the intersection of your career and the real world, it's important to see things as they are, not how you believe they should be.

As an aside, if you want the inside story on why I went through this publisher, the answer is less glamorous than you might think. They're in New York and I needed a good pizza connection.

Regardless of what the real you deep inside needs, whether it's the adulation of the masses or just a decent paycheck, the path to success begins with the same first step. Know thyself.

Working for a Living

While not the only form of validation, money is one that provides a number of benefits. If you can make a living purely through your creative passion, it buys you freedom. Even if you just want to do it part time, it'll certainly buy you a pizza. Many creatives are happy with nothing more than an audience, and that's hard enough to obtain as it is. If you want to enter the world of commerce, it involves additional considerations. As you might expect, the first and foremost is the definition of your desires.

Do you want to be rich and famous, a member of that tiny elite who has more money than a Third World nation, and a face that appears on every media outlet on the planet? It might surprise you that not everyone does. Don't get me wrong, I like a good mansion as much as the next guy, but that's way too many rooms for me to clean. Before robots came along, I had a hard time just keeping the living room vacuumed.

If, like me, you're content to make a living doing the things that you love, your career path will have a distinctly different set of steps than those who are driven to appear on the world stage. Whether you want to be an international superstar or just an everyday creative creature, the choice is good as long as you're being honest with yourself. The important thing is to know what you want so that you can plan effectively.

If your heart's desire is to be a megastar who makes blockbuster movies, it's wise to assume that you may not get there in one single step. How long it takes depends on talent, planning, and a healthy dose of sheer dumb luck. With that in mind, you should give thought to what life will be like between point A and point B. In other words, once you're involved in a major motion picture, your financial situation should be in good shape. Until that time, however, how are you going to pay the bills?

If you're not practical about this, you stand a good chance of being miserable for however many years it takes to reach stardom. I see no need for you to endure that. The key to avoiding such unpleasantness lies in incremental goals. If you're a broke waitress dreaming of the big time and thinking of nothing else, you may be slinging hash for many years before you get your big break. As someone who's flipped his fair share of cheeseburgers, I can assure you that this isn't a particularly gratifying place to wait for fame and fortune.

Even though for a time I wanted to be a rich and famous rock star, I found over the years that I really enjoyed playing bars for a living. Sure, it has its less-than-glamorous moments, but I get to be in a room making music with my friends, surrounded by a lot of people who enjoy the experience. When I walk off stage, I get to hang out with the crowd and make even more friends.

Back when I was pursuing music as a career path, I wasn't on the cover of *Rolling Stone* and I didn't sell a million albums. However, I was paying the bills without working a day job, and it was a lot more fun than flipping cheeseburgers.

There are just as many opportunities for our hardworking waitress. There are local theater shows, commercials, voice-over gigs, and many other opportunities that will not make you rich and famous but will keep you out of the local diner until your big break comes. Could you find happiness in such an interim scenario, or some variation on the theme? It's well worth considering. If your spirit doesn't require an all-or-nothing approach to life, there's no reason you should have a bad time on the road trip to glory.

How Much Is Enough?

Whether you're biding your time or you're just happy doing a few gigs here and there, one of the things to include in your considerations is an evaluation of your baseline monetary requirements. In other words, how much is enough?

My best friend was a working-class musician all his life. He preferred jazz but played every type of music, and his gigs included bars, weddings, country clubs, and more than a few Holiday Inns. These were not glamorous events. I know. I played many a job with him. He always lived in modest apartments or houses, and we both gave our share of blood in order to eat. For many, this would be a dismal life that would feel like complete failure. For him, it was success. As long as he could make music and pay the bills, he was happy.

When I lived in New York, I rented a guy's bedroom. There was a shared bathroom and my kitchen was a hotplate that sat on my dresser. Two cots were lashed together to make something that resembled a full-sized bed. I was playing six nights a week in a band that was booked into the biggest rock rooms on Long Island. I wasn't making a lot of money, but I had an absolute blast.

What about you? Where's your threshold? You need to know whether you require a particular standard of living to enjoy the experience or can be just as happy with a bohemian lifestyle. Once again, there is no right or wrong answer. All that matters is that it's a truthful one.

What do you want out of your creative career? Luxurious digs and raving fans; the ability to do what you want at any moment in the day; or simply to have food, a bed, and an audience? It's your choice, but it's important to know what you want so that you'll know when you've succeeded.

Up to now, we've been speaking in terms of full-time employment, but that's not the only path to fulfilling creative work. The world is full of artistic souls who want the stability of a steady job, good insurance, and a nice house in the suburbs where they can raise a family.

You don't have to choose between working for a major corporation and pursuing your creativity. In fact, one of my oldest friends is an excellent example. A talented musician, when I met him he was working full time at IBM. On the weekends, he played keyboards for one of the hottest soul bands in town. He got paid for both.

These days, he's a project manager for a software company and is a happily married family man, something that he'd always wanted. He also travels the world as a freelance photographer, has written a book on gorillas and society in Central Africa, and just got back from New Guinea, where he was doing missionary work. No matter what your creative desires, trust me, you have options.

If you're looking for part-time work, you have a different set of things to consider than do those who depend on their gigs to pay the bills. You'll have much more flexibility in terms of income. Your creative revenue can be a supplement to increase your overall standard of living, or, if you're already doing okay in your day job, it can be an extra bonus that you can spend on pure fun.

Life is ever the exercise in trade-offs, and part-time work is no exception. Even if you do not require top dollar or a minimum number of jobs per month, you will have to juggle a more complicated schedule. Right off the bat, if already you work a nine-to-five job, you're limited in the additional days and hours that will available for taking on creative gigs. Whether you're living with the love of your life, raising kids, or are just in the middle of a budding relationship, you'll also find that people require time and attention. As you consider pursuing your creative fulfillment, you'll also need to factor in how much of those things you'll have time for.

Full or part time, it's also worth doing a quick reality check on how much work is actually out there. If you're an actor who wants to do nothing but the works of Shakespeare, you'll doubtless find opportunities in a local theater no matter where you live. That might be enough to satisfy you if you're only seeking part-time work. If you're set on full-time employment, however, you may need to do extensive travel in order to work on a regular basis. If you're not single, you have additional considerations. Some relationships can handle extended absence on a regular basis and remain strong. Others, not so much.

All of these factors contribute to the overall picture of your lifestyle. Once you have a firm grasp of what will make you happy, you'll be in a position to consider the practical details of how to bring that dream to life. Knowing what you want out of life in terms of comfort, stability, travel, relationships, money, and all those other little details of the human experience gives you power. When you have a detailed understanding of your desires and their implications, the steps you need to take in order to achieve them become much clearer.

By the way, these are all things that I still think about on a regular basis. I've been fortunate enough to do a lot of creative things. However, as I mentioned earlier, there's always that next mountain to climb, and so my self-examination never ends. Sometimes, in the midst of all this naval gazing, I experience a bit of blank-page syndrome.

I've found it helpful at such times to simply look at the world around me. From the scandalously wealthy to the part-time pole dancer, whatever you want to do, someone else has probably done it. Consequently, I draw inspiration from the lives of others. I may not take the exact same path, but there's nothing like a real-world example to get you back on track.

The Perfect Gig

As you delve deeper into what you want, the questions become both more specific and easier to answer. Whether you're looking for full- or part-time work, once you have a strong sense of what you want out of the experience, you can begin painting the picture.

If you're a graphic artist, there are a wealth of opportunities for employment. Consequently, asking yourself whether you want to work as an employee or be self-employed is a sensible question. Other forms of creativity have a fuzzier picture when it comes to finding work.

If you're a drummer who likes to play country and bluegrass, the thought of being an employee might seem inappropriate. Musicians tend to think of being an employee as sitting in rush-hour traffic en route to a day job. Nonetheless, if you play in a band, someone is responsible for paying you, even if it's you.

A band can be a collaborative effort, which is much like a company with several partners. It can also be a sole proprietorship where one person who is in charge, books the gigs, and pays the players. Do you want to be

Have Fun, Get Paid

a business partner, a sole proprietor, or an employee? We're each suited for different roles. You won't be happy unless you choose the one that's right for you.

Once your position is clarified in your mind, it makes finding work that much easier, because you have a smaller and more well-defined set of considerations to manage. If you don't want the responsibilities of being in charge, you can narrow your search to working with bands that have a strong leader, that are in need of a drummer, and that play the style of music you prefer. If you don't like being a passenger but also don't want the pressure of being the only guy to scare up the money, you can seek out a more collaborative experience. If you're an alpha personality, you put the word out for players and start your own band.

No matter which option you choose, you're now looking for the kind of work that will be gratifying for you. Because you know exactly what you're looking for, it will also be much easier to find. At this point, we'll circle back to the beginning of the thought process and once again ask, What is success?

Now that you have more details about what you want, you're in a position to start visualizing the perfect scenario. While many of the principles we have considered are common to all artistic endeavors, at this point in the process the details will be very closely related to your specific art.

There is a very long list of creative disciplines. Some, like software development or graphic design, seem so close to the business world as to appear at first glance to be more job than art. That's an illusion, of course, as they're first and foremost a way of expressing creativity and only monetized as an additional consideration. Other arts have the exact opposite problem. If you love writing poetry, few would question its artistic merit but many would have difficulty seeing it as commercially viable.

In reality, they're all art and they all have monetary potential. It's worth reiterating that commercial enterprise is not the enemy of art, nor does it diminish its legitimacy. It's simply a phrase that means you get paid for what you love to do. If you want money for your creation, that's commerce. Those who pay the bills in such a manner will be quick to point out that when the rent comes due, commerce is indeed your friend.

Now that you know the type of work you want to do, how much income you need, and the lifestyle adjustments you're willing to make, you can start thinking about the types of gigs you would like to do at this point in your career.

If you're a graphic artist, you may be able to work in the digital domain, the physical, or both. Chances are good that you'll have some preferences. Some will pursue work on comic books and graphic novels. Others will sell their creations as an entrepreneur. Another group will interact with the corporate world, designing graphics for software and the Web as either a full-time employee or a freelance artist.

These are just a few of the options, but it gives you an idea of how to look at your own situation. Artistic people seem to come factory equipped with blinders preinstalled. If I love this, everything else must therefore suck. I've fallen prey to this thinking myself in earlier years, but over time I found that it was limiting.

It's a very helpful thing to take a couple of steps back and view your entire artistic discipline, not just the subset of it that you're currently obsessed with, and give each little subsection a closer look. If you can do so with an open mind, you might be surprised to find additional areas of interest and opportunity that will expand both your artistic expression and your bank account.

I'm a hippie musician who came of age in the 1970s and '80s. We're all heavily influenced by the cultural tides that are prevalent when we're young adults. The 1970s was a period of spiritual seeking. In the 1980s, we just wanted to have fun. In that decade, I also spent time teaching sales and found a love of helping people improve their lives as a result. Just before the 1990s showed up, I discovered software development. I found that creative process to be very similar to tales I'd heard of heroin addiction. It also allowed me to sneak into the corporate world through the side door. All of these experiences have left an indelible mark on who I am as a creative creature.

In addition to my love of rock-and-roll, I'm also a writer. When I first started putting pen to paper, my head was still wrapped up in spiritual seeking, the quest for the meaning of life. Consequently, that was the only kind of writing I wanted to do. It didn't matter if I possessed talent for any other form. I simply wasn't interested. Had you asked me to write a business book, I would have run screaming out of the room covering my ears.

When the dial flipped to the year 2000, I'd been paying the bills for quite some time in the world of software. It was fun, but I was looking for additional things to do, so I thought I'd try writing books. As a working-class programmer, I had some street cred in that area. However, most software books are essentially geek manuals that teach you the bits and bytes of how to use a particular technology. Yuck. That might be fun for some, but it sounded like factory work to me.

About that time, one of my geek friends was running a very popular Web site for programmers and asked me to write a column, not about the bits and bytes but about the business, the people, and the real-world aspects of managing a career. He also said he would be paying for me to be the wise ass that he knew me to be. Who could refuse? Writing those columns led to writing my first book, *The Career Programmer*, which addressed those very things along with occasional references to the night watchman's attack Chihuahua.

A couple of years later, I wrote the first edition of *Unite the Tribes*, which is a book on leadership and thus spoke to the corporate world. Both *Career Programmer* and *Unite the Tribes* came after my experiences of teaching sales, working in software development, witnessing the mind-numbing stupidity of many corporations, and other such adventures.

In the 1970s and '80s, I would not have enjoyed writing a book that taught geeks how to survive their career or leaders how to bring out the best in their people. I wanted to write about spiritual seeking. All you need is love, yeah, yeah, yeah. I still had the mindset that what I wanted to do was good, and therefore everything else sucked. As the years went by, I began to see life through a wide-angle lens and because of that, I've had some fun creative experiences. I'd still love to know the meaning of life, and it would be great if all we needed was love, but I'm no longer constrained to that perspective. Today, I enjoy the practical side of life as much as the artistic, and I have a much wider range of opportunities that I enjoy as a result.

View life through a wide-angle lens that brings in other views and perspectives. New opportunities are bound to come your way as your interests evolve.

It's very likely that your interests will evolve and expand as you go through life. Because of this, it's worth taking a step back and reaching for the wide-angle lens. The things you weren't interested in a decade ago may now have newfound appeal. With every new aspect of your art form that you embrace comes new opportunity. That means a wider range of gigs to choose from.

You also have more flexibility. Today you can spend time in the studio as a painter. Tomorrow you can design a logo for a big corporation. On the weekend you can work on graphic novels. You don't have to be just one thing, and neither do your gigs. All that truly matters is that you know which types of jobs you enjoy. From there, the opportunities become much more obvious.

How Badly Do You Want It?

Although we've been considering what you want, that's not the whole story. It doesn't matter what type of creativity you're drawn to. You're going to have lots of competition. The room was crowded enough before the days of a global computer network. Now, thanks to the Internet, you compete for work with every other person on the planet. Regardless of how you define success, it's not going to just fall in your lap. You're not only going to have to work for it, you're going to have to work very, very hard. This is not an arena for the faint of heart.

If you want to get paid, you're going to have to step outside of your comfort zone. It's not enough for you to sit back, do the fun artistic things, and expect someone else to make the work magically appear. You have to actively engage, or that work will go to someone who does. This brings up an entirely new set of things for you to consider as you contemplate your naval.

If you found considering the topic of validation uncomfortable, you may also find our next foray into self-examination difficult. They're deceptively easy to answer until you dig deep and commit yourself to total honesty. They fall into another one of those areas where parroting what you think is expected of you won't be of much use. That's because you won't just be answering questions. You'll also be making commitments.

Building a career of any description requires effort above and beyond improving your creative skills. How many hours a week are you willing to work at it? For most of us, doing all that businesslike stuff of beating the bushes and looking for work is unappealing to say the least. Without that effort, however, you simply won't get any results. No pain, no gain.

You need to be honest with yourself about how hard, and how consistently, you're willing to work on the noncreative side of things. Only then can you put together a plan of action based on reality, which is the only kind that ever succeeds. If you tell yourself that you'll spend four hours a night, five days a week, to address the career aspects of your art and base your strategy on that, what happens when you find that you can barely force yourself to spend two hours once a week?

It's not just the total amount of hours that will be affected. In planning, things often depend on the step that was taken before. Remove those steps and your world becomes chaos. A plan based on two hours a week, consistently executed, is far more effective than ambitions of twenty hours' worth of work that never gets done.

In addition to the amount of effort, you need to think about your capacity for enduring rejection. When you're out there trying to make things happen, you're going to hear no nine times for every one yes that you get. Rule number one of sales is developing the ability to build a wall around your emotions that you can erect at will. If you can't do this, each and every no is going to hurt.

We're all capable of building this barrier. Even so, some defenses will be stronger than others. Consequently, you need to have a realistic understanding of how much work you're willing to put into building a thick skin and how effective it will be. This will then tell you how much rejection you can endure without being damaged. Plans based on a realistic evaluation of this will subject you to no more than you can handle, and thus you'll be able to execute them consistently over the long haul.

You'll also have to endure other discomforts and sacrifices. While I've slept on more than a few floors in my life, I'm not a big fan of suffering for my art. I don't believe that it's a requirement. However, if I want something bad enough, I'll put up with some inconveniences, up to a point. That said, I have my limits. Do you know what yours are? You may have to live on less money, sleep in less-than-optimal surroundings, and give up time with family and friends. That's just the short list, of course. The pursuit of creativity comes with no shortage of potential discomforts.

As with your capacity for rejection, you need to have a firm and honest understanding of exactly what you're willing to endure for the sake of your dreams. It doesn't matter if the guy down the street gets all macho and belittles you because your efforts aren't as Herculean as his. You are two different people. What works for him may be a disaster for you. On the other hand, if you each approach your career in harmony with your nature, you'll each make solid and consistent progress.

As you evaluate your capabilities and boundaries, you'll also need to weigh the trade-offs. Paying jobs mean expectations. The person paying you gets to call the shots. Sometimes you'll both be on the same page. Other times you'll have to make artistic compromises in order to secure the work. Where you draw that line is an individual matter. Greater freedom of expression often means less opportunity for income. It doesn't matter whether freedom or expression is more important to you, only that you know where the line is so that you can be happy with the work you get.

Job security is a closely related consideration. It's difficult to verbally describe a cartoon, but I think this one is worth it. In the very early years of the cartoon strip, Garfield appears in an animal shelter as the masked avenger, there to rescue the poor, captive animals. As he throws the cage doors open, he proclaims, "You're free! You're free!" The animals all cling to the inside of their cages in terror. He then observes that they must not be terribly into freedom these days and proceeds to slam all the cage doors shut, reassuring them, "You're secure! You're secure!" One person's castle is another's cage. Do you know which yours is?

We touched on relationships in the context of travel a bit earlier, but romance occupies an entire area all its own. Having a husband, wife, boyfriend, or girlfriend is challenging enough as it is. Were that not the case, everyone on the planet would be living happily ever after even as we speak. If you're passionate about your creativity, you're going to dedicate a significant portion of your life to its pursuit. That can leave the person you love feeling a little left out.

Because the pursuit of art often creates conflict with loved ones, many creatives avoid both serious relationships and raising children. You don't have to sacrifice one for the other, but know that a balanced life requires hard work. Be prepared to put in your fair share.

I'm the poster child for this particular mistake. I've been deeply immersed in my creative projects my entire adult life. While there was a brief period in the early rock-and-roll days when I lived with promiscuous abandon, I'm really a one girl kinda guy. And I've had serious, long-term relationships with some really great girls at that. Lots of them. In other words, I'm apparently not very good at balancing the creative drive with the needs of another real, live human being. Whatever value they might find in me, there's very little of it if I'm not around.

If you think meeting the needs of one person is a challenge, you can imagine what happens if you're raising a family. That takes things to an entirely new level. The person you fell in love with might understand. The kids won't, nor should they. They are completely dependent on their parents, both physically and emotionally.

As with creative compromise, there is a line to be drawn in terms of relationships. Whether it's closer to the creativity or to the romance is a personal matter, but you'd better know where that line is or you'll experience one emotional disaster after another. Of course, for the married-with-children crowd, decisions regarding the raising of small human creatures transcend the domain of preference and enter the realm of responsibility.

Knowing my nature, I made a decision very early in life to not have children. When I was young, people just assumed that I'd grow out of it, but I was quite serious. As a middle-aged man, I still feel the same way and know that it was the correct decision for me. That said, if you think such a choice limits your opportunities for interaction with the females of the species, you're not far from the truth.

We all learn, evolve, and grow as the years go by. There are also aspects of our nature that are likely to remain constant. I know who I am, and being a creative creature isn't something I can turn on and off at the flick of a switch. Would I like to find true love and artistic gratification all rolled into one? You bet. And I'm not dead yet, so I haven't given up on that dream. As I plan on ways to do that, however, I remain unflinchingly honest with myself about my art, my nature, and the consequences for relationships. Only when you're truthful with yourself in these matters can you chart a course that won't put you at the bottom of the ocean.

If you're driven by a creative urge that won't be denied, you're going to have to work hard to have a successful career at it, whether you're a weekend warrior or a full-time artist. It's going to require a great many compromises and hard decisions, forcing you to take a close look at your priorities and to plan based on reality rather than wishful thinking. I've had a great time with life thus far, and it only looks to be getting better. You can, too, but only if you're willing to do the hard stuff.

You Gotta Believe

Some of the things I've pointed out might sound a bit discouraging. At the very least, I've advocated a lot of hard work and urged you to delve into areas that may well be outside of your comfort zone. There are people who create because it's a passing interest, and there are those who are simply wired that way, unable to be anything but the creative creatures that they are. If you fall into the former camp, all this truth-and-consequences talk may scare the pants off of you. If that's the case, there's no need for you to stop doing the expressive things that you love, but you should definitely stay out of the career end of the pool. It gets deep in a hurry, and there are no lifeguards on duty.

On the other hand, if your DNA is indelibly stamped with the mark of the artist, leaving you no happiness in life without the pursuit of your dreams, you're in luck. You don't need a lifeguard. Swimming really isn't that hard to learn.

Of all the things we've evaluated thus far, the one thing I haven't mentioned is belief. It's a word that gets interpreted in many ways. Some consider it to be akin to faith, accepting a precept in the absence of proof. Others view it as a matter of self-confidence. I would imagine there are a number of other perspectives as well. If you're trying to work in your chosen field, I think they all apply.

Without a doubt, you have to believe in yourself. Those who lack your talent will often try to tear you down, driven by their own insecurities and inadequacies. Others will tell you to give up on your dreams and pursue a nice, safe, predictable life where the bar is set much lower. They'll do it out of love and concern for your future, but it's a limitation just the same.

You'll have competing talents in addition to the person holding any paying work telling you that you're not good enough. You may also have the landlord telling you that you're out at the end of the month unless you cough up the rent. Without self-confidence, these forces will grind you into a very fine powder.

Perhaps that's where faith comes in. Whatever your belief system, from the pragmatic scientist who looks out the window and sees billions of galaxies to the spiritual person who bonds with forces yet unseen, sometimes you just have to have a little faith that things will somehow work out for the best.

Assume things will work out. The more you believe they will, the more effort you'll put into bringing your dreams to life. Optimism and practicality are an unstoppable combination.

I don't pretend to understand the mysteries of life. The closest I'm likely to get to explaining the larger forces that surround us is by quoting Yoda. All I know is that there have been many times in my life when the only thing that kept me going was the irrational belief that I was going to somehow land on my feet. The fact that I did can be attributed to many factors, but one thing is certain. Without a little faith, I would have just given up, thus guaranteeing failure. If a Jedi master would like to drop by and explain why it all worked, I'll have the tea kettle waiting. In the meantime, I'm just going to keep the faith. When things get crazy, it's the only thing that keeps me sane.

Being a creative creature is a wonderful experience. You'll also be delighted to know that the overwhelming majority of your competitors out there don't want to know anything at all about this pesky business and career stuff. That means you're in a much stronger position than you realize. It is absolutely possible to build a solid and gratifying career doing what you love. You just have to know what you want. And you gotta believe.

CHAPTER 5

Think Like a Start-Up

You are not a ballerina. You are not a programmer. You are not a poet. You are a start-up company. If you want money, that pesky little substance required by all who wish to pay the bills, you have to think like a business.

There is no word in the English language that generates fear and loathing in the hearts of creative creatures the way business does. For some, it is the antithesis of everything they believe in artistically. For such deluded (and typically broke) souls, the domain of commerce is devoid of passion and meaning. In it, they see nothing but cold, hard cash and the transactions that generate it, a world lacking both beauty and art.

In defense of the artistically pure, it's true that the titans of industry are concerned first and foremost with profitability, not art. That said, if you can't bring yourself to deal with the realities of the business world, then you will forever be a hobbyist, someone whose creativity is an expense rather than a source of revenue.

There is nothing wrong with having a creative hobby. Personally, I think the world would be a better place if every man, woman, and child on the planet had one. However, my audience is not the hobbyist but rather the creative person who wishes to pay all or some of her bills through her expressive talents. You simply can't do that without intersecting with the business world.

While I'm defending things here, I'd also like to point out, as I have earlier, that money is not evil. True, some people do evil things to acquire it and others use it to achieve unethical results. There are also people who do terrible things with hammers.

I once knew a construction worker who was a bit on the rowdy side and prone to getting in bar fights. When he went drinking, he'd wear his tool belt, which included a hammer hanging from a convenient loop. If you think that the common hammer can't be employed with devastating effect, I'd like to remind you that it was Thor's weapon of choice.

If you do bad things with construction tools, they're going to put you in jail. I will nonetheless be an ardent supporter of hammers everywhere. People used them to build my house. In a similar fashion, money can be the cause or the tool of evil. If you do bad things with it, or to obtain it, they will lock you up. That's not going to stop me from utilizing it as a beneficial resource. Simply put, if you have hang-ups about money or business, get over it or get used to being broke. You have no other options.

Fortunately, if you can manage to get past the twitch factor of interacting with the business world, the rest is fairly straightforward. In fact, once you've realigned your perspective, you'll find that the pursuit of business is a creative art in its own right. All of those products and services that you enjoy didn't just spontaneously appear in a puff of smoke, although I'm sure the marketing department would be delighted were that the case.

What you're holding in your hands right now started out as an idea. I'm not talking about my words but rather the physical medium you're experiencing them through. Perhaps it's a printed book, but it could just as easily be a desktop computer, a dedicated e-Reader, a pad, a music player, or even your cell phone. Products start with imagination, but the creative process continues until it's something tangible.

When you want to build an audience for something, whether it's a new product or a dance recital, you have to find a way of getting people's attention. A huge amount of creativity goes into that. Why do you think the people on Wall Street spend billions of dollars annually to hire creative entities like the Madison Avenue advertising agencies? Devising a strategy to build your audience, secure more gigs, and advance your career is great fun in its own right once you see it for the blank canvas that it is.

As long as all you think about is art, all you'll get is art. If you want money, you have to think like a business. The two are not mutually exclusive. You can, and should, do both. Whether you're just getting started or have been in the game for a while, the best mindset you can adopt is that of the start-up company. They always have the most innovative thinkers because they have to elbow their way into a crowded landscape and convince people that they're worth considering.

Start-ups are also an excellent source of inspiration. Apple is one of the richest companies in the world. It started out as a couple of guys in a garage. The industry-dominating player it was up against was IBM. Think about that the next time you complain about having a hard time getting work because the competition is too tough.

You Are the Product

Apple started out selling computers. That was its product, and that's the way most businesses are run. The product or service is separate from the people who run the company, unless of course you happen to be a hooker.

For most of the creative arts, the abstraction between product and purveyor doesn't exist. If you're a performing artist, you are the product. Even if you're a graphic artist or fashion designer, there's a deep emotional connection between you and the product. In a very real sense, it's an extension of you.

This is why so many talented people freeze like Bambi in the glare of a freight train's headlamp when the topic of business comes up. In the previous chapter, we talked a bit about the individual need for validation and how fragile that area of the personality can be. It's very similar to what it feels like to sell yourself as a product. Our lively and confident ladies of the evening have made peace with this, but for the rest of us it can be an awkward and uncomfortable experience.

The artistic world is no stranger to huge egos and arrogance powerful enough to launch a probe to Mars. As often as not, these qualities are usually attached to those who merit them the least, and we tend to view those people as shallow, phony blowhards. Most of us are more sparing with self-praise. In fact, because so many of the egotistical come across as fools, the last thing we want is to look like them.

Even if that weren't an issue, we must each do battle with our personal demons and dragons, who most often appear as a less-than-accurate self-image. It doesn't matter how many times you stand on stage and hear the crowd roar. If you don't believe you're really all that talented, the audience isn't going to convince you otherwise.

In the world of business, you start with a product and then proceed to promote it. This means that we, as creative creatures, must in effect stand on a platform and tell people why we're great. For most of us, myself included, that can be an uncomfortable experience.

If the audience approves of what I do and applauds, that's appreciated. If they tell their friends the next day that they heard me speak and it was great, I'm okay with that. If someone writes a review and says they enjoyed a book I wrote, I'm grateful.

These are all forms of promotion in their own way. The only difference is who's doing it. If you say something nice about my art, I can graciously accept it. If I say it about my own work, I sound like a pompous jackass. At least that's what it feels like to me, and I know I'm not the only person who experiences this.

Your art, whatever it is, won't sell unless you promote it. It's as simple as that. So suck it up and get on with it. As you get better at it, you'll start to make money doing what you love, at which point you'll enjoy the marketing more as well. Success is always fun.

Nonetheless, if I play in a band, I'm expected to spread the word. If I'm speaking at an event, part of my job is to bring in a larger audience. If I write a book, it's my responsibility to do interviews, sign books, and anything else that would help both me and my publisher succeed. I am the product. Waving my own banner feels egotistical. On the other hand, a very fundamental rule of business is that products do not sell without promotion. Therefore, if I want to make money with my art, I have to suck it up and do my part with the hopes that people will see what I'm doing as spreading the word about something I believe in rather than an exercise in self-aggrandizement.

Tech Start-Ups Are a Great Example

Once you've done enough naval gazing to get over the twitch factor that inevitably comes with self-promotion, it's time to start thinking like a start-up. I have a natural bias toward the tech industry since I've spent so many years in that world. These days, though, you don't need to be a professional techie to be included in that sphere of influence.

Most of us spend at least a little time on the Internet and with our computers and mobile devices. We've heard of the dot-com boom and bust, where fortunes were made and lost in the gold-rush atmosphere of the early Internet craze. Because of this, the notion of a tech start-up is more familiar to us than the inner workings of IBM would have been to the average creative person fifty years ago.

Even though Steve Jobs and Steve Wozniak started Apple in a garage, they're not the best example of a modern start-up for our purposes. They were in the hardware business. The geeks who launched a thousand Web sites, on the other hand, were in the software business. Both are technical and have their challenges, but software in many ways is a much easier business to launch.

I can sit at home in my bunny slippers and create a Web site with nothing more than my computer and a text editor. In fact, I have done so on many occasions. Were I to have hardware ambitions, I would be faced with not only the design but also the expense of supplies and manufacturing, the logistics of shipping and order fulfillment, and a great many other complications. If there were a design flaw, I wouldn't be able to just push a new version of the product to the Internet. I'd have to throw away physical products and pay to build them again.

Of the two, software development is much closer to the nontechnical arts such as music or dance. You have an idea. You do it. You build an audience. You get rich and retire to an island in the Caribbean.

In fact, that's the desired career trajectory of those who launch a tech start-up. The goal is to get rich through their artistic talents. They start with a vision and bring together the creative creatures they need to bring it to life. More importantly, they understand that their audience isn't going to create itself.

The successful entrepreneur knows that a business venture like this is a team sport. It requires software developers, graphic artists and designers, writers, testers, and others to build the product. It then requires an equally diverse and talented group of people to market and promote that product so that customers will be willing to spend money on it.

Once sales are happening and money is rolling in, there is also a need for accountants, administrative personnel, customer service reps, and others to support the infrastructure. Put it all together and you have a business with a good shot at growth.

Depending on your artistic discipline, you likely won't have even a tiny fraction of this staff at your disposal. Instead, you'll be wearing many of these hats yourself and delegating the others to people you contract with for the task.

For example, I don't employ a marketing rep or hire a PR firm. I teach myself how to do those things. On the other hand, no way am I going to do my own taxes each year. If it was just me working a salaried job and filling out a 1040, I'd be fine with it. Since I run a small business, I have both corporate and personal tax returns to file. I don't want to become an expert in corporate tax law, but I do want to stay straight with the IRS.

Consequently, each year I call my accountant, give him the appropriate paperwork, and pay him to do the job for me so that I know it's right the first time.

Like any successful entrepreneur, you'll need to assess the various jobs that need to be done and then put some thought into how to accomplish the work. Since artists are rarely flush with spare cash, it's in your best interest to make use of the many educational resources at your disposal and learn to do everything you can yourself. If you hit a wall and simply don't have the skills to do a job, allocate a portion of the money you make to hiring someone qualified who can. Think of it as just the cost of doing business.

Tech Start-Ups Are a Terrible Example

Everything I've just said about the world of geek enterprise is true, at least for some companies. Tech start-ups are also the worst possible examples you can follow. In order to truly appreciate the folly of their business practices, let me give you a quick overview of the landscape and a little background.

There are a great many reasons that the dot-com crash happened at the turn of the century, but there was a central theme to it, which, surprisingly, lives on even today. Even though the Internet, being nothing more than a global computer network, had been around for decades, it was only in the 1990s that it hit the public consciousness. When it did, everyone proclaimed it to be the way of the future and countless people rushed off, mining tools in hand, to make their fortune on this new frontier.

Because it looked like there was serious money to be made, venture capitalists were investing wildly in anything that even smelled like a Web site. For those who don't know, a venture capitalist is someone who invests money in your start-up in return for partial, though often massive, ownership in your company. From a business point of view, it's legalized gambling.

If you look up venture capitalist in the dictionary, you'll see a picture of a shark. They are often involved in highly predatory operations. However, in a rather karmic turn of events, the shark, in this case, ended up being the prey.

The model for a Web site start-up, both in the midst of the dot-com craze and today, is simple. A developer has an idea for a cool site. It's new. It's shiny. It sounds like something people would want to use. However, developers need to pay the rent, so they go in search of someone to invest in this great idea. That's where our fin-wearing friends come in.

The idea might be a social-media site, a new way to share pictures, a blogging platform, or anything else that sounds popular. Everyone agrees that yes, this is very exciting. The masses will love it. Invariably, the plan is to launch as a free service to build an audience. The investors invest. The developers develop. Ultimately, the product is launched.

I know it's impolite to give spoilers, but I'm going to tell you how the story ends. The audience grows. The developers burn through the cash. There's still more to do, so the investors pony up more money. This goes on for as many cycles as the money men are stupid enough to tolerate. Eventually, someone wakes up and discovers that there's no clear path to monetization. That's business speak for, "Whoops, we forgot to figure out how to make money with this." The company goes out of business. The developers move on to the next sucker. The venture capitalists write the loss off on their tax returns. The audience they built is left out in the cold. Rinse and repeat.

In simpler terms, these people have decided to create something that's very cool from an artistic point of view. They immerse themselves in the process of bringing it to life. Finally, they come up for air, proud of what they've created, only to face the harsh reality that no one has the slightest idea of how to make money with it. This is very much like putting a polka band together, rehearsing for a year, and then realizing that there's not a bar in town that wants to hear a polka.

Before you plunk down your hard-earned money to launch a business, be absolutely certain there is a market for your offering. Even really smart money lenders forget this part.

You should take the best from the world of tech start-ups, but there's also great value to learning from their worst. If I walk down the same unlit street each night, it would be useful to know where the potholes are. If I break my ankle by stumbling into one, I gain this information the hard way. If I see the guy in front of me break his, I learn the same thing, but without the pain. With apologies to my now-limping friend, better him than me. Experience is the best teacher. That doesn't mean it has to be your experience.

Business Plans

If you reach a point where your career is doing well and you really want to take it to the next level, there is no end to the educational resources at your disposal to help you become a better businessperson. To get you started, however, let's take a tour of the basics. This won't earn you an MBA, but it will get you thinking about the various career options you have and how best to approach them.

A business plan sounds very official, and in fact gets tossed around quite a bit by the MBA crowd, usually over expensive martinis. (The people eavesdropping from the next table are probably venture capitalists.) In reality, a business plan is exactly what it sounds like—a plan for running a business. From that perspective, it's not really that intimidating, is it?

Since you are your own business, you need a plan. To start with, you need to know what path you're taking. There are three basic options. As an employee, you work for a company and are provided with a fixed salary. Depending on the kind of company, you may also receive benefits such as health insurance. Taxes are withheld by the employer, and at the end of the year the money is applied to the taxes you owe Uncle Sam. You may break even or pay a little extra, or you could get a refund.

The next option is working as an independent contractor. You do a job, you're paid for the job and you're done. Maybe they hire you again, maybe not. It's up to you to find gigs and set your prices so that it's a profitable experience. Any expenses you incur are yours to bear, so what you get paid isn't necessarily what you take home. Additionally, while you're still responsible for taxes each year, no one manages that for you. It's your responsibility to put a portion of each dollar earned into savings so you can pay the tax man when the bill comes due. The IRS doesn't want to hear that the dog ate your checkbook.

A more fully realized version of the independent contractor is running a full-on business. You may do this as a sole proprietor or with partners. The number of employees you have is also a variable. While there may be a few more moving parts, conceptually this is just an extension of contracting. You offer products and services, you pay your expenses, you pay your taxes, and you keep the profits.

Technically, working for someone as an employee isn't a business. I've listed it among three possible business plans because at a higher level we're looking at the three major categories of making a living. Each of these has benefits and challenges. What's important is choosing the one that's the best fit for you. A high-paying job that sucks is still a job that sucks. A lesser-paying job that's a joy to do makes for a happy life. I'm going to make a stretch here and assume we're going for happiness. With that in mind, let's take a more detailed look at your options.

Help Wanted

In many arts, this is the most stable and safe approach. You get up each day, go to work, go home after it's time to clock out, and get paid on a regular basis. Managing your finances is greatly simplified because you know how much money you can count on each month. If you get benefits like health insurance, they'll typically cost you a great deal less than they would were you to pay for them yourself. Best of all in the minds of many is the fact that you don't have to do any marketing. You just show up and do your thing. Keeping the business profitable is someone else's problem.

There are also trade-offs. The same sense of security that gives you peace of mind can feel like a prison to some. You're told when to be at work, when you can leave, how much time you can take for lunch, and even how you should dress. If that's not enough to make you twitch, you'll also have much less artistic freedom in the work you do. You're working for someone else and consequently it's their vision, not yours, that takes precedent. If you choose a company that's in line with your own vision, there may be very little conflict in this area. Choose poorly and it can be extremely frustrating.

It's also worth mentioning that job security is an illusion. In the mid-1900s, it was common to go to work for a company, spend your entire career there, get a gold watch when you retired, and then live out the rest of your life with a decent pension provided for you.

Today's world is much more volatile. Companies are constantly going out of business or buying each other, with many people losing their jobs in either scenario. Even in a business that's relatively stable, it's not at all uncommon to see corporate reorganizations or other such sleazy tricks designed to get rid of people before a pension has to be paid out. The days of the gold watch are largely behind us.

Expensive wrist jewelry notwithstanding, life as a salaried employee can be a good gig as long as you keep your eye on the weather and make sure you've already secured a new job before the storm hits your old one. Commonsense is your friend no matter what career path you choose.

Employment opportunities are more common for some creative arts than they are others. If you're a dancer or musician, you'll be looking for media and entertainment oriented companies, and there are not as many of those around as there are businesses selling widgets.

Graphic artists and software developers have a wealth of opportunities, not just in the tech sector but in the corporate world at large. Most companies need marketing materials and other image-building artwork. A great many also have internal software systems, even if software isn't the business they're in.

There are also openings for creative arts that you might not normally consider business oriented. For example, if you're a poet, you might assume that you're destined to spend your life in hip coffeehouses working for tips. What you don't realize is that every marketing department in the world depends on the cleverly written word.

It's also worth noting that should you choose the employee path, it's not a decision you're locked into for life. You can change careers as many times as you like. There are no rules.

Taking a job with an organization doesn't have to be "Prison with pay." You can get out whenever you'd like and do something else, with more money in your pocket for the experience. Four walls can also be enjoyable if they surround a good vibe.

Hired Guns

In the corporate world, they refer to temp workers as contractors. Another common term for this sort of work is freelancing. Either way, it means the same thing. It's your responsibility to find the work, and you're the one who negotiates the compensation.

This is a life of much greater freedom than the salaried employee. As you would expect, this means a life of less security, at least in terms of a guarantee. When a client hires you to do a job, you have a source of revenue for just that gig. The life of a successful freelancer is built on reputation and relationships. Do a good job and you're the very first call that the client will make when there's more work. Generate positive word-of-mouth and that same client will also tell her friends to hire you. You can't predict how much money you'll make each month like you can as a salaried employee, but when you do it right, the pay is every bit as steady.

As a freelancer, you also have the ability to build a large client base. An employee has to put all his eggs in one basket. As a rule, people only work one full-time job and most companies take a dim view of you skipping work a few days a week so that you can make money with someone else. A contractor, on the other hand, is expected to have multiple clients. In fact, the more you have, the higher your perceived value as long as you're giving each one the attention he deserves. After all, if that many people are hiring you, you must be good at what you do.

Another benefit of working as a mercenary is freedom from petty office politics. You'll find that most of this gossip and currying of favor is driven by individual ambition. Since you're not trying to climb the corporate ladder, you don't have a dog in that fight. This allows you to quietly opt out of much of the negativity and backstabbing that you encounter. A word of warning, though. It's wise to sleep with one eye open whether you have a stake in the politics or not. You're just as dead from collateral damage as you are from an intentional strike.

Of course, along with these benefits comes the responsibility for putting food on the table. You're the one who has to look for work. While you may get a referral from clients here and there, those who do well with this approach aren't passive about it. Rather than sitting back and waiting for the work to roll in, they're actively engaging their clients, asking if they have any friends, whether or not they've heard of new projects, and in general doing all they can to generate the referral.

The efforts required to market your services can run the gamut. At one extreme, you'll find yourself doing everything the average small business does, including such things as advertising, generating media coverage, performing search engine optimization to drive more traffic to your Web site, and a host of other such tasks.

Depending on your skill set, you may have additional marketing options. Many industries have a healthy pool of recruiting agencies whose sole purpose in life is matching up contractors with the companies who need them. Generally speaking, they bill the company, receive the payment, and then pay you after taking a cut for their efforts. Sometimes they'll work for a percentage that's discussed up-front. In other cases, such as gigs that are paid by the hour, they'll negotiate your hourly rate, bill the company a higher rate, and make their money on the margin.

If the fixed-percentage scenario sounds a lot like a booking agent, you're right on target. Either of these can be a good source of work for you. If you go with this approach, it's important to look at things with the proper perspective. I've known a great many people who get snippy about the cut their agency is taking. Unless you're flat out getting screwed, which is very rarely the case, this attitude is both unprofessional and stupid.

The rules of engagement were well defined when you signed up. Whining about it afterward makes you look like an irresponsible amateur. As for stupidity, chances are good you're going to want a gig when the current one is complete. Do you really think they're going to work with you again if all you did the last time was behave in a petulant and resentful manner? These folks need to make a living just like you, and they provide a valuable service. They've earned their money.

Personally, I love paying commissions. If someone's charging me 20 percent, the remaining 80 percent is money that fell into my lap. I didn't have to chase it. The gig came to me. Don't like the cut they want? Everything in life is negotiable. If you left money on the table because you haven't bothered to refine your skills, that's your fault, not theirs. If you don't like the offer, don't say yes. If you agree to the arrangement, take it and be happy. Should you find out later that you could've made more, don't be negative about it. Be grateful for both the job and the education, and next time bargain a little harder. It's allowed.

In addition to marketing, you're also on the hook for any other paperwork that's required to keep your contracting business in a legitimate state. You might want to set up a simple business entity so that you can keep your company and personal checking accounts separate and more easily manage your funds. It will also be easier to manage legitimate businesses expenses by paying through the company and keeping those receipts separate from your personal purchases.

If you go the solo route, it might be wise to set up a simple business entity. (Talk to an accountant or advisor about which might be best in your situation.) Then, open a checking account for the business. Pay all bills and deposit all receipts into this account. A little work up-front will save you hours down the road when it's time to do your taxes. You'll also appear more professional to the outside world.

It's also wise to keep a separate business savings account and deposit the appropriate portion of every dollar you make into that bucket for the purposes of paying your taxes at the end of the year. Being disciplined about this means no panic at tax time. You fill out the forms (or hire an accountant to do so for you), pay the money you owe out of the savings account, and life goes on without a ripple. You even earn interest on the money throughout the year.

The list of opportunities for contracting will look very much like those for employees. However, this approach is also practical for work beyond the corporate and small business clientele. Actors, dancers, and musicians are just a few of the artists who regularly get work through a booking or talent agency. Though you may never have thought of yourself in this manner, you are in fact an independent contractor. You're getting your work through an agency who charges you a commission. Painters and sculptors may find representatives to help them sell their wares, again on a commission basis. In general, if you have something to offer that's worthwhile, there's a good chance that an industry exists to help you both make a buck off of it.

Small Business

You might not think that life as an artist is compatible with the notion of running a business. In fact, it's not only a very viable opportunity; it's one that can really save your bacon as your career evolves. Let's address the pork first.

Many art forms are very youth oriented. This is especially true in the performance arts. Musical trends change about once a decade. The previous generation's music is thrown out as tragically unhip stuff played by tired old people, and the industry ushers in a new sound devoted to, and played by, the next herd of young people. In this world, old doesn't mean some ninety-year-old guy hobbling around on a cane. It's a label you acquire when you turn thirty.

Actors are hired based on physical appearance as well as theatrical talent. Often, the former is the most important factor. If you want to see institutionalized sexism, you'll find that this rule applies much more to women than men. With the passing of years, a guy gets more distinguished looking. A girl just gets old. This, of course, is the perception embraced and promoted by Hollywood and based on the fact that male audiences are attracted to beautiful young women.

The world of dance is harsher still. Sexism isn't the enemy that accompanies age in this industry. The antagonist is none other than the human body. The world of dance is extremely demanding from a physical perspective. When you think of Bob Fosse, it's more common to recall his work as a choreographer. If you've ever seen him dance, however, it's poetry in motion. Unfortunately, male or female, age diminishes the body's physical capabilities. As with the world of professional sports, there comes a time when they get rid of aging dancers and bring in the young. Of course, aging is defined as someone in their thirties.

Chances are good that you're not planning on dying on your thirtieth birthday and will likely be a creative creature until you really are that wobbly ninety-year-old with a cane. What are you supposed to do for the next sixty years in an industry where you're no longer wanted? In a word, teach. That's where the small business comes into play.

Fosse transitioned from dancer to choreographer and enjoyed huge success. In a sense, he was following the path of a freelancer more than that of a small business. If you're a dancer, however, you'll be hard-pressed to live in a town where there's not at least one school teaching dance. In a major metropolis, it can seem like there's one on every street corner.

Furthermore, it's not a one-size-fits-all proposition. Some will teach tap, others modern jazz. There are ballet schools, clogging schools, square-dancing schools. There are even those schools that throw tradition out the window and teach their own style. The one thing they all have in common is that they're functioning as a small business.

To run a school, you need to rent space, hire instructors, advertise to bring in customers, find suppliers of merchandise whose wares you can sell at a profit, and take care of the paperwork. If you're successful, you can open additional locations. This means hiring and training branch managers as well as doing more paperwork.

Teaching is a time-honored method artists use to continue their work in the business, have fun, and get paid.

Though you many not appreciate the comparison from an aesthetic point of view, a successful dance franchise is exactly like McDonalds from a business perspective. That's not a bad thing. It's an American success story.

Actors, musicians, and other strange creatures of the night also have these opportunities. If you've made a living in the arts, it's because you were good at both your craft and managing your career. These are things that the next generation needs, and they'll pay you for it. Another very reliable source of revenue is from parents of young children. Going to dance class or an acting coach is fun and a good part of a child's upbringing if they have the interest. It doesn't matter if your daughter is planning on being a billionaire CEO when she gets out of college. When she's a kid, she might enjoy dancing for no other reason than the fun of it.

Teaching isn't the only path to the land of small business. The world is also full of music stores, typically run by musicians. It's another way of staying in touch with their passion and paying the bills. Theater companies are rarely run by career accountants. Instead, you'll find seasoned actors at the helm.

The considerations for running a small business are essentially those of a contractor on steroids. You're the leader and manager. You're the marketing-and-promotions guru. Depending on how many people you can afford to hire, you may also be the clerical staff and janitor. The deeper you get into the world of business, the more you'll want to dig into those resources that businesses of every industry study, including sales, finance, and all that other official-sounding stuff. By the time you're to that point, you're already a well established business owner, so your path will be clear to you.

There's no rule that says running a small business has to be the second or third generation of your career. For many, it's a natural evolution. However, you can also jump right into the deep end. There's a lot of money to be made in the advertising industry, and many graphic artists are quick to launch their own agencies. As we've discussed, the software world often seems like little more than a breeding ground for tech start-ups, and these are just a couple of examples. In short, this is America. If you have something of value, you have an opportunity.

Master Your Mindset

Thus far, we've been talking about practical, nuts-and-bolts issues. It doesn't matter how much you think about something; nothing happens until you get up off the couch and take action. There is, of course, another part of this equation. If you want to be successful, it all begins with attitude and the proper mindset.

The world owes you nothing. Your dreams aren't going to show up on a silver platter just because you have talent. It may shock you to discover that in a country populated by several-hundred-million people—and a planet with over seven billion—there's quite a bit of talent to be found. If you want to live life on your own terms, you're going to have to work very hard for it.

Successful start-ups know this and conduct themselves accordingly, taking nothing for granted and pursuing every opportunity they can find. On the other hand, the ostrich is the patron saint of creative creatures everywhere. One mention of business and most of them immediately stick their heads in the sand. Aversion and wishful thinking are rarely the beginnings of an effective strategy.

Your first and quite possibly most difficult challenge on the road to career freedom resides between your ears and in the pit of your stomach. It's always a bit scary doing something new. It's even more uncomfortable when it's something you'd rather not be doing in the first place. Like most challenges, however, the first hurdle is the hardest. Once you clear it, you'll realize it's not nearly as bad as you thought. You'll also enjoy newly found confidence. There's nothing like the feeling of controlling your own destiny instead of your career being at the mercy of others.

Without a doubt, you're going to make a lot of mistakes in the beginning. A friend of mine teaches the classical Japanese martial arts. He once told me that it was pretty much a given that you were going to be cut in a knife fight. The key to success, he said, was the willingness to take a cut to a nonfatal area in order to prevail. That may sound a bit grim, but it's really no different than diving into the business aspect of the arts. You're going to screw up. It's a given. However, as long as your mistakes aren't fatal, you'll keep improving over time and ultimately, your success will be assured.

While we're speaking of martial subjects, you may not be aware of the fact that many businesses study classic books about military strategy in order to be more effective in the marketplace. Most of us in the creative world would doubtless prefer to avoid the world of violence, and yet there's a lesson for us here. Just as businesspeople study *The Art of War*, so too should we study the art of commerce.

CHAPTER 6

Image Building

No matter what creative arts you pursue, there are constants that span all disciplines. Chief among them is the power of your image. Your creativity will not be judged in a vacuum with its aesthetic quality the only consideration. The perception of your audience will be colored in part by how they see you, the artist. If you produce serious, high-caliber results but are considered by most to be a buffoon, your art will never be seen in its best light regardless of how deserving it may be.

In a similar fashion, when you're looking for paying work, your persona speaks much louder than your art. The people in a position to hand you money are in business, and nothing improves your chances of landing a gig like professionalism. As is the case with many of the things we've been considering, perception is reality. The best way to be treated, and compensated, as a professional is to act like one.

Your First Hurdle Is You

There are a number of reasons why we don't put as much effort into managing our image as we should. Some of us get caught up in the illusion that the quality of our work is all that should matter. From this lofty perch, high atop the ivory tower of unrealism, we convince ourselves that an emphasis on image indicates a meaningless and shallow creator.

It's not hard to look at the world of commercial products and see marketing that's run amok, producing products of terrible quality and selling them hand over fist through the use of hype and sensationalism. I can use a screwdriver to pound in a nail, but that doesn't make it a hammer. Misuse of a tool doesn't invalidate its purpose in life.

If cheesy self-promotion is the only way you can peddle your wares because they're simply not very good, there's a case to be made that you should consider a different line of work. On the other hand, an excellent painting looks even nicer in an elegant frame. Don't disregard a useful tool just because some don't know how to wield it properly.

An even greater challenge for many is the demons and dragons that lurk just beneath the surface of the average creative person. There are artists in the world who are supremely confident and believe that their efforts are the greatest thing since sliced bread. Some are modest. Some are not. For many of us, however, self-doubt and insecurity are not strangers. Regardless of how many people fawn over our latest creation, we cringe inwardly and fear that someone may discover us for the fraud we truly are.

Since people come in all shapes and sizes, not everyone experiences this to these extremes. Demons are versatile little creatures and can grow or shrink to suit the nature of their victims. In my own case, I don't grapple with the intensity of feeling like I'm a phony who might be uncovered at any moment, but I've known many who truly did. They were wonderful people who did great work. Unfortunately, they were never able to see this with their own eyes despite many admirers who could.

For me, the vehicle for self-doubt is not a Harley but rather a penchant for merciless critique. As an example, I just finished writing the second edition of *Unite the Tribes*, a leadership book I penned a decade ago. The core material was still relevant, and the only update I needed to make to focus it specifically on the needs of the technology sector. The plan was simple. I'd write a few new chapters to set things up and then just make a light editing pass through the remainder.

When it was all said and done, I'd completely rewritten the entire book. The only thing that remained was the chapter titles and headings. A friend asked me why I shoved the first edition into a shredder and rewrote it from the ground up. I told her that the writing was so bad I just couldn't live with it. She gave me the same look that our true friends offer when they're trying to decide if you're on drugs or just fell and hit your head really hard.

She told me that she still has her copy of the first edition and had really liked the way I wrote it. She's smart, a friend of countless years, and I trust her, so when she told me it wasn't the crap I perceived it to be, I knew she was telling me the truth. My personal demons, however, weren't even remotely interested in what she was saying. I think they were too busy sipping martinis to be bothered with anything as trivial as reality.

I share this rather embarrassing story of my own for a functional reason. One of the common aspects of housing demons and dragons is the sense that you're alone in your struggle. For some it can be a paralyzing experience. In milder cases like my own, it only causes a lot of extra effort, along with the teeth marks that come inevitably from gnawing on your own ankle.

> Many creative people harbor secret fears that they lack skill and will soon be discovered as frauds. Just tell the gremlins inside to just shut up when the din gets too loud. Over time, your anxieties will diminish and your art will flourish.

Either way, it's easy to feel like we're screwed up and stupid for having internal issues while other, decidedly more normal, artists are immune to this affliction. In reality, I've met very few creatives who didn't have at least some degree of self-doubt. And I've certainly never met one who was normal.

By realizing that you're not alone and that those late-night, martini-swilling parties going on inside of you are not at all uncommon, it can make it at least a little easier for you to shout down the stairwell and tell them to shut up and turn the loud music off. There is strength in numbers, and the creative world is a pretty big crowd.

Of course, in my case the harsh critique was turned inward. It doesn't take much imagination to realize that there are plenty of people out there who are quick to offer a searing criticism of your work rather than focusing on their own. If you're a little tender on the inside to begin with, this can sting quite a bit. It will certainly fuel any feelings of inadequacy that you may already harbor.

The first step in building a positive and professional self-image that will get your work taken more seriously and make it easier to get a gig is believing in yourself. This isn't exactly a novel suggestion, but sometimes it's worth trotting out life's little truisms for no other reason than the fact that they're true.

It's very likely that the single greatest obstacle between you and the image you deserve is currently deep down inside of you, doubtless making another martini. There are plenty of great resources out there to help you work through these feelings, and it's important that you do. You can't consider the second obstacle in the race until you've cleared the first hurdle.

Avoid the Cult of Ego

Another practice that's harmful to your personal brand lies at the exact opposite pole. It's still driven by personal demons, only this time they don't swill martinis. It's more likely that they shoot tequila, since that has a tendency to make you feel ten feet tall and bulletproof. It's hard to imagine a world of creativity that doesn't contain those boorish and overbearing souls who believe that they're the most spectacular talent in the known universe.

Some people are truly this deluded. It's worth noting that a self-aggrandizing nature may well accompany a gifted person. Nonetheless, egomania is always a delusion, regardless of the quality of your work. None of us are superior enough to look down on our fellow humans. More importantly, to do so makes you look like a jerk. That's never good for business.

A raging ego isn't always indicative of an exaggerated sense of worth either. Occasionally it's exactly the opposite. Personally, I deal with my demons by opening the basement door and dousing them with a fire hose. It probably doesn't change much, but at least it screws up their martinis. We take our little victories where we can find them. Others, however, will turn self-doubt on its head and cope with it by convincing themselves that they're superstars and then acting the part. On the outside, it looks pretty much the same as massive overconfidence and has an identical effect on your career.

It's actually not that hard to fall into the cult of ego when you live the creative life. After all, we exist to have an audience and, if we're any good at what we do, we're going to have at least a few people telling us that we're great. If looking into the basement is uncomfortable, it's far more appealing to embrace the praise you receive and immerse yourself in that.

A variation on the egomaniac is the aloof artist with an often subtle but no less irritating sense of superiority. This is the hipster who has to sit at the cool kids' table rather than hanging out with us lesser mortals. He doesn't connect with his audience so much as he endures them, those little people who just don't understand the purity of his art. It's not difficult to see the problems this can create for you. Being unapproachable makes you exactly that. Those with gigs to offer will simply approach someone else.

It's important that you develop a sense of confidence. Without it, you'll never get very far. However, there is a balancing act between confidence and arrogance. It can feel like living life on the high wire without a net, but it's crucial to find that center point, believing in yourself without being obnoxious about it.

Up there on the wire to keep you company are humility and self-doubt, an equally precarious combination. To believe in yourself without becoming a jerk, you need humility and perspective. Go too far in that direction, and you're in the basement. Watch your step in all that water. I haven't mopped the floors in a while.

It can be tricky maintaining your balance, to be sure. For what it's worth, I've been actively fighting these battles my entire life. As you might imagine, I see more road ahead of me than I do in the rearview mirror. Even so, I've learned that it's well worth the effort. Everything about my life, and certainly my creative career, is far better today than it would be if I didn't put forth the effort in areas that are uncomfortable for me, although I do have to admit that the fire hose is fun. Keep at it. You'll get better as you go.

Rejection Is Part of the Game

Another thing that's a little hard on the self-image is the experience of being rejected. It doesn't take a postgraduate degree in clinical psychology to know that this can be painful. Very few of us go through life without someone pushing us away, but nowhere is it more common than in the arts.

For most of us, the entire point of creating is to share with others. While some may have difficulty accepting that they have a need for validation from their audience, look deeply enough and you'll find that it's present. You may have to wade through some water and step over a couple of empty tequila bottles to find it, but it's there.

To create is to expose a very important part of our soul to a crowd of complete strangers, trusting that they'll understand how vulnerable we are in that moment. Such trust is often misplaced. Mathematically speaking, the larger the audience that you draw, the greater the likelihood that some will criticize your work. When it happens, you're not going to care much for the experience.

The potential for rejection has always been a part of the artist's life, but the Internet takes it to new extremes. Above and beyond the sheer number of people who can interact with you is the fact that a significant portion of them will be trolls, those malevolent miscreants who enjoy making fun of others. It's almost impossible to imagine a comments section on the average Web site without them. Moderating their musings can become a full-time job in and of itself. It matters little that these mean-spirited posts are coming from disembodied voices associated with fake names. It hurts just the same.

Of course, trolls aside there will be others who simply don't like your work. They can be regular people who are a part of your audience or industry figures who give you a bad review. Getting panned by a critic is no fun because they're supposed to be an authority on the matter. Therefore, if they say you suck, your inner demons will raise a glass and heartily suggest that you agree.

Pay no attention to the trolls on the Internet or in other parts of your reality. There's a reason they hide behind fake names and false bravado. Keep putting one foot in front of another and those disembodied voices will eventually be drowned out by the applause of your fans.

In truth, critics reflect not only their own personal taste but a very specific vision of what they feel does and does not qualify as art. While they're busy judging you based on the ivory tower criteria of the art school they graduated from, thousands of screaming fans are loving what you do. That's often a loud enough noise to make demons and dragons run for cover.

There's another kind of review that's commonplace these days and in many ways much more relevant. It's rare that I buy something from Amazon without first glancing at the reviews for that particular product. This is the voice of the people, your true audience. They're the ones who just ponied up the money for your latest work and thus have the right to an opinion.

I know that there are some creative people who are totally immersed in what they do and are driven by the art itself, not the response of the consumers. Such creators can be immune to the opinions of others. As for myself, regardless of the medium I work in, I'm just not one of those legendary Michelangelo-type figures who grace the planet every few-hundred years with important work. While it's true that I create based on what I feel rather than what I think people want to hear, ultimately I'm a big fan of my audience. Without them, there's not much reason for me to be creative at all.

While I respect the opinions of critics and others who are educated well beyond my meager pedigree, the voice I care about is the voice of the people, the audience who takes the time to consume what I produce. Naturally, it makes the Amazon reviews a bit more relevant when it's my own work under scrutiny. However, even though they're supposed to be the opinions of those who actually read the book or consumed whatever else it is I have out there, it is still the Internet and some fundamental rules apply. If you keep them in mind, it can help you maintain the proper perspective.

It's common in sporting competitions to have a panel of judges who throw out the highest and lowest scores and then average what remains. It's a fairly reasonable approach to eliminating bias in either direction. This is useful when considering reviews as well. Some people will love you no matter what you do. Even if you have a bad moment and put out something truly beneath your normal standards, they'll give you five stars. Trolls exist in reviews as well, and they will be a good source of single-star reviews.

It's also worth noting that business is business, and it's neither fair nor nice. Some of your competitors will trash your work to make their own appear more appealing. The unethical will pay for positive reviews to pump up their status. As if this wasn't enough, there's also good old-fashioned human nature to consider. If you have dozens of five-star reviews, someone's going to ding you just because they think you need to be taken down a notch.

I've also noted that with noncreative products, there's the idiot factor to consider. This is produced by the people who buy a toaster and then give it a one-star review because it didn't heat up when it wasn't plugged in. I'd love to think that every person on the planet is intelligent, perceptive, and has a valuable opinion. Reality dictates otherwise.

Of course, I'm just using Amazon as a working example. These principles apply across the board, from online retailers to brick-and-mortar stores and from the vaunted words of critics to the mass of enthusiastic bodies at your latest performance. There's no way you can be a creative person without exposing yourself to rejection. However, if you can learn to see it for what it is and take it with a grain of salt, it'll be much easier to survive the experience with your self-image intact.

Be Who You Want to Be

Up to this point, I've spent a fair amount of time talking about the difficulties of maintaining a positive self-image in a world that's often hostile to the concept. You can't build anything lasting on a shaky foundation, so to be seen as who you want to be it has to start from the inside and work its way out. You can wear all the right clothes and hang out at the trendiest spots, but if you don't believe you're cool, no one else will. They may not even know why. It's just one of those things we sense.

Now that we've mopped up all the excess water and walked the empty tequila bottles to the recycle bin, it's time to turn our vision outward. To be successful as a creative creature, regardless of what your interpretation of success may be, you have to know what the end result looks like. It goes along with knowing what you want from life and so requires the same amount of effort.

Too often we imagine ourselves standing in the bright spotlight and nothing more. You have to see things more clearly than this. Look down and see the duct tape and stains on the well-worn carpet of the stage. Peer into the first row and see the faces of the people in the audience. Look in the mirror and see what they see. You have to paint a completely realistic picture in your mind of what you're creating before you can create it. That goes for more than just your art. It applies to your career as well.

Chapter 6 | Image Building

It's hard, but do your best to see yourself as others see you. Image is an important aspect of your artistic career. Face it—people don't want to see their favorite hip-hop artist in a three-piece suit sans jewelry. Adapting to the expectations isn't easy, but it can be fun if you approach it as yet another creative endeavor in your life.

If you're the philosophical sort, you'll probably consider the deeper meaning inherent in visualizing your goals in great detail. I'll leave advice on such matters to more qualified people. For our purposes, we're going to focus on the practical aspects that accompany this approach. Simply put, you can't hit the target if you don't know what you're aiming at.

Since a great deal of success is influenced by your image, both in the eyes of the professional community and that of your fans, you have to become active in creating what you want them to see. This isn't a matter of being phony or deceptive. In fact, it's quite the opposite. If the world is to perceive you as a talented and successful artist, you need to stand up and be exactly that.

I'm a blue jeans and sneakers kinda guy. It's not uncommon to find a fair degree of wear and tear on both. For what I do, that works fine. If I'm playing guitar in some smoky bar, it's reasonable attire. If I'm doing a speaking gig, I'll wear nicer jeans, put on a pair of biker boots that are actually polished. I might even throw a sports coat on over my T-shirt. This is also appropriate, as it takes it up a notch in terms of professionalism without losing sight of my image. I'm not a conservative businessman who works at an investment firm, and those aren't the people in my audience. If I showed up wearing a tie, they'd probably hang me with it.

Now imagine how this would work out if I were a fashion designer, trying to get my line of extremely elegant clothing taken seriously by the leading voices of the industry. I could hire the best models for the runway, but what would people think when I showed up to the party afterward looking like I'd just stumbled out of Joe's Bar and Grille? No matter how trendsetting my designs, and regardless of the professional allure of the models who displayed them, every serious industry professional in the room would immediately consider me a buffoon with no taste.

As in our earlier examples, people often form these opinions at a subconscious level without ever thinking about it. From an idealistic point of view, all that should matter is the quality of my designs. I have good stuff and I presented it in the proper light. How I personally dress should be irrelevant. I'm not a runway model.

All of these points are true. None of these things should matter. But everyone at the party will leave with the sense that something's just not right with this picture. After all, if I have no sense of fashion in my own attire, how serious a player could I be in the world of international design?

If I were invited to speak at a black-tie affair, I wouldn't show up in blue jeans and a T-shirt. I would either decline the gig if I thought I wasn't a good fit for the audience or I'd hit the nearest tuxedo-rental store. Back when I played music full time, I often had to take whatever work I could get. This included country clubs, weddings, and other such decidedly non–rock-and-roll affairs. I needed the work and took the gigs, so I showed up looking like what they expected to see. The jeans were in the car, ready for a quick getaway, but for the job I presented the appropriate image.

These days I'm in a better position to pick the kinds of creative work I take. As a result, I have the freedom to be who I want to be and build on that. I write and direct video projects and film. I play guitar in a band. I develop software. I do public speaking and also take on the rare consulting client when I think he's worth the effort. Many of these creative outlets could play to a variety of audiences, so I cultivate the ones that I want.

Nobody cares what the director looks like on a movie set. The computer is equally apathetic about my attire when I'm programming, but some of my clients have dress policies. If I'm working on-site instead of remotely from home, I dress accordingly. Because of this, I've been known to decline gigs if they wanted me to show up in a suit and tie. When I'm speaking, I direct my efforts to those events in which the people will enjoy me for who I am. If I happen to be singing and playing guitar, my apparel depends on the gig. I don't mind putting on shiny clothes for a fancy rock-and-roll show. On the other hand, if I'm playing blues at Billy Bob's Biker Bar, the grungier the jeans, the better.

In each of these cases, I'm able to make the right call because I understand the image I'm trying to present as well as what the reality of the situation dictates. Having a firm grasp of such information is the key to your success in this area.

It's well worth taking time on a regular basis to consider all of your creative dreams and break them down, as I have above. For each of them, who do you want to be and how would you like others to perceive you? In addition to your desires, you also have to know what the situation requires. I'll emphasize that you should be aware of how things really are, not how you think they should be. Once you're a big star, perhaps you can set new trends. For now, know what it takes to get the gig.

It's essential to know what it takes to "get the gig." That means different things in different circumstances. Though you'd always like to dress "like an artist"—as you do at gallery openings—can you tone it down a bit to get a teaching job? The chameleon has great power.

This thought exercise should extend beyond just making a list of attributes. You're a creative person. This will work best as an exercise in connecting with that nebulous, indefinable thing that runs through all our artistic endeavors and comes out as inspiration. Allow yourself to daydream, fantasize, and become immersed in the world you wish to enjoy. That's always fun. Just keep your notepad at hand so that you can keep track of what you learn in as much detail as possible. See the vision of who you want to be, then paint the picture.

Learn the Language

When I was a beginner in the world of professional musicians, my best friend and mentor was a guy who was twelve years my senior. As generation gaps require, we had different tastes in music and culture, but that didn't stop a bond from forming. It also didn't stop me from learning a great deal from him. All that was required was an open mind and the willingness to occasionally translate concepts from his world into my own.

One of the very first things he taught me is something that seems obvious today but was anything but at the time. If you want to be treated as a professional, you have to be perceived as a professional.

I was a long-haired rock-and-roll singer who spent a lot of time playing in garage bands. For those of you who aren't of the musical persuasion, a garage band isn't a description of where your rehearsals take place. It means a band who does nothing but play in garages because they can't get any paying gigs. My friend, on the other hand, worked most nights of the week and paid the bills with that money. In short, he was a professional. I was not.

As a reminder, the term commercial does not mean selling out. It has to do with commerce, the act of getting paid for your art. In a similar vein, professionals are people who pursue their art as their profession. It's how they make a living. I didn't come to these conclusions on my own. They were patiently explained to me by a friend who wanted me to understand that if I wanted to be a professional musician, I should probably understand what the phrase meant.

As I warmed up to the idea, I began to see that there are certain mannerisms that serve as cues to show the working musicians who's a pro and who's not. Much of this has to do with attitude, although that turned out to be a different kind of attitude than I was expecting. I was all wrapped up in the countercultural statements of youth, rebellion, and the part rock-and-roll played in it all. As it turns out, when you're looking for paying work, the people who are in a position to hire you aren't terribly impressed with this sort of thing.

There's a common language among working-class musicians regardless of genre. In fact, much of this language transcends artistic boundaries altogether and is understood by the painter, the dancer, and the actor with ease. The first thing I learned was the effectiveness of subtlety. As any who know me can attest, this is not something that comes naturally.

As it turns out, one of the quickest ways to spot the amateur in the crowd is to note who's making the biggest claims in the loudest voice, those having strong opinions in areas of little experience. The guy who's making a fuss is generally trying to puff himself up artificially because he has nothing in his background to do it for him. The person who's working six nights a week playing the bar down the road has a completely different demeanor. Sure, there are egos aplenty in this business, but the working-class musician isn't bragging about how he's a star. It's more likely that he's trying to get a cute girl to buy him a drink.

The world of the working artist is focused less on being a superstar and more on being able to eat this week. You'll see that reflected in their conversations. Instead of the garage band mentality of discussing grand and glorious visions, the singer looking for a gig will simply ask you how often your band is working and how much it pays.

The power of such questions is shockingly deceptive. Simple and innocuous, they nonetheless communicate that you're a pro with professional concerns on your mind and you're wondering if the band you're talking to is in the same league. If they're not working, you politely excuse yourself and move on to the next opportunity. If they are, you've accomplished two things. You've validated this as a solid lead for work, and you've given them a subtle cue that you're the real thing, not some starry-eyed wannabe.

When I moved to New York, it was at the invitation of a girl I'd met while she was visiting Florida to pursue a relationship that we both wanted to explore. As we all tend to do from time to time, I didn't really overthink the matter. I just packed up and hit the road. Of course, this meant that my first order of business upon arrival was looking for a gig.

At that time, most cities had local papers for the creative arts, and that's usually where musicians would advertise that they were looking for players or bands. With one of these papers as a resource, I remember one night making a number of phone calls while my girlfriend looked on. Most of these conversations were polite but brief. We'd exchange a couple of pleasantries, and then I'd ask the person how often the band was working and how much the gigs usually paid. The response was typically zero on both accounts.

After a number of such conversations, my girlfriend looked at me and patiently explained that I was being completely unrealistic. You don't, she told me, just show up in town and immediately step on stage with a gigging band. You have to pay your dues, which means spending a lot of time rehearsing in someone's garage for no pay. Eventually, you'll get lucky and get a chance to play live, usually for free, but in time you'll start to get paying work.

It's worth mentioning that she was a great person and very intelligent. She was also not a musician and had no experience whatsoever in this world. The conventional wisdom she passed along was learned through association with friends who played in garage bands.

My little universe has always had a decent sense of humor, which is why the very next phone call I made after her explanation went differently. I asked how many nights the band was working and the answer was five, sometimes six. There was also a quick and straightforward answer on how much the jobs paid.

After determining that we knew a lot of the same songs, he invited me to the club the band was playing the next night so that I could sit in and sing a few songs for an audition. I did exactly that and was hired on the spot. I worked with them for quite some time and it was a great gig. Of course, my girlfriend had heard the entire conversation. When I hung up the phone, I certainly didn't point out to her that I'd just showed up in town and would immediately step on stage with a gigging band. I'm not an idiot.

While this example is in the realm of music, you'll find that it holds true for every paying art form. As you spend time with the working class, pay attention to the phrases they use and how they talk about their trade. Some of the topics will be creative in nature but others will be about business.

Hang out with artists who get paid for their work. You'll learn way more than you would spending time with entitled wannabes expecting the world to discover them. The professionalism of the working-class creative will seep into your psyche over time, eventually turning you into a paid artist as well.

When you're in conversation with your more gainfully employed friends, don't overdo it or try to be something you're not. Just learn the subtle language of those who get paid for what they do and adopt it in your own mannerisms. If you've never worked a paying job in your life, be honest about it. Credibility is important. However, even without practical experience, the fact that you have a professional attitude about things will encourage others to give you a chance. If you have talent and are easy to work with, that's all you need.

Understanding Touch Points

Presenting yourself as a professional extends to more than just conversation. It happens at every level, any place where there's a chance for interaction. It also involves more than just your peers. Success requires not just business sense but interaction with people who are willing to shell out their hard-earned cash for what you create. How they perceive you has a lot to do with whether or not they feel the transaction is worth it.

In order to build an image as a professional, perhaps even one well on her way to stardom, it's important to reflect the proper image at every step of the way. You do this by paying close attention to the quality of your touch points. These are the places where you, the creative creature, come in contact with someone else. They include the realm of personal interaction as well as things like promotional materials, conversations with the media, and other such things.

A great example is your Web site. In today's connected world, fans and potential employers alike will expect to be able to find you on the Web. There are many ways to accomplish this. Because one of my creative pursuits is technology, I have an advantage in this area because I actually get paid to do Web site development for clients. This means I can handle my own site with ease.

Of course, most people aren't professional geeks. Because of this, they often rely on a social media site or some art-specific venture to produce a few Web pages for them. A graphic artist might post work and have a profile on a site devoted to that type of creativity. A musician may post songs on a similar site devoted to bands. At best, doing this will allow you to have a presence on a public site that's at least on topic. At worst, you rely on a generic social media site. Either way, your visitors aren't coming to a site that's dedicated to You, Inc. They're visiting the pages of a technology company. You're merely a squatter.

What kind of image do you think this conveys? Think of your favorite superstars, the people in your field whom you most want to emulate. Chances are good that they've paid someone to set up their own site, one that's about their work and nothing else. They're not borrowing some dusty corner of a tech company's offerings. They're professionals, and they look the part.

You don't have to spend a lot of money on this. You can register a Web site domain name (mine is ChristopherDuncan.com) for less than twenty dollars a year. There are countless companies out there who will host your site for ten bucks a month. If you don't have any geek friends, you can find a great many free resources out there that will give you prefabricated templates for your site layout. All of which means that for a little effort and for less than the cost of a cheeseburger and fries each month, you can have a professional looking presence on the Web. In business terms, that's called a competitive edge.

Your Web site is only one example, of course, but it's a good one. Some people you do business with will want to use e-mail. Nobody's going to take you seriously with an AOL.com address. When they reply to one that ends in YourWebsiteDomainName.com, you look more credible, like someone who takes their profession seriously.

Your business cards, letterhead, pictures, brochures, and other such bits of physical paraphernalia are subject to the same rules. If you're a sculptor and you just photocopied some grainy snapshots of your work, how impressed do you think the gallery down the road is going to be?

Everything connected to you—your image, your Web site, your business card—reaches a potential paying customer or fan. Make sure it reflects your skill and professionalism.

The same can be said of other such demo tools. If you're a dancer, they help to show people how well you dance. If you give people a link to a video of you prancing around in your living room, it doesn't exactly scream prima ballerina.

You can get surprisingly good quality from a cell phone camera if you pay attention to lighting. Find a background that looks appropriate. Beg your way onto a high school stage on a weekend, or get some creative friends to throw together a reasonable looking backdrop for you. You're not trying to sell some clumsy attempt at deception, hoping viewers will believe you're on stage at Madison Square Garden. You merely need to show that you have a sense of professionalism.

Technology is cheap and ever present in our lives today, and you don't have to be a working-class geek to use it. Find the resources you need, look at the results the pros get, and emulate that in your demo materials. You'll be surprised at how much this makes you stand out from the herd.

The best starting point is to take stock of all your touch points. How many different ways does your creativity and personal image intersect with the professional world as well as that of your potential fans? Catalogue each and every one of the ways, and then set out to insure that no matter where people encounter you, the experience is first class.

Emulate Success

One of the mistakes that many people make when building their image is operating on their own preconceived notions rather than tuning in to what the pros are doing. When immersed in your art, you should be true to yourself. When you're building an image and looking for work, it's equally important to be true to your environment.

I'm not a big fan of the color brown. I'm sure it's a fine shade and has many respectable qualities, but it just doesn't excite me. That said, if I were to look for creative work in an industry that was dripping with shades of brown, I would completely disregard my love of blue and make sure that my promotional materials had every bit as much brown as those of the most successful people in the field. In other words, one of the easiest ways to look professional is to observe what the pros do and emulate them.

If the artistic purist in you cringes over what you may consider to be a copycat performance, take heart. This isn't an exercise in pretension. It's all about understanding boundaries.

When I'm working on a book, I have my preferred approach to writing. I'm casual and speak in a conversational voice, much as I would were I talking to someone in person. I can get away with this provided I don't stray too far from the accepted norms.

When I'm writing for a business audience, as I did with *Unite the Tribes*, I can be casual but only to a point. If I stray too far into slang, profanity, or examples that are far removed from the world of tech start-ups, readers will stop taking me seriously and I'll lose them. Because I read business books and pay attention to what respected authors do, I'm familiar with the norm. It tells me where I can push the envelope a bit and where I need to paint within the lines.

If you find such considerations to be artistically unacceptable, you're going to be a garage band creative for the rest of your life. If you want to get paid, regardless of the discipline, there are rules. Some can be bent and others fractured. Some are completely inflexible. As the old saying goes, you can't break the rules until you know what they are. A corollary to this is the fact that you can't play the game if you don't know the rules. This isn't about conforming. It's about being someone who fits into the business model of your art form and is thus a candidate for being paid.

Chapter 6 | Image Building

Want to get paid for your work? Know the rules before you break them. There's a business model that exists to make it easier for consumers of your art to find you, buy your wares, and come back for more. Know that model intimately.

With that in mind, you should spend a great deal of time studying those who are making a living at what you want to do. However—and this is where people tend to make the next big mistake—don't look at the rock stars exclusively, or even predominantly. Your best role models are the people who are doing the average day-to-day gigs. They're not rich and famous. They may even struggle to pay the rent when they hit a bump in the road. They are, however, working on a regular basis.

Superstars make lots of money, so they can afford all sorts of wardrobe, PR departments, and managers to keep them looking like stars. Try that on your macaroni and cheese budget and you're not going to get very far. Furthermore, if you try to emulate that as best you can at your own level, you won't look like a superstar. You'll just look pretentious.

This concept applies to your search for jobs as well. If you're an actor looking for steady work, take a look at what's in your area. Sure, go ahead and audition for that Hollywood blockbuster with the famous director. You can't win if you don't play. When you're done, go look for something that will buy you dinner tonight. Make note of all the theater companies in your area. Find out how much work there is for commercials. See if there's a good indie film community where you live. Look for every possible paying gig you can find that doesn't require you to be a superstar in order to be considered.

Once you have a notion of where the work is, start paying attention to the people who get it. How do they dress? What do their promotional materials look like? What auditions do they go on? Look at their Web sites and other PR materials.

Perhaps they work through an agency. Since securing a good agent is often harder than getting an actual paying gig, find out what work they've landed without the guiding hand of a manager.

These people are paying the bills by doing what you want to do. Find out how they conduct themselves and how they're represented in each of their touch points and you'll learn the secret of their success.

In addition to emulating those who are going somewhere, it's also worth reviewing those who aren't. Another of my many pursuits involves a camera. When I first started out with video, one of my interests was in how things came together in postproduction, where elements both real and imagined are stitched together to create a believable scene. With the same bar band mentality I just described, I didn't focus on blockbusters who spent millions on graphic artists. I watched B movies as well as a lot of things on the Web. Often, I wasn't looking for the really cool shot. I was looking for the disaster, the scene so phony and unrealistic you wonder how it ever made the cut.

I remember watching an action adventure that had a bit of sci fi in it. There was a fair amount of green-screen work, scenes where actors are shot against a solid green fabric so that they can be replaced later with a background shot somewhere else. In this movie, the composited backgrounds never really worked. Instead of looking like they were in a lush forest, the actors more closely resembled a ransom note, where scraps of a magazine are cut out and pasted onto a white piece of paper. The actors looked fine. The forest looked fine. In no way did they look like they belonged together.

By analyzing these scenes, I started to home in on the problem areas. In one case, it was the edges of the actors' bodies. They were sharp and clean-cut in contrast to the background. I then learned about a technique called light wrap, which is based on the fact that the lighting of our environment bounces off the edges of our bodies in a way that brings the two together. By learning how to emulate this effect, I got better with my own green-screen work. The benefit didn't come from looking at completely perfect Hollywood movies. I improved my skill by looking at the mistakes others made and learning how to avoid them.

In your creative circles, there will be plenty of people whom no one takes seriously. They don't get hired because they're obvious amateurs. If you study how they present themselves and compare that to how the working class go about their business, you'll begin to see many glaring mistakes. By focusing on them and learning to avoid doing the same yourself, you'll continually polish the stone of your own image, making it look ever more like the gem of professionalism.

While this can be an extremely productive exercise, there's one cautionary note. As you do this, it will be very easy to develop a sense of superiority, looking down on the people making mistakes and eventually falling into a pattern of ridiculing them. Remember, everyone has to start somewhere. A few years from now, these same people might be quite successful after learning the hard way those same lessons that you can glean from observation. More importantly, however, is this: No one wants to work with a jerk who looks down on others. Don't let yourself fall into this way of thinking or you'll seriously impair your chances for success.

Chapter 6 | Image Building

Fake It 'Til You Make It

If you act like a professional for long enough, eventually you'll become one. When you're first starting out, you might feel like you're just pretending. You are. However, when done properly, it's okay. Think of it not as being phony but rather as rehearsing your part to perfection. The people who are working act professionally. Those who don't have difficulty staying employed. You want to study and emulate the pros so closely that anyone you meet will feel confident in hiring you, knowing that you're not just talented but are someone they can depend on to produce quality results.

Believe it or not, part of the path to success is actually avoiding certain gigs. If you want to play in a garage band for the pure fun of it, there's absolutely nothing wrong with that. There have been periods in my life when I was focusing on other areas of my creative career and didn't have time to play with a steadily working band. However, I was still a musician. My solution was to find some friends, open a beer, and crank up the guitar on a Saturday night for no other reason than the joy of making music. A garage band was fine in this scenario. It would have been a waste of time when I was trying to pay the bills with my music.

If you're striving for full-time employment through your creativity, you're going to follow up on a lot of opportunities in search of the ones that pay. In the process, you'll encounter more than a few that are the equivalent of garage bands in your own art form. If you're talking to people with whom you would collaborate, and your first questions beyond the courtesies are professional in nature, they're going to immediately blow you off if they're not ready to work. In other words, by acting professional you will have immediately taken yourself out of consideration for the gig. That's exactly what you want to do. The more time you spend with people who can't get paying work, the less you have to find those who can.

You'll also need a bit of a thick skin from time to time. Those who haven't yet made the transition from idealism to the working class are often insecure and sensitive about the fact that they haven't yet been accepted into the world of paid gigs. Such rejection is frustrating, and they'll often take those feelings out on you, berating you for being callous and commercial instead of believing in their pure artistic vision. In effect, by framing the conversation in a professional manner, you'll be implicitly rejecting them. That never feels good.

If you keep that in mind when you get the occasional negative response from people, it'll take a little of the sting out of their reactions. It's also worth it to develop a high degree of diplomacy and graciousness in the way you deal with people. There's never any benefit to making others feel bad. There are also practical considerations. You're going to be in this business a long time. The amateur you have a conversation with today might be a superstar ten years from now. Maybe chance will bring you together again in the future. Maybe it won't. Either way, people remember how they were treated and people talk.

There's power in repetition. The old street slang "Fake it 'til you make it" is based on this principle. It's not about being phony. It's about repetition. A professional athlete performs rigorous exercise on a daily basis in a regimen designed to improve her skills. A dancer will execute the same difficult move over and over again until he can do it flawlessly without thinking.

In a similar fashion, if you continually act as though you're a professional even before you are, it will become habit. No matter what situation you find yourself in or how spontaneous the opportunity, you'll instinctively conduct yourself as a pro. The image that others have in their mind of you will reflect this. When there are a dozen qualified candidates, everyone will immediately point to you as the one they want to hire because it's clear that you operate at a higher level.

In the arts, image is a powerful tool. Give this area constant attention in your career and you'll gain more than just a respectable appearance. You'll have transformed yourself into the professional that you want to be.

CHAPTER 7

Spreading the Word

As we've already discussed, nothing strikes terror into the hearts of creative creatures like marketing. Performing artists who shine onstage shrink into a corner when confronted with the need for self-promotion. Visual artists capable of creating the most compelling promotional materials run screaming in the opposite direction of these most basic business needs.

Across the board, those who pursue a life of creativity find the world of sales and marketing to be distasteful at best. These are the same people, by the way, who complain the loudest about always being broke. No one ever said the artistic mindset was logical.

In the highly competitive world of artistic endeavor, no one is going to give you a break. There's only so much attention to go around, and everyone is competing for it. To make matters worse, technology and the Internet are empowering every man, woman, and child, and more than a few house cats, to become creative creatures in their own right. It's a very crowded room. If you stand quietly in the corner, no one is going to notice you. From a financial perspective, it's hard to get paying work when no one knows you exist.

There are probably more marketing books in the world than you can read in one lifetime. This isn't one of them. If you're having trouble getting the word out about what you do, the problem probably isn't a lack of educational resources. It's your unwillingness to utilize them. With that in mind, my goal is not to give you a comprehensive education in marketing but rather to take the teeth out of the beast and show you that he's not as scary as you originally thought. If you can take that one small step, your chances for a giant leap are boundless.

The Attention Business

The most common thing that comes to mind when people think of sales and marketing is our friend, the obnoxious used-car salesman dressed in an equally tacky plaid sports coat, hammering on you with a high-pressure sales pitch for a low-quality automobile. We don't hold such people in high regard.

In fairness, I spent a chunk of my life teaching these salespeople how to pay the bills. Some of them were every bit the caricature that comes to mind. For the most part, however, they were just regular people. One of the things they shared in common with the creative crowd is that neither of them want to work a real job.

The world of marketing is like that of any other profession. Over the years, people have discovered what works and what doesn't through the process of trial and error. In other words, there are certain rules and principles that you can count on for predictable results. No matter what you're selling, you can break it down into a few basic concepts.

If the thought of promotion makes you cringe, it's helpful to look at it from a different perspective. One of the first and most important concepts of marketing is that you can't make a sale unless potential customers are aware that your product exists. Consequently, once you've established a professional image, this awareness is what you need the most. In and of itself, it won't guarantee you paying work, but it's the largest contributing factor in achieving that goal.

No one will buy your product or attend your performance unless they know it exists. The need to publicize your work is therefore fundamental and unavoidable—that is, assuming that you'd like to get paid to have fun doing what you love.

If you want to build a better career, you don't have to become a used-car salesman. You just need to do what you're already good at. You create in order to share your inspiration with your audience. In other words, you want people to notice and enjoy your work. From that perspective, one could say that you're in the attention business. That's also how I would describe the world of marketing and PR. It's really no more complicated than that. You're simply trying to get the attention of your audience.

Once you look at it in this way, the thought of spreading the word about your art becomes much more natural. When you do something cool, you have no problem telling your friends about it. If you've built a following, you're equally comfortable telling your fans that you have something new to share. Taking your career to the next level and expanding your audience through the basics of promotion is no different than what you're already doing. It simply occurs on a larger scale and with better organization.

The Internet Is Not Life

If you've dipped your toes into the waters of marketing, chances are good that the first thing you did was spend some time searching for resources on the Internet. For many of us, the first thing we reach for when we're researching something is a Web browser. It's immediate, and it's free. It's also a mixed blessing.

When you talk to people about marketing, the first words you'll hear will be ones like "social media" and "search engine optimization" (SEO). The latter is the art of making your Web site show up at the top of the search results. Without a doubt, the Web can be a very useful marketing tool. There's just one catch. Shocking though it may be, not everyone spends large chunks of their day on the Internet. In fact, it might surprise you to learn how many people there are in the world who aren't wild about technology in general.

When you're building an audience, do you want to limit yourself to that subset of the population that is technically savvy or do you just want a large following? There is more to life than the Internet. A great many of your potential fans are out there living it.

I mention this not to discourage you from employing every technical advantage you can find but rather to keep you from limiting yourself. There are a great many ways to spread the word about what you're doing that don't require a computer or cell phone. Were this not the case, no company would ever have made a sale before the silicon revolution of the 1980s and '90s. This means that Internet-based promotion should be only one aspect of your efforts.

It's also worth noting that while much of what you can do on the Internet is free, it's also a very crowded space for that very reason. If you want to optimize your Web site so that it shows up on the first page of search results, you can probably do it, but it won't be easy. There are countless competitors trying to do the same thing. Some of them are even paying marketing firms to better their chances.

All of this adds up to one inescapable conclusion: Use the technical resources you can find whenever possible, especially the free ones. However, don't put all your eggs in one basket. Your best approach is a balanced one that combines as many different elements as you can pull together.

Explore Your Options

I remember reading an interview with a big rock act that was touring in support of their latest album. They had a single that was at the top of the charts, which meant you couldn't twist the dial on your radio without hearing it every five minutes. It was a big hit, so naturally people wanted to hear it live. Having attended their show, the person conducting the interview found it curious that they opened the show with this song, and I thought the band's response was brilliant.

The singer pointed out the obvious, that everyone wanted to hear the radio song. Because of that, the people in the audience weren't going to notice anything that was played before it. They were too preoccupied, impatiently waiting to hear that one popular tune. Since the band wanted to share an entire evening's worth of their music, they played the hit song as the very first number. The crowd went nuts because the band gave them what they wanted. Having been satisfied, fans were then open to hearing other things.

You can't talk about marketing without encountering the inevitable obsession with the Internet. It's what everyone expects you to talk about. Consequently, I got it out of the way first so that we could focus on matters that are actually more important. People who want to promote their work rush to the Web, do a few simple things they read about on a blog, and then sit back to wait for the bucks to roll in. Not surprisingly, they're frequently disappointed, and for good reason.

You can't do effective promotion until you have an intimate understanding of your product and its market. Just as you can't play even the most simple three-chord rock song until you know a few basic guitar techniques, so too is a marketing initiative a complete waste of time until you first consider the fundamentals.

Before you can make money, you have to know how to monetize your business. This means jotting down the components and making sure you have a detailed understanding of each. You'll be tempted to gloss over some of these steps because they seem obvious, but in this particular case, accepting the way things appear on the surface doesn't offer much benefit. It's worth digging deep even if you don't always come up with anything new. The times that you do will make it worthwhile and expand your capabilities.

You'll start by defining your product or service. This is, of course, the easiest place to roll your eyes and assume that you already know the definition. Because I'm often the poster child for the stupid and presumptuous creative creature, I'll go first. Since I engage in a number of artistic endeavors, I'll just pick writing as an example.

Have Fun, Get Paid

The first time I did this exercise, I thought, "Yeah, yeah, I write books." Done. However, when I dragged myself back to the drawing board to take a deeper look, I saw more. "Yes, I write books. However, because of my background in marketing, I also have some skill with commercial copywriting, doing things like marketing brochures, Web site copy, and so on." That opened up another stream of revenue.

As it turns out, before you can produce a film, TV show, or other such video production, someone has to write a script. I'm a writer, so I did what I always do. I jumped head first into the world of video production, writing a script and then bringing the show to life. It didn't make me any money, but that particular show wasn't meant to be a source of income, merely an educational experience. When I was through, I saw that it was something I had a knack for. This opened doors to everything from a feature film that's currently on the drawing board to commercials and other client video work. These are all marketable services that expand my income potential.

Because I write books and have a long history as a professional entertainer, speaking engagements are yet another source of revenue. I also have a high-tech audio and video recording studio that I designed into the lower level when I had my current house built. This means that I have the ability to create a series of audio and video training materials to sell from my Web site, at the back of the room after speaking gigs, and anywhere else the opportunity presents itself. While I haven't pursued that project thus far, it is nonetheless another set of potential products that could bring in more income.

In the minds of many, if you've published books you must be an authority on the subject. While I don't consider myself the ultimate guru in much of anything, we once again find that perception is reality. People are at least willing to entertain the notion that I know what I'm talking about since I write books. Because of this, I also have the option of taking on consulting clients, something I've done from time to time. This is, of course, yet-another source of revenue.

Define what you do in great detail. A writer who writes books or articles, for example, may also write screenplays, marketing copy, audio scripts, and so forth. There are usually dozens of ways you can monetize your skill.

I could probably dig deeper and come up with even more products and services, but this list should be sufficient for the purpose of illustration. When I sat down to do this exercise for the first time, I almost glossed over it because I was sure that I already knew all that there was to know about my products and services in the area of writing. I write books. Duh. What's the point of digging deeper?

As you can see, once I forced myself to sit down, shut up, and give it a chance, I discovered a wealth of opportunities, many of which I'd never have given much thought to beforehand. What about you? Think of your creative talents, especially the obvious ones, as the trunk of a tree, then explore the possibilities as each branch buds out into a few branches of its own.

In my case, I'm not pursuing each and every opportunity that I have at the moment, but that doesn't mean I won't in the future. It's nice to know that they're there. It's the same for your situation. You're in the safest place in your artistic career when you have as many options as possible. Whether or not you want to pursue them at any given moment is a separate consideration. What's important is that you know they exist.

Once you have an in-depth understanding of the products and services you have to offer, you'll be able to consider another important question: Who is your customer? If, like me, you end up with a long list of things you could offer, and you probably will, you won't have just one definition of your customers. The potential buyer for each of your products or services will have her own unique characteristics.

Another important question to consider is why money should change hands. It doesn't matter how cool your offerings are. People will only part with their money when there's a perceived value in doing so. In other words, if you want someone to give you their cash, you have to ask yourself what you're doing for them in return. As with our in-depth exploration of products and services, you'll find that just beneath the obvious answer will be a wealth of less conspicuous ones.

Understand Your Business Model

If you start a conventional enterprise, you need to know your business model. In other words, you need to be fully aware of what you're selling, who will buy it, and how the transaction will occur. Without these very basic bits of information, you simply can't do business.

If you have decided to open a clothing store that specializes in custom-tailored creations, you'd probably want to have a physical storefront. If you're creating custom stage clothes, for instance, you'd want to meet the performer in person so that you could measure her body, consider her contours, and interact with her to arrive at the perfect result. You couldn't do this exclusively on a Web site. This means that as part of your business model, you would need to specify that you need a traditional brick-and-mortar store.

Because you're meeting in person, you would be able to accept not just credit cards but also cash and checks. That's another aspect of your model. When and under what conditions you would require payment is another consideration. Do you get a deposit up-front before beginning the process? You might charge an initial fee for sitting with your client and discussing her desires. You would also need to have a policy on when final payment is due as well as any money-back guarantees you might offer should the client be dissatisfied with the result. All of these things are a part of your business model and are highly dependent on the specifics of your industry.

If you are a graphic artist, you might have decided that you want to get into the T-shirt business, selling your custom creations. In this scenario, you could design the shirts and sell them exclusively on the Web.

You might choose to order a large quantity of a particular T-shirt as a way of getting lower prices. Alternatively, you could use a print-on-demand service that allows you to order one shirt at a time when you make a sale. In this case, your profit would be lower and delivery time might be a bit longer. There are pros and cons to each approach. You will need to decide which choice you would go with, which will then become a part of your business model.

Ordering with an on-demand model would also give you more storefront options. You could rent space in a local mall or sell the T-shirts exclusively on a Web site. In the latter case, your payment options would probably be limited to just credit cards, as checks are less convenient in that scenario. For online sales, you'd need a way to fulfill and ship the product, so those considerations would also be a part of the model.

All this talk of order fulfillment and business models might sound a bit too conservative for some members of the artistic crowd, but it's a part of our world nonetheless. We just don't think of it that way. It's one thing to sell T-shirts. If you're a performing artist, however, you might have difficulty making the connection. It's really no different though. It simply requires looking a little deeper in order to understand the components.

Let's say that you play in a band. This means that you're in the entertainment business, offering a service that involves the live performance of music. Your primary customers are probably nightclubs, and you want them to hire you. Your potential clients make money by selling food and drinks. The more people in the house, the more money they make. Therefore, the benefit you offer is the ability to draw in a larger clientele through your entertainment services and keep them there longer. Payment is negotiated in advance and paid in full upon completion of the job.

If you sell T-shirts, CDs, or downloads of your songs, you also have products. In this case, your customer is the person in the crowd watching you perform. Your merchandise could be sold directly to people at the gig as well as from your Web site. In the club, you would accept cash only. On the Web site, you would only accept credit cards.

In addition to securing your own work, you might contract with a representative to get more gigs. You pay him something like 20 percent for each job he procures. The nightclub pays your rep, who in turn pays you after deducting his commission. In the music business, such people are known as booking agents, but this model also exists in a great many other industries.

All of these things combined define your business model. It's really not that complicated once you break it down. As you can see, before you can mount an effective marketing effort, it's important to understand how your business works. A global, Internet-based promotion wouldn't be very useful to a business that operates out of a single storefront in one city and caters exclusively to walk-in traffic. Therefore, first know your business, then figure out how to spread the word.

Know Yourself

Because your creativity is the asset that is being marketed, in a very real sense you are the product. If you spend much time in the world of promotion, you'll also find frequent reference to the concept of personal branding. It's a sensible notion in our case.

If you were going to sell a box of cereal, you'd invest in a design firm to come up with a snazzy-looking logo and box to make it sell better. If all that mattered was the quality of your cornflakes, where the best-tasting cereal was the one consumers consistently choose, the entire supermarket would be filled with nothing but plain white boxes.

It costs a lot of money to come up with these marketing materials. Corporations never spend a dime unless they think they can get fifteen cents in return, so you can be sure that colorful packaging has a proven effect on product sales. With that in mind, it's important for you to have a well-defined brand of your own, one that's both appropriate and easy to represent.

Your artistic skill is, essentially, your product. That makes it important to think of yourself as a brand. What will make a consumer choose your creativity over that of another artist? When you can answer this question, you'll be adept at marketing. It's really that simple.

I know many creative people who think that the quality of their art is all that matters. Remember, regardless of how cool you think your creativity is, presentation is a crucial consideration. Your local grocery store has very few plain white boxes. If it ruffles your artistic feathers to think of your lofty offerings being on par with a box of cornflakes, get over it or get used to being broke. The laws of physics do not bend because you wish them to be otherwise, and neither do the laws of commerce.

With that in mind, it's time to consider what your brand should be. You'll be delighted to know that it's all about who you truly are as an artist. We're not going to stuff you into a colorful box and put you on a shelf next to the frosted sugar bombs when you're really more of a granola kinda guy. In fact, it's imperative that your brand match your image, something we've put a fair amount of effort into defining. Your image, in turn, is driven by what you offer, and that comes down to your inner workings as a creative creature. In other words, relax. This won't hurt a bit. Here, have a magazine.

Knowing who you are as a brand is a combination of defining your creative work, identifying the image that arises from it, and understanding the marketplace that's receptive to your wares. However, it also has to do with your personality. In order to spread the word, you have to be willing to get up off the couch and take action. You can come up with the most sensible branding and strategies in the world, but if they don't mesh with who you are on the inside, you'll be uncomfortable with them. Unless it's at gunpoint, we rarely do the things we're not comfortable with.

This means that you don't have to force yourself to be someone you're not. In fact, it's imperative that your branding be in sync with what you feel good about. The combination of those two aspects will create an effective campaign that you'll eagerly embrace. Take a stroll over to the nearest mirror and think about who you see.

If marketing and promotion is something that feels alien to you, take heart. Your brand only works and sways others if it's who you truly are, so amplify that. If you do it right, you'll be entirely comfortable with the image you project.

Are you shy and introverted? If so, creating a brand that's lively and outgoing would be a disaster. You'd be much better off emphasizing your subtlety and the intimacy of your art. If you're wild and crazy at heart, presenting yourself as a conservative businessperson who shows up in a suit and tie would make you miserable. Your customers would also be dismayed to find that they didn't get what they thought they were paying for. By taking the time to know who you are, you'll be able to build a brand that's in harmony with both your work and your spirit. That's the path to both financial success and an enjoyable life.

Now look past the spotlight and into the crowd, performing the same exercise with them. Who are the people, your fans, your patrons, and the collection of humans, who enjoy your offerings? What's their collective personality? You need to understand their spirit just as intimately as you know your own. When you do, you'll see where the two intersect, and that's where the magic happens. The key to your brand is finding that common ground that makes people want to be a part of the muse within you.

Almost all art falls into genres, styles, or categories. This means that your audience also enjoys the work of many others, not just your own. Unfortunately, they have only so much disposable income. How do they choose where to spend it? When it comes down to you and several others who all work in a similar style, it's important to know how to be the one who's most appealing when it's time for your customer to make a decision.

In the business world, a marketing term that gets kicked around a lot is the unique selling proposition, or USP. It addresses this exact need of distinguishing yourself by conveying what's special about your offerings. In other words, what can your customers get from you that they can't get from your competitors? If you can define this and make it a part of your personal brand, you have a reason for people to patronize you rather than someone else. It's a competitive advantage.

Creative people tend to think simplistically about these things. If you're a painter, you might think that your USP is obvious. You're the only person who produces your paintings. If you let yourself think in those terms, you quickly become a generic commodity, which is never an advantageous place to be in the business world. From such a perspective, your business is just another bunch of paintings. Big deal. The world is full of paintings. Yours are red, but the other guy has red paintings, too. While it's true that only yours have that carefully crafted signature on the bottom, that's not much of a distinguishing factor.

I don't know much about the visual arts, so I can't have an intelligent discussion about the techniques or influences used by the various artists. I'm just a consumer. However, as the old saying goes, "I know what I like." If you visit my home, you'll find several prints from Frank Frazetta, a legendary fantasy artist who was known in the 1960s and '70s for images of wild-eyed barbarians, battle scenes, and the occasional voluptuous women. Among other things, he painted covers for books like Conan the Barbarian.

When I see his work, I find it emotionally stirring. It evokes feelings of ancient times, real or imagined, and fiery, passionate experiences. I have no interest in being a collector, and neither do I care to be seen as an art aficionado. I have Frazetta prints on my walls because of the way they make me feel. Lots of people paint barbarian warriors. None of them have this impact on me. That emotional reaction was Frank Frazetta's USP, not the fact that he was the only person who could create a Frazetta painting.

Move beyond the thing that you create, be it a product or a performance. Look deeper and discover what it is that your audience experiences as a result. Find that place inside them that only you can touch in a certain way. That's what makes you unique.

Your "unique selling proposition" isn't the product of your creativity per se. Other people offer work that's similar to your own. Your USP defines that special something unique to your art and presents it as a value that your audience can only get from you.

Know Your Customers

We tend to think of our audience and our customers as one and the same, but very often this is not the case, at least not exclusively. If you're an actor, you perform to a theater full of people who paid for the privilege. Are they your customers? An easy way to answer that question is to look at your paycheck and note the signature. I suspect it will be the name of the production company, not the guy sitting in the middle of row fourteen.

As a businessperson, the client is the one who puts money in your bank account. As a creative creature, you also have an audience, those people you entertain or enthrall through your artistic endeavors. If you sell T-shirts out of the back of your van after the show, your audience then becomes your customers as well. The important thing is to know the distinction between the two so that you're addressing the right people when you're seeking income.

Just as we walked through the exercise of defining your products and services, you must also perform the task of determining where the work is for each source of revenue in your line. Dancers and actors will most often be paid by production companies of one sort or another, be they in theater, film, or commercials. Musicians will be paid by venue owners and promoters, but they can also book gigs with individuals who are throwing parties or getting married. A graphic artist might find a gig with an advertising agency while creating graphic novels on the side. Both of those creative endeavors derive income from companies. However, our artist also has the option of creating and selling prints directly to fans.

These are just a few examples, of course, and the answers will be different for each person. In fact, as you go through the various products and services at your disposal, your answers will probably be different for each one.

Once you know where the work is, it's equally important to understand who the authorized buyer is. In sales parlance, this is the person who has the final authority to make the purchase. Getting to the heart of this matter is not always a straightforward proposition.

If you attempt to book your band at a local bar, you may be told that the manager handles all entertainment. You might even meet with him and be told that he's the one who makes the decisions. After several frustrating weeks of vague responses from him, you eventually discover that he does all the grunt work of auditioning acts but only makes recommendations to the owner of the club. In this case, the owner is the authorized buyer because only she has the power to hire you. If you make your case to her and she likes you, you're in. If you waste time with the manager, the owner may never even know you exist.

Perhaps you create jewelry. Your work is highly regarded, elegant, and expensive. It's also exclusively for men. If a well-to-do married couple shows up at one of your shows admiring your work, you might give the husband a lot of attention since he's the one who would be wearing your work. However, if the wife is the one who manages the household finances, including discretionary purchases, you're not going to make a sale unless she's on board. In this case, while the husband is the audience, the wife is the authorized buyer because she controls the checkbook.

You'll find this to be an important consideration no matter what you're selling. If you spend your time courting someone who doesn't have the authority to make the purchase, you're wasting your time. Whether you're looking for gigs or selling your wares, the marketing you do must address the appropriate people or you simply won't make any money.

Once you know who your potential customer is, whether it's a tech company, an advertising agency, a production company, or just the owner and patrons of Joe's Bar and Grille, you're ready for the next step. In order to spread the word about your products and services, you need to let your prospects know that you exist and why you're worth doing business with. Of course, you can't do this unless you know how to get in front of them.

For each type of customer that you have, you need to do your homework and learn everything you can about them. In simple terms, you can think of this as finding out who they are, where they hang out, and how you can get in front of them. Each answer helps with the next question.

If you create arts and crafts that you sell exclusively to the consumer, your first step is to make a profile of your average customer. This can include marital status, whether or not she has kids, how much money she makes each year, and what hobbies and other interests she has. If you can get a clear enough picture, you'll also know what magazines she reads, which Web sites she frequents, and the social hot spots around town where she's most likely to congregate. Armed with that information, you now know who she is and where she hangs out. This in turn tells you how to get in front of her.

Understand that the consumer of your art isn't always who pays you. The main customers of a large book publisher, for example, are the bookstore chains and online retailers that it must please first. The customer for your dance troupe might be whoever controls scheduling in the local dance venues. He, in turn, serves the people who sit in their seats and clap for you. To get gigs of any kind, know who your customers are and then show them how they will benefit when they do business with you.

Equally important is the value that you provide. This goes hand in hand with your USP but extends it into an important area. It's not enough to say what's special about your work. You have to show your customers why they will benefit from doing business with you. If you're an established actor with a good following, the benefit that you bring to your audition is the fact that your already-sizeable audience will make a significant contribution to ticket sales should you get the gig.

By digging deep and gaining an understanding of who your customers are, where they hang out, how to get in front of them, and what they'll care about when you do, you're in a good position to increase your income. You'll also be well ahead of your competitors, as most of them won't put in this level of effort.

As I mentioned in the beginning, my intent is not to give you a comprehensive education in the area of marketing and promotion but rather to show you the various pieces of the puzzle and how they all come together. If you're willing to get serious about this, then self-examination is important, but it will take you only part of the way down the road.

There are countless books, blogs, Web sites, and other resources that will teach you about branding, promotion, and marketing. Don't limit yourself to the ones that address the creative arts. Marketing is marketing. While the techniques will vary based on the specifics of your situation, the basics never change. If you learn them, they'll serve you well no matter what your products and services may be.

The Buddy System

I'm well aware of the fact that I don't have the average creative background. While I've slept on floors and given blood in order to supplement my meager existence as a working-class musician, I've also been a serial entrepreneur, running a number of small businesses over the years. Additionally, one of those ventures was a consulting company that taught sales and marketing. Because of this, I'm much more comfortable with promotion than most creative creatures.

Make no mistake, I've met some brilliant promotional minds who were as artsy as they come. In terms of sheer numbers, however, they have always been the tiny minority. Most artistic people just want to do their thing and hope that making a living will magically follow. Promotion and marketing is not something that comes easily to them. If you find yourself in a similar frame of mind, you can still do a great deal to help yourself.

It's common for people in the arts to congregate, not just with those of the same discipline but with the artistic community as a whole. In this melting pot of diverse talents, there is great opportunity.

As you've seen thus far, building an image, defining your brand, understanding your marketplace, and following up to promote your art is a lot of work. It also requires a great many skills. Some will come naturally to you. Others you'll have to work harder at. This is where your friends and acquaintances in the arts come into play. You'll find that most of them are in the same predicament.

A graphic artist may be a natural at designing a Web site but have no knack with words. As a writer, you may not be of much use when artwork is required but certainly know how to craft an eloquent phrase. Why not pool your efforts?

This one simple example can be replicated countless times for all the needs you have in your promotional campaigns. Share the talents you have with others who need them and can fill in your gaps with their skills. This will expand your capabilities immensely, allowing you to do high-quality marketing without spending money or trying to acquire skills in areas that aren't natural for you. As an added bonus, you'll be helping others where they're weak. Generating goodwill is always a good promotional effort.

This doesn't get you off the hook, of course. Most of the work we've discussed thus far has to do with deep thinking and truly understanding your art, your market, and what you present as a result. No one can do that but you, and it's an effort you must complete before you approach someone for help in the implementation of your promotional campaign.

In fact, I'd heartily recommend not even mentioning collaboration to others until you've done your homework, only because it's too easy to let yourself get caught up in brainstorming with friends in order to avoid doing the harder work that you really don't want to do. Show a little self-discipline and take care of the internal matters first. Doing that not only ensures that the work will get done; it also demonstrates to others that you have your act together when you approach them for a joint effort. There's a lot of empty talk in this business, so people are always hesitant to engage in what could be a complete waste of their time should the other party turn out to be flaky.

I'll offer one final note on working with others, and it may seem a bit harsh—but reality is often an unforgiving soul. You're going to be tempted to lean heavily on others when it comes to things you don't like doing. With the right people, this can be a great arrangement. However, people aren't always dependable. If this is true in life, it's even more accurate in the flighty world of the artistically minded.

Building a mutually beneficial arrangement is a great idea when it works, but you have to be prepared to go the entire road alone, doing every task as best you can. Only then are you truly in control of your own career. When working with others, keep an eye on how consistent and dependable they are. If you see early indications that they're more prone to delivering excuses than their fair share of results, pull the plug quickly and politely. It's far better to salvage a good friendship than maintain a bad business relationship, and trust me, if they're not taking care of business, bad feelings will arise.

No matter how many friends and supporters you have, when it's all said and done you are the only person responsible for your career. Take that responsibility seriously and you'll be greatly rewarded.

CHAPTER 8

Going the Distance

One of the most effective networking techniques you can employ has nothing to do with attending meet ups, honing your elevator pitch, or trying to impress a roomful of complete strangers. Not only is it easy to do; it's something that even the most marketing averse can comfortably embrace. The best way to enhance your image and spread the word about your art is by helping others in your field.

Reputation is a volume business with a long-term payoff that continues to grow over time. When you lend a hand to others, don't expect an immediate payoff. In fact, don't expect a benefit at all. Doing so will diminish the value of your actions in the eyes of others, and thus the effort will do little to help you. Rather than being seen as a really cool person who takes the time to help others, people will see you as a crass and calculating manipulator who's just using them for your own benefit. They'll be correct.

By now, you might be wondering why you should bother helping others, at least from a marketing point of view, if you're not going to get anything in return. After all, the time and effort you spend showing another artist how to improve her career could be more productively spent on your own. The value of this approach is more clearly evident if you once again reach for your wide-angle lens and look at your career from beginning to end.

Life Is Long

No one knows how many years they have to live. Some don't survive for long, particularly in the arts. However, if you look at the total number of creative people and average out the lifespan, you'll find that very few die

Chapter 8 | *Going the Distance*

in their twenties. With the continual advances in science and medicine, we're living longer than ever before. We're also much healthier as we age and thus able to live life to its fullest well into old age. People living into their nineties is nothing unusual these days.

Stan Lee, the legendary creative force of Marvel Comics, was born in 1922. I watched the Hollywood blockbuster movie *The Avengers* in 2013. As is often the case with superhero movies, he had a brief cameo. That same year, he was involved in a host of creative projects including a YouTube series and personal appearances. If you have your pocket calculator handy, you'll note that this was all done when he was ninety-years-old.

The fact that he's successful and famous doesn't make longevity any less relevant for the rest of us. We don't suddenly lose all creative urges when we turn thirty. I mention this particular age because the creative arts, from music to software development and all points in between, are very youth oriented in nature.

When you don't have much life experience behind you, it's easy to get caught up in the perspective that comes from living in a bubble. In their song "My Generation," The Who famously wrote, "Hope I die before I get old." That's the view from a young person who sees old age and creativity as mutually exclusive. I saw The Who perform at the Super Bowl halftime show a few years ago. They'd changed the line to, "Don't want to die. I want to get old."

I grew up in the shadow of the Vietnam War with a possible future involving M-16s and dangerous jungles lurking just over the horizon. I was lucky enough to graduate high school the year they were airlifting the last Americans off the Saigon embassy rooftop, so up to that point, I can assure you, getting old was something that was very appealing to me. It seems The Who reached this same conclusion, even if it took them longer to figure it out.

If you start your creative career at the age of twenty and then find yourself, like Stan Lee, still very much active at ninety, that's seventy years of making a living in the arts. For the geeks among you, that's 25,550 days, the occasional leap year notwithstanding. The amount of time you spend in your twenties is trivial by comparison. As you've probably already figured out at this point, that's excellent news and paints a very bright picture for your future. It gives you a very long time to figure things out and build a solid, reliable career.

You can have a long artistic career, so don't assume the fun ends at thirty. Picasso, Dali, and Monet worked well into their eighties. And the good news for middle-agers: you have plenty of time to make a name for yourself.

Fresh out of high school and entering the working world for the first time, you probably thought fifty was old. In fact, mathematically speaking, if you live to one hundred, it's the literal definition of midlife. At that point, you're only halfway through the game. Unlike a few centuries ago, we're no longer cane-wielding men and little old ladies at that age. We're out playing racquetball, riding motorcycles, and producing some of the best work of our creative lives thus far.

All of these age-related considerations are important to your career. One area where the implications come into play is reputation building. Suddenly, getting an instant return on your investment of time and effort is less important. If you do some work today that won't produce any benefit this week, that's okay as long as it will at some point down the line. Today, you want fame and fortune, or at least enough money to eat something besides noodles. Three decades from now, you're still going to enjoy fame and fortune as well as the occasional meal that doesn't include cheap pasta.

Consequently, sometimes you work for today; other times you invest in the future. Building a reputation among your peers by being the one who's always ready to help them out is therefore no different than putting your money into a long-term savings account. The investment keeps getting more valuable with each passing year.

Lend a Hand

The mechanics of how you can help others are as varied as the arts. In general, they're easy enough to understand by looking at your own career. You'll find many areas where you're confident and competent. It's likely that you'll also find a number of things that you struggle with, whether it's due to a lack of the requisite skill or just an aversion to doing stuff that you don't enjoy. Either way, things still need to get done and you've probably wished that a guardian angel would show up, wield a magic wand, and solve all these problems.

If you look around and see the careers of your friends, you'll notice that they also have areas of weakness. The more extroverted of them may actually reach out for help, asking you or others to help them accomplish something that they're having trouble with. Others may not directly ask for your involvement but will certainly share their frustrations with you.

Unless you're omnipotent, you won't be able to help everyone. Some will struggle with the exact same shortcomings that plague your own career. Others will have needs that exceed the amount of time you're able to give at the moment. In the midst of all of this, however, will be a subset of people who are weak where you are strong and whose need doesn't exceed the time you're able to give.

When you see opportunities, don't wait for an engraved invitation. Wait for the opportune moment and then raise the subject. I encourage you to consider your timing for a simple but important reason. People can be proud—and those in the arts doubly so. If you walk up to someone while they're in the middle of a conversation with their fans and raise a topic they're struggling with, they may feel that it makes them look stupid in front of others. It doesn't matter if this is true or not, only that the person feels this way. It will make them uncomfortable and defensive, accomplishing nothing for either of you.

If you wait until it's just the two of you and then suggest that you might be able to help them, you'll get a completely different reaction. We're rarely opposed to someone giving us a hand if we think the reasons are sincere.

What sort of things should you offer to do for others? That will naturally vary with both you and those you reach out to, but they fall into two basic categories. You can help them grow as an artist and you can offer assistance with the mechanics of their career. You can break those down into further subdivisions, but these are the two main branches of the tree.

As with the timing and surroundings of offering help, it's also worth noting that talking to someone about improving their art can often be seen as an offensive gesture. That's not surprising when you consider that our creative efforts come from deep inside us and thus we're emotionally attached to them.

One of my artistic endeavors is playing guitar. I've been doing it for a while now, and though I'm an average player, I still might have worthwhile insights that would help someone who just started playing a couple of years ago. Were I to offer this advice unsolicited, it could be translated as my saying that the person's playing was inadequate. Nobody's going to respond well to that.

If I saw a guy having trouble with a technique that I was comfortable with, I could mention that it was a tough lick to figure out. If his reply indicated that he was open to help, I could offer that I'd been through the same struggle and ask if he'd be interested in what I came up with. If it was clear that he wanted no interference, the moment would pass and no harm done.

Business and marketing topics, on the other hand, are much easier to broach. It's an area most creatives don't want to deal with in the first place. If you're talking to someone who has difficulty keeping her accounting straight, you'll find a receptive audience should numbers be your thing. If she also struggles with putting promotional material together and you know some things that would make her life easier, it's unlikely that she'll be offended by your offer of assistance.

These are just a couple of examples, of course, but they open up an entire world for you in terms of building a reputation as someone who's a great person to know. Seeking out opportunities to help others is time well spent. You shouldn't do so much of it that you don't take care of business in your own life, but it's a rare person who can't find at least a little time for others.

See the Entire Show

The value of this approach becomes even more evident as you look at your entire career. Like a play, your life consists of multiple acts, hopefully more than three. Naturally, your reality is quite different in each decade of your life. At twenty, you may spend a lot of time hanging out in bars and howling at the moon. At thirty, you may find yourself married with children, listening to howling of another sort. At forty, you could be ushering your kids off to college or careers of their own, leaving you more free time for creativity. At fifty, it's likely that your kids are the ones who are married with children and your role as a grandparent leaves you vast amounts of time for your art.

As it turns out, your audience isn't planning on dying anytime soon, either. They may spend a lot of their time going to work, raising a family, and doing all those other things that normal people do, but they still need entertainment. In fact, if you've ever had the experience of working a job or raising a family, you'll know that pleasant diversions are most welcome.

The implications for both you and your audience are encouraging. What you have to say as an artist will change over time, as will the needs and taste of your audience. Leaving your twenties behind doesn't mean the end of creativity. It merely changes how you create, usually for the better. The experienced journeyman does much better work than the new apprentice.

In some cases, your initial audience will follow you throughout the decades, since the cultural perspective you have as you age will often stay in sync with that of your fans. However, they're not your only following. Increasingly, doubtless due to the way the Internet has of exposing us to so many slices of life, younger generations are more open-minded than ever before.

I remember one night when I was shooting scenes for a Web series I was directing. I walked into the main studio and heard one of the twenty-year-old interns singing a Kansas song. This was a band that was popular in the 1970s, before he was even born. I'd seen a lot of age-related prejudice in my youth and had a fair dose of it myself. Music created by the young was good. The work of older people was bad, even embarrassing. So I asked him why he was singing something that came from old-timers. He looked at me as if he didn't understand the question, shrugged his shoulders, and simply said that good music was good music.

As you age, don't fall into the trap of assuming that younger people won't like what you do. The new generations are smarter and more accepting than ever before. Create something cool and you'll find them to be some of your greatest supporters.

Kids today are far more open to art created by people much older than themselves than the youth of the 1960s or '70s were. You may find them among your most enthusiastic supporters.

Just as your art and audience evolve over the decades, so too do your opportunities to help others. Your twenties will be a time of much discovery. Your creative abilities will expand in leaps and bounds. You'll also learn a great deal about the business of your art, much of it the hard way.

Given that you're still looking at over half a century of living, growing, and learning yet to come, you might think that you don't have a lot to offer your peers at this point. However, that's not an accurate outlook. You don't have to be the wise, old master on the mountain to be of value to others. All you need is one thing that you can do better than the next guy, and a willingness to share it.

Once you cross the decade boundary into your thirties, you will gain not only the benefit of experience but also the street cred of being an elder. It doesn't matter that thirty is far from old, only that—to those in their twenties—you're no longer one of them. While being in an older age group is sometimes met with prejudice, when it's time to extend a hand it translates instead into gravitas. Whereas it might seem presumptuous for a twenty year old to offer to mentor another twenty year old, if you make that offer at thirty-five, it seems sensible and generous.

As you work your way through each decade of your life, you're going to have an increasingly effective arsenal at your disposal to combat the difficulties of life as a creative creature. Your perspective will be different at each stage, as will be those of your contemporaries. You'll also see the potholes in the road behind you more clearly, making you all the more valuable to those about to break an ankle.

Additionally, you'll be accumulating more wealth, at least in terms of your reputation. If you helped someone out last week, it was a nice gesture. If you've been doing it for three decades, you're a respected figure in your art. Even if you live and work in a single city your entire life, others travel and word gets around.

In the movie *Rock Star*, a singer in local a metal tribute band gets his big break by being asked to join the rock group he idolizes. The introduction comes by way of two female fans of his tribute band.

Rather than treating them in a dismissive manner, like groupies who merit no respect, he interacts with the girls as friends. They end up going backstage at a concert and getting to know the famous band and thus make the introduction. Connections are made in ways that you can never predict. People talk. What will they say about you?

Avoiding Displacement

Age is a double-edged sword. As it increases, we gain experience, wisdom, and expertise. In the youth-oriented culture of the creative arts, however, it's also a liability. Industry moguls are often looking for the next new thing. They assume that this can only come from the young and thus dismiss anyone who isn't that. Advantage: youth.

That's not the end of the story, however. Ask any young person who's just starting out about the difficulties that they encounter and you'll hear a common refrain. The room is always crowded, filled with the existing players who have established themselves and thus get all the really good gigs. The young have no track record, no connections, and more often than not, no street smarts when it comes to how things work. You'll hear constant grumbling about how tough it is to break into the business. They're being pushed aside by the older players who have learned how to protect their turf. Advantage: age.

As you can see, it's not a completely unbalanced game. Nonetheless, you will one day elbow your way into the room, which will result in someone else being pushed out. When you're just starting out, this is good news. You made it into the room. However, as the decades go by, you'll become increasingly aware of the younger elbows that come perilously close to your personal space.

In fact, there's a common curve to the career of a creative creature. It starts at zero, where you have no connections and no gigs, only talent and desire. As you learn the ropes, things progress in a skyward direction. Whether you hit the big time or plateau at the local scene, you may hang around there for quite some time. Eventually, however, it's common for the curve to trend downward as you continue to age. You can very easily end up back at zero even though you have many more decades of artistic work still in you. In short, you've been displaced by others.

The most amazing thing about this scenario is that we tend to get better and better at what we do the longer we do it. You would therefore assume that the curve would instead be a straight line that always went up, to match your ever-increasing abilities. Instead, what we find is that a songwriter is brilliant this year. Two decades later, even though she's that much better, she's nowhere to be found. The industry has swept her aside, the implication being that her music is no longer good enough to sell. Logically, it makes no sense. Unfortunately, reality is rather apathetic to the pleas of logic.

The average career curve is common, but it's not an immutable law. The Rolling Stones began life as twenty-something kids immersed in the rebellious, youth-oriented culture of 1960s rock-and-roll. They're still working today. Mick Jagger is seventy. To those who believe that rock is a young man's game, the thought of someone's grandfather prancing about onstage will elicit an unsurprisingly prejudiced response—"Ew, gross." Those are the battles and preconceived notions you'll face in later years as you attempt to work in a genre that has a bias toward youth.

Obviously, it's a fight you can win, or the Stones would have long since faded into obscurity. Most of their contemporaries from the 1960s did exactly that. Being rich and famous is no guarantee of longevity. There were a lot of bands from that era who were at the top of the charts and sold lots of records. Today, they're nowhere to be found.

There is no single explanation for the success achieved by Stan Lee, the Rolling Stones, or any other such survivor. It's often a combination of influences. There are, however, things that tilt the scales in your favor. If we come down out of the clouds, leaving behind the world of rock stars, and look at the local scene, we can filter out some of the factors that might obscure our vision. Without fame, fortune, and millions of fans, we're left to consider the simple day-to-day things that can help us eat next week.

When you reach the top of the curve and are looking at a potential downward trend, how will you protect yourself? Much of this depends on what you did along the way. An old adage known to all in the artistic community aptly observes that the same people you meet on your way up are the ones you'll see on your way down.

If you've been a completely self-centered, egotistical jerk during your rise to the top of the heap, what sort of help do you think you're going to get when the gigs become slim? Not only will there be few willing to do you any favors, many will enjoy watching you crash back to earth with a sense that you're finally getting what you deserve.

Now consider what life looks like when you've spent decades going out of your way to help people, asking for nothing in return other than the fun of seeing others learn, grow, and do well. It's likely that the people who benefitted from your actions and advice are on the curve behind you, still on their way up. Additionally, if you're still living the way you always have, you're reaching as far behind you as possible to give someone else a leg up.

If your art suddenly falls out of favor and jobs become scarce, what sort of reaction do you think your friends will have?

People aren't perfect and not everyone is a noble spirit. There will be plenty of times in your life where you'll do something nice only to find down the line that a recipient of your efforts won't even take your phone call. We'll write off this predictable percentage as nothing more than the cost of doing business. Everyone else is going to see that you're having difficulties and be inclined to do what they can. Introductions will be made and opportunities will be offered.

Sometimes you'll do valuable things for people that ultimately go unappreciated. Don't take it personally. Consider it a cost of doing business. That's all the more reason to help others without the expectation of return. When you give from the heart, you'll never be disappointed.

In some cases, the people you helped will have no power to return the favor. That won't stop them from talking about you, and word gets around. A gig that came about through the friend of a friend of a friend is a gig nonetheless.

People Power

It's not what you know, it's who you know. We've all heard that time and again, probably because it's so true. You can be tremendously talented and watch the work go to lesser souls. The business world isn't fair, and that doesn't change just because we're talking about creative pursuits.

It's worth reiterating from time to time that this is business. People don't give you money out of the kindness of their hearts. They pay you because they receive something of value in return. In the case of a bar, theater company, advertising agency, or any other such commercial enterprise who hires you, they do it because they're expecting to make a profit in return. Therefore, you must first and foremost be a resource that will benefit those who have the money. Without that, all bets are off.

However, even if you have sufficient qualities to be a marketable commodity, your success is far from assured. You'll encounter plenty of instances where you would have been just as good a choice, or perhaps even better, but someone else got the gig. How can this be? The answer lies with our old friend, human nature.

A business exists to make a profit. However, businesses are run by people. As humans, we're not always logical about how we go about things. Our emotions are involved and we each have our own agenda as well. These are but two factors relating to the complexities of the human species. The complete list is long enough to keep the psychiatric profession occupied for many years to come.

When deciding who gets the gig and who doesn't, it often comes down to whom we feel the most comfortable with. There are a great many talented people in the world, so it's usually not difficult to find someone who can meet the current needs. That leaves us with the X factor, those considerations beyond someone's talent that help us make the final hiring decision.

You could be the nicest person in the world—and even a damn fine artist—but if promoters, gallery owners, or agents can't find an audience for you, they won't return your calls. After all, they're in business to make a profit. Take an active approach to your career. If you can show them how to make money by working with you, they'll have your number on speed dial.

Should you find yourself in a position where you're considering three equally qualified candidates but one of them is a friend, who are you going to hire? If all other things are equal, you can't be accused of favoritism. After all, your friend was just as qualified as everyone else. The fact that she knew the right person is just the way it goes.

Of course, not everyone is concerned with matters of ethics, so you'll also find plenty of cases where the other candidates were in fact more qualified but the gig went to the friend just the same. How can someone get away with that? People get away with unethical things all the time. That's life.

Assuming you possess enough talent to make you a good choice for whatever work you seek, the person with the work is going to need a tiebreaker. That's where relationships come in, and there's absolutely nothing wrong with that. If you've spent your entire career making friends and creating bonds because you have gone out of your way to help others, there's actually a certain amount of justice in you landing the gig. After all, if you built bridges while others were content to simply walk on them, why shouldn't you get special consideration?

Once again we find that reputation is a volume business. Sure, you can make one friend and ultimately end up catching a break because of it. However, you're going to be in this business for a long time. Therefore, the more friends you have, the better your overall odds in good times and bad.

The Benefits of Benevolence

I have mixed emotions on many philosophical matters. It's true that I came of age at a time when social trends embraced spirituality, peace, and love. I'm a fan of all those things, and it would be great to live in a world where we could all just hold hands and be nice to each other. I'm also a fan of practicality. For me, it's not enough for a concept to sound appealing. It has to actually work out here in the real world, where life isn't fair and people are less than perfect, or it quickly loses me. Perhaps that's a character flaw. Heaven knows I have enough of them.

I mention this because I've heard lots of advice over the years that was noble in spirit but unwise in practice. If you spend a lot of time thinking positive thoughts, you're going to have a positive attitude. That's a practical benefit. However, if you sit in your living room doing nothing but thinking, it's likely that *nothing* is exactly what's going to happen in your career. You have to get out on the streets and take action.

Even so, advising you to go out and be nice to other people might also sound like a bit of a "Don't worry, be happy" philosophy. As you can see, however, there are practical benefits to benevolence when done in the proper spirit. That said, I'm aware of the fact that this requires a leap of faith for some. I'm suggesting that you go out of your way to help other people without requiring, or even expecting, something in return, all with the promise that it'll work in your favor over the course of time. When put that way, it's almost enough to make me question the effectiveness of this approach myself.

Fortunately for my own sanity, there is indeed an X factor to assure me that I'm not just selling snake oil. The magic ingredient is experience. I've been around for a few years and have a fair amount of road behind me. What I lean on when I question my own thinking is empirical evidence.

I've seen cause and effect, in my life as well as that of others, enough times to know that the long-term payoff to benevolent living really does exist. I've landed plenty of gigs because a friend I'd helped out in the past called up to do something nice for me. I've watched others encounter what to all the world looked like a lucky break when I knew that it was simply the payoff of a good reputation. Consequently, I'm willing to live with my inner demons whistling "Don't worry, be happy," even when they're not in tune.

If, like me, you find value in a long-term approach to career building, you might be tempted to reach for the nearest social media outlet and limit your activities to that domain. While you should use every tool at your disposal, it's important to recognize that a significant amount of networking that takes place in such scenarios is really little more than a meaningless computer game.

No, you really don't have 243,817 friends. That's just the number of people that pushed a button on a Web site. You probably have had very few intimate, or even significant, interpersonal interactions with most of them. There's nothing wrong with using the Internet to expand and connect with your audience as long as you don't mistake the practice for something that it's not. Anonymous interaction with thumbnail images on a computer screen is not an adequate substitute for connecting with people in the real world.

Social media isn't as social as you may think. Nothing takes the place of human interaction in the real world. That's where you can do, and receive, favors that will boost your artistic career in many ways. There's nothing like hanging out with real people to brighten your day.

In a similar fashion, those extroverted souls who go to all the networking events aren't much closer to the mark. Yes, there's absolutely a benefit to increasing the number of contacts that you make in life, as long as you don't confuse it with making real connections. As with Internet-based experiences, there's no rule that you can't do both. It's only important that you know the difference.

While there's value in both physical and computerized networking activities, reaching out even this much is difficult for many artistic people. That's where making a personal connection with people you actually know turns out to be a powerful tool that's also easy to employ.

A guy who's self-conscious about walking around the room and introducing himself to a bunch of strangers has no trouble tossing back a couple of beers with a few friends. The girl who has no desire to spend time on a computer still has a good time having dinner with the people she sees on a regular basis. In both cases, it's easy because there's no pretension, no sales involved. You're not forcing yourself on someone else. You're talking to people you know. Consequently, it's easy to do. The things that are easy get done. We tend to avoid those that aren't.

Helping someone you know is also more powerful than having anonymous interactions. There's a personal connection, and that's the sort of thing people remember. Posting an inspirational message on your Facebook page isn't quite the same.

Now I'm going to completely contradict myself, or so it may initially seem. There's great value in building relationships with people over the Internet. If you think I just spent the last few paragraphs saying exactly the opposite, go back and read them again. Or, if you're as impatient as I usually am, I'll give you the shortcut. The keyword here is relationship.

Tweeting to the masses or posting a bunch of photos up on a sharing site is spreading the word, but it's not building relationships. They're two different things, each with their own value. Of the two, the latter is far more powerful. It's also something you can do while sitting at a computer.

Like many people, I hang out on a few Web sites dedicated to my interests, usually participating in forums. People often come to such places with questions. I usually don't have the answers, but when I do, I enjoy sharing. However, it often goes beyond throwing out an answer and then diving back into the tall grass. Conversations take place, I get to know people, and on many occasions we'll get together via e-mail to continue our friendship in a more direct manner.

Even though I've never met some of these people in person, I nonetheless consider them friends. In many cases, I give them the same kind of help that I would were they sitting on my living room couch having a beer with me. They do the same for me, as is the case among friends.

The key distinction here is getting to know people on a personal level. It's possible to do this on a social media site, in a crowded roomful of networking strangers, on a topic-specific forum, at a gig, or at most any other such venue. A hit-and-run approach that leaves behind nothing but your elevator pitch and business card won't build a friendship. Getting to know people, understanding the difficulties they have in their careers, and helping where you can will build relationships that last.

If you put time and effort into connecting with others, you'll benefit in a variety of ways. You'll certainly generate good karma. I wouldn't even attempt to quantify that nor could I readily explain it, but I've seen enough instances of good things coming out of the clear blue sky to acknowledge that something more than sheer dumb luck is at play.

A benefit that I can certainly explain, and have explained at length, is an enhanced reputation. The more that people know you as a good spirit who takes the time to help others build their careers, the more status you earn. With that comes the goodwill of others, often when you need it most.

There's an additional perk to this kind of living that's specific to the creative crowd. Like good karma, it's a bit difficult to explain. When you practice benevolent living on a regular basis, it becomes a habit and your life resonates with it. Inspiration often comes from an indefinable source, but I've found that the more I'm helping others, the more that part of me opens up. I get new ideas, greater motivation, and a stronger creative urge.

Perhaps more scientific minds could elaborate on the mechanics in a nuts-and-bolts fashion, but when it comes to the muse, I don't require an explanation. All I know is that when I help people I feel good, and when

I feel good, I'm at my most creative. Simplistic, perhaps, but I'm a simple creature. Sometimes all that matters to me is that things work.

Don't wait for someone to ask. Actively look for opportunities to make someone else's life better. You'll gradually gain a good reputation, along with much love and respect in your field. This is a volume business, and one that takes time to yield results. Even so, people talk. When opportunity arises, who do you think they're going to share it with?

CHAPTER 9

The Power Behind the Throne

Anyone who's been around understands that it's the assistants who rule the world. They decide what calls get through. They have countless contacts. They handle all the daily details. Simply put, if you want to get something done, chances are good that at some point in the process you'll have to go through an assistant.

Many people dream of being discovered, that magical event that will transport them to a life of fame and fortune. Others have a dream that's less unrealistic, if only by a small degree. Rather than waiting passively for some important person to walk through the door, notice their work, and sign them to a gazillion-dollar deal, they go big-game hunting.

Promotional materials and demos in hand, they make the rounds trying to get in front of top executives in their industry. As you might suspect, they meet with very few high-level players. They do, however, encounter a lot of assistants. If you've ever heard any of these tales from your friends, the people at the front desk are rarely referred to as anything but an obstruction, a roadblock to success that they were unable to pass.

While it's doubtless a frustration to pin your hopes on meeting someone powerful enough to grant your wishes only to be denied, the people between you and this exalted figure get an unfairly bad rap. They're not the enemy. In fact, they're some of the best friends you could possibly have.

Chapter 9 | The Power Behind the Throne

"Gatekeeper" is usually used as an insult. In truth, the person standing at the gate can be a boon to your career, swinging the gate open at just the right time. But only if you're nice.

The Pyramid Effect

To give you an idea of how these people fit into the grand scheme of things, it's useful to take a field trip to the corporate world, where we can see some of their relatives in their native habitat. Don't stick your fingers inside the cages, please. They're not as tame as they appear.

We'll start by looking at a map. In the business world, that's the org chart, corporate slang for the collection of boxes and lines that document who reports to whom. It looks very much like a pyramid, even if it doesn't have a snazzy-looking sphinx guarding it.

At the top, you typically have a position like president or CEO. The few boxes just under that are senior staff, which continues onto the parade of C-level executives, such as the CFO, CIO, and COO. They're the chief-financial, information, and operations officers, and they're at the top of their own little pyramids for their respective departments. They don't have a sphinx, either.

From there, it expands out in a similar fashion, with vice presidents, directors, managers, and so on, each reporting to someone above and having a few people who directly report to them of their own. Not represented on the typical org chart are the working class, the people who do the actual work of the business. In a manufacturing facility, those who design the products and work the assembly lines to create them don't get their own little boxes. Instead, they're represented merely by the box of their manager.

Representation and man-headed lions aside, this accurately sums up the way most industries work. At the highest level, you have the ultimate decision maker. Responsible for the entire organization, the CEO doesn't have time to get into the details of each and every issue. Instead, she depends on those who report to her for a summary of that information.

Travelling down to each successive level of the chart, the story is very much the same. However, with each level you go down, more detail work is required by the person in the box and the decision-making power is more limited. When you get to the very bottom of the pyramid, that invisible level not represented on paper, you have the working-class stiffs whose jobs entail zero decision making and all detail. In other words, they do the work and have no say in the matter.

Assistants don't live on the lowest level. Instead, they occupy a position of virtual authority that's part illusion, part reality. For example, the CEO doesn't answer her own phone nor does she type up her correspondences. For these details and many others, she relies on her executive assistant, often referred to as an EA.

Virtual Power

Naturally, it would be most inconvenient to have a CEO with an office in the penthouse suite while the EA has a desk in the basement of the building. That's why you'll find the assistant right up there with the CEO. The desk won't be as fancy, and it might even be in a cubicle. It will, however, be up there in the penthouse.

While it's not how the world really works, for a moment let's imagine a skyscraper filled with workers. From the basement to the penthouse, each floor makes a little more money and has a bit more status than the floor below. When viewed from this perspective, you have an EA whose actual pay scale would be in the lowest third of the building. And yet, his office is in the penthouse because that facilitates easy communication between him and his boss.

Then there's power. While officially, the assistant has no more authority than his salary would indicate, there are different types of power. Middle managers many floors above him make much more money and have absolute power over the people they employ. They're certainly higher up on the food chain than our assistant. He merely answers the phone and does the paperwork for an executive.

Therefore, on paper the assistant is much less powerful than the middle managers. In reality, however, it would be a very foolish mistake to act on this assumption. I know. I spent a lot of years in the corporate world and watched many step on this landmine without realizing how stupid it was.

If you're a big, hotshot manager with an ego to match, you may not feel the need to show respect for someone's hired typist. In fact, you may consider him quite beneath you and treat him accordingly. Technically, there's nothing the EA can do, as he has no authority over you. Meanwhile, back in the real world, he spends all day, every day, interacting with the CEO, who is the most powerful person in the company.

We're all accustomed to the idea that if you want to see an important person, you make an appointment with her assistant. This also applies to the passing of information. Rather than leaving voice mail, people will instead explain the issue to the EA with the expectation that it will be summarized and compressed into a message that fits the executive's busy life.

In short, these administrative workers, who are often treated as lowly clerks, do a great deal of filtering, interpreting, and other subtle tasks that have a significant effect on what you're trying to accomplish. The power is implied, not explicit, but it exists just the same.

As an example, imagine that there are three managers who are all competing for control of a project. The CEO will ultimately make the decision, and each of them are eager to make their case and impress the boss. One of them also treats the EA with consistent disrespect.

Through long association, the EA knows that by the end of the day the CEO is tired, a bit frazzled, and often very impatient. We all have our little quirks. When the time comes to schedule meetings for the managers' big presentations, the two who are nice to the EA will get early-morning slots, when her boss is fresh and in the most receptive mood. The jerk will get a time slot wedged in at the very latest point in the day.

If all three managers were equal in every way, which one is now at the greatest disadvantage? The guy with the late appointment will have to work much harder to impress, and may well fail no matter how good the presentation.

In short, he got screwed. In fairness, he brought it on himself. While I advocate treating all people with respect just because it's a nice way to live, I certainly advise against being rude to the people who stand between you and what you want. It's just bad strategy.

Worker Bees

I hope you all enjoyed your brief tour of the corporate world. Please be sure to deposit your empty popcorn bags in the recycling bins located conveniently near the exit.

While some creative careers do in fact intersect with the traditional world of business, most of us aren't going to be talking to the EA of a major executive. If we get anywhere near the penthouse suite, it's a pretty good bet that security will be involved. This doesn't imply that we don't deal with the assistant class. It just means that they have different titles and perform duties beyond the clerical. Beyond that, the same rules apply. Ignore them at your peril.

Whether it's a Fortune 500 company or your local art gallery, the pyramid effect is always present. One aspect of this is the top-down organization of decision making. Another part of the picture involves the knowledge and capability required to perform low-level tasks. In fact, you might say that the degree of hands-on expertise is inversely proportionate to the position of authority.

Have Fun, Get Paid

The pyramid power structure is most visible in the corporate world. But it operates in scaled-down form in nearly any organization you can think of. With a little practice, you'll see who stands behind the throne whispering in the queen's ear.

The higher up you go, the less likely you are to find someone who knows how to pop the hood of a Corvette and rebuild the engine. Instead, they know how to manage people who have these skills. Both have an important role to play in the grand scheme of things, but if I want to beef up the engine of my 'Vette, I'm not calling the manager unless it's to get the number of the mechanic. I want the guy who knows how to turn wrenches.

While it's true that some people rise to the top by working their way through the ranks, it's not a requirement. Additionally, spend enough time in the upper levels and you can lose touch with the day-to-day details that your people are handling for you.

In the world of film and video, production assistants, commonly known as PAs, perform a wide variety of tasks. In fact, on lower-budget productions that can't afford to have an official person in every slot, a decent chunk of the details are done by PAs, making it a bit of a catch-all job title.

Need coffee? An assistant will grab you a cup. She may also be the person who snaps the slate in front of the camera before each shot and then quickly sets it aside to grab the script and feed the actor his lines. When the lighting director needs gels or a fixture moved, it may be the PA who does the work. Can't afford a boom-pole operator? No problem. You just teach the PA how to hold one.

Long before your production was ready for shooting, it may have been the PA who performed the script breakdown, the tedious and detail-oriented task of cataloging all the production elements implied by the script. In a hundred-page movie script, you need to know how many locations there are, what equipment needs to be rented, and many other such details. All of these things need to be first identified and then later managed.

In this case, I'm talking about the world of video, but you can see this played out in every industry. There will always be detail-oriented tasks to be performed. Sometimes, you can afford to hire a person dedicated to each job. Many times, you can't. In the latter case, it's always the assistants who pick up the slack. This means that these helpers will frequently have a lot more expertise than their title implies. Need to get something done and don't know how? Ask an assistant.

Even if they don't know how to perform a task personally, they have another virtue that comes with the territory. When the director needs set designers, electricians, recording engineers, and several other groups of people to perform specific tasks, he doesn't spend an evening on the phone. He gives his needs to the assistant, who does the research, places the calls, and either hands out the job or gives the recommendations back to the boss for final approval.

If you're getting the idea that these people make a lot of contacts, you're beginning to see another example of their power and utility. Need to get something done and even your assistant doesn't know how to do it? No problem. She knows someone who does.

Another example of what this class of people can do for you was illustrated in the long-running TV sitcom M*A*S*H. The de facto administrative assistant was corporal Radar O'Reilly, who did the paperwork, handled the phone calls, and dealt with other such mundane work.

He was also a power broker by virtue of his bartering network. Since supplies were often hard to come by through official channels, he would get on the phone to the assistants in other camps, telling them what he needed and finding out what he could trade in return. If you wanted to get something done, you didn't call a general. You called Radar, who would call the assistant to the general and work out a deal.

This is exactly what happens in the creative world. Those who populate these supporting positions have their finger on the pulse of the industry. The phone calls and correspondences go through them. They hear their bosses talking about the high-level problems. They know who's getting what work and why. While their bosses work with each other across the country and spanning the globe, the assistants do the same, building relationships with people in numerous industries. They are the Radars of the creative world, and every bit as powerful.

Those who seem the most powerful on paper—the director, the CEO, the music mogul—would be lost without the assistants who know how to get things done. A CEO might issue an order, but it's the well-connected assistant who makes it happen.

R-E-S-P-E-C-T

We're accustomed to treating powerful people with respect. Surprisingly, for all the influence that they subtly wield, the assistants of the world get very little of it. They do a great deal of the work, are paid on the lower end of the scale, and have the least status. They're treated dismissively by those who go through them to get to their superiors, and often by their bosses themselves.

Much of our behavior in life is learned by watching others. You might think that a wolf howls at the moon because it's natural to do so. However, just the other day I saw a delightful picture of a wolf, surrounded by small pups, throwing its head back and howling. The pups, emulating the parent, did the same. It was captioned, "Howling practice."

If wolves teach their young how to howl, it's not surprising that we pick up our cues on social behavior by watching others. While this is often beneficial, it can occasionally result in acquiring bad habits. If you see people treating assistants with casual contempt, or, at the very least, mild disrespect, you may find yourself emulating that behavior without even thinking about it. Other times, we act the same as others because we want to fit in. Either way, when you give up the right to do your own thinking, you also relinquish your ability to control a small portion of your life.

These seemingly unimportant people who schedule the meetings, take the calls, and act as your interface to someone more important are not to be taken lightly. As we've seen, they possess a wealth of information and are also well connected. Another thing that people often forget about is the mobility factor.

Yes, this guy is an assistant today. He's also twenty. Where will he be in his career at forty? If he's good at what he does, he may well rise to become an important person in his own right, capable of granting your wishes and keeping you working. You can gamble on his not remembering how you treated him early in his career if you like. It's a bad bet.

Excellent assistants get promoted, over and over again. The twenty-five-year-old you dissed in 1994 now runs the show, and you can be sure that you won't be a part of it. However, it works both ways. We remember those who treat us with kindness and respect. If this is the kind of reputation you have, that same person will open doors for you that you scarcely knew existed.

So far, we've talked a lot about assistants and not much at all about you, so let's turn the tables for a moment. If you understand that these people are far more influential than is apparent at first glance, how can you benefit from this knowledge?

This goes back to what we were considering in the previous chapter: Building relationships is one of the most powerful, long-term strategies you can adopt to improve your career. When it comes to assistants, you'll often see positive results in the short term as well.

In their position, it's common to be treated as unimportant. That means when someone like you comes along and shows respect, they notice. It makes you stand out from the crowd. As is always the case, sincerity is paramount. It's not a matter of treating them with shallow flattery. That sort of thing is transparent and obvious to everyone but the person offering it. If, instead, you're actually nice to them and treat them with the same respect you'd show your friends, it comes across as intended and never fails to make an impression.

I once worked for a major corporation in a fancy-looking office building. Several times a day, I'd take the elevator down to the lobby level and get a cup of coffee from the shop there. The same woman worked there all throughout the week. When things weren't busy, I'd take the time to hang out for a few minutes, hear about her day, and just enjoy a little conversation.

Often I'd step to the side as some important-looking person rushed in to place an order. They were invariably impatient and brusque with whoever was at the counter, treating them as little more than flesh-colored robots requiring no courtesy whatsoever. They'd get their coffee and just as quickly blow back out the door. More than once, I'd ask my friend how she put up with this all day. She'd simply shrug her shoulders. That's just the way it is, what are you gonna do?

One day I came to get my coffee, and she reached over the counter to hand me a yellow T-shirt. She was a graphic artist and had been to a trade show over the weekend. She snagged a few giveaways and thought I'd like the shirt, so she brought it for me.

There was no romance, and we didn't socialize outside of our daily coffee encounters. Neither did I treat her with friendship and respect because I wanted something in exchange. It's just the way I am, and she was a nice person who was fun to talk with. I was surprised by the gesture, and while neither of us made a fuss about it, I valued the gift greatly. While I never saw her again after my job at that building ended, I still have the T-shirt to this day.

To everyone else who came through the door, she was just some anonymous part of a business transaction. I treated her like a regular person, with friendship and respect, and she made a gesture to show me that friendship goes both ways.

How you treat people doesn't go unnoticed, especially when they're in a position that's accorded little value in the eyes of many. Take the time to make someone's world a little brighter, even if it's nothing more than offering patience, a smile, or a little casual conversation to distract her from an otherwise-hectic day.

Doing so improves your reputation and establishes you as someone worth knowing. When opportunities are being considered, you'll often be mentioned because you fit the bill and you're a really nice guy. Sometimes they'll pass along a tip that can help you out. They may tell you that they don't have any work right now but will offer the number of a friend, or perhaps someone a friend works for, who does.

There are many ways you can benefit by treating the working class with respect. It's also one of those things you can do to improve your career that has no downside. You're never going to be at a disadvantage because you treated someone with kindness.

Motivation Matters

How you approach your interactions with others is important, so this bears emphasizing again. Being kind to others isn't a transaction, and if you approach it as such, it's going to do you more harm than good. This, of course, after I just said there's no disadvantage to being nice. When you're just yanking someone around because you think you can flatter them into helping you out, that's not kindness. It's manipulation, and it will justifiably make you look bad.

If you're a shallow, callous, and insensitive person who has no desire to be otherwise, none of this is going to help you. People will think you're a jerk, and they'll be correct. You can try to hide it, but every time you talk with another human being, your true nature will come out and there won't be much you can do to disguise it.

Fortunately, it's a pretty safe bet that this description doesn't fit you. Professional jerks aren't terribly interested in reading materials such as this and wouldn't have made it past the first chapter. You're here because you want to improve your career and you'd like to enjoy yourself, and the company of others, in the process.

The admonition to keep an eye on your motivations and how they affect your approach is valid nonetheless. If you're sincere about building a better livelihood through your creative talents, you're going to work hard and do your best to put these things into practice. It's perfectly understandable if you therefore approach others with a voice in the back of your head reminding you to show respect, value the person you're talking to, and so on. Since your motivations are doubtless sincere, a word to the wise should be sufficient.

What you're really doing is becoming more adept at making friends. They're nice to have regardless of the career benefits that may arise. At the very least, every time you're standing in your booking agent's office talking to the receptionist, it's going to make passing the time an enjoyable experience rather than a tedious wait. If it turns out that making friends also improves your livelihood, you get the best of both worlds.

When you get right down to it, this is very easy to do. It doesn't involve public-speaking skills, dollars spent on a Dale Carnegie course, or any other type of formal and rigorous training. It all comes down to very simple actions. Be nice. Be real. You'll make friends.

Get a Grip

Assistants aren't the only power behind the throne. In fact, the working class of every industry is full of people who can be helpful to your career. Most of them you may never have even noticed.

On a Hollywood movie set, grips (the show-biz term for people who do manual labor) are often treated as the lowliest of creatures. After all, they're just a bunch of guys swinging hammers, building sets, carting equipment across the parking lot, and other such glamorous chores. And yet, they know an enormous amount about production.

When the lighting director decides to set up a particular type of fixture in a certain location, it's often the grip who drags it across the room, braces the stand with sandbags, attaches the appropriate gel, and manages the focus. On some productions, there are lighting technicians dedicated to these tasks, but when the budget is low or there aren't enough people to go around, you can be sure that someone will ask the grip for a hand.

Sure, it was the lighting director who made the decision and gave the directions. Even so, how many years of paying attention, following instructions, and performing the tasks does it take to constitute a formal education? The lighting guys get the credit. The grips learn how to do the work.

"Grips"—or laborers—exist in all arts-related organizations. These people know a lot about making movies, books, software, and more. After all, they've been doing these things for years. Therefore, don't hesitate to ask how to do something, like set up stage lights or use a rarely employed feature in Photoshop. Not only will they be happy to help; they'll remember you as someone who treated them with respect.

There are countless examples such as this where the guy who shows up on the set for the purpose of doing labor ends up acquiring a lot of valuable skills. How do I know this? One of my friends is a grip, of course. Recently retired, he spent his career working in New York on high-profile productions ranging from blockbuster movies to long-running TV and cable series.

Have Fun, Get Paid

I met him through conversations in a video-related forum when I was directing a sitcom I'd written. This was a garage band project, something I did for the pure fun of it and released on the Web with no intention of making money. Above and beyond the enjoyment, it was also a learning project for me. Making movies was yet another creative art form I wanted to pursue, and I learn best by doing.

Because I never worked in the Hollywood or New York movie scene, I didn't care about the social pecking order. To me, this guy was just a friend who was very generous about sharing what he'd learned with a rookie director. Each week, I'd tell him about this challenge or that problem that I was having difficulty overcoming. Not only did I lack years of experience, this project was being funded out of my back pocket. I didn't have a lot of money to throw at solutions the way a major studio could.

Time after time, he'd tell me how he'd seen problems overcome on the job. It surprised me to learn that very often it had nothing to do with money. Instead, it was the result of a bunch of guys who were on location and had to get creative in order to get the job done.

He told me more than once that even in his world of professional filmmakers, nobody was impressed by the fancy gear that you showed up with. All that mattered was getting the shot. If that meant standing on top of an apple box balancing a street sign on your nose so that the cameraman could shoot a wiggling stop sign, that's what you did.

I found lighting particularly daunting at first. Much of my education came from his tales of what he learned by dragging lights at the direction of others. There were other surprises as well. One day, UPS knocked on my front door bearing several six-foot cardboard tubes. I had no idea what they were.

Turns out they were filled with partial rolls of lighting gel. On big sets, it's the labor cost that's the most expensive, so rather than trying to keep up with leftover supplies, they just chuck them into the dumpster. My friend had collected a lot of this discarded material since it was still perfectly usable. Knowing I was just getting started, he bought some shipping tubes, packed them up, and sent them to me without saying a word.

While you may not get unexpected deliveries, if you get to know the people who are doing the everyday work of your art, you'll be amazed at how much you learn. Stage hands, roadies, art supply dealers, and even the guy who sweeps the floors at the local dance school are all embedded in the daily reality of their art form. All it takes to benefit from their years of experience is a pair of ears and a desire to make new friends.

When we were finishing up my sitcom, I listed my friend as a technical consultant in the credits. Pretty silly, of course, when you consider the multimillion-dollar projects that his name is on, but it was just my way of saying thanks. I mention this because there's one other thing that's important when you learn from the working class—gratitude.

Never pass up an opportunity to express your gratitude.

They're Everywhere

Speaking of monster movies, our administrative and other working-class friends could star in one of their own—*They Live Among Us*. As with Godzilla, they're not the villain at all, just underappreciated for who they truly are.

They're not that hard to spot, no matter what little corner of creativity you call your own. If you're in the performing arts, you'll find them in every venue. They're the people who work at bars to the stage hands of your local theater company. They've also been known to hide away in the back office doing computer work, paying bills, and ordering supplies.

Speaking of supplies, as I've mentioned before you'll often find that the people who sell you paint, canvas, guitar strings, or dancing shoes are creatives in their own right. Even when you visit a coffee shop, you may discover that the person handing you a latte turns out to be a graphic artist. However, many times the people who work for suppliers aren't artistic at all. They're just regular people who have a job at the store you patronize. That doesn't stop them from being a wealth of information, resources, and referrals, at least for their friends.

First contact isn't just a term used in science fiction movies. It also describes the person who greets you when you walk into the office of talent agencies, publishers, and other such enterprises. From the receptionist to the executive assistant, these are often people who have the ear of the king. They're also well informed on the things that you care about since they're plugged into the industry.

The working class is an incredibly rich source of technical knowledge. They're also not the sort of people who end up in the spotlight, at least as long as they're working in their current capacity. Not only are they among the best educational resources out there; they're usually a lot of fun to hang out with. Free from the pretense and ego that can accompany the rock stars, they're just regular people making a living in an art form that they enjoy. You know, just like the rest of us.

Learn to recognize them wherever you go and take the time to get to know them. By cultivating relationships, you'll build a powerful network of secret allies, not to mention a formidable knowledge base. It's also worth remembering that people rise through the ranks. Today's assistant may be running the farm and doing the hiring tomorrow.

CHAPTER 10

Paying the Bills

Each field has its own opportunities for making money. Even so, they tend to fall into common categories. Whether you're looking for full-time or part-time work, your options are much the same, as are the rules of the game. Naturally, not all of the opportunities we cover here will apply to you, but even those that don't may serve as inspiration for other jobs that you might pursue.

It's also good to cultivate multiple streams of revenue whenever possible. This might be based on a combination of performing, selling merchandise, getting a teaching gig in addition to your main job, or even cultivating corporate clients along with selling directly to your fans, just to name a few.

Most creative types are surprised to learn that the quality of their art is only a small part of the equation when it comes to who gets the work. As with all things where people are a factor, the secret to success lies in developing an understanding of what's important to the person doing the hiring. It's often not what you think.

With that in mind, let's take a walking tour of the various sources of income available to the average creative creature. I'd recommend a comfortable pair of sneakers, but I suspect you're already wearing them.

Being Discovered

In the entertainment business, the most common approach for those who seek fame and fortune is to hone their craft and then hope that they're discovered by some scouting agent. As stereotypes go, the magical person they're waiting for will see the artist's work, recognize his star potential, and then whisk him and his mates away in a long black limousine to a life of fabulous prosperity.

Even in the days before most of the creative industries suffered an Internet-induced meltdown, this was fantasy of the highest order. The fact that the scenario I just illustrated actually happened on rare occasion is a terrible thing, as it encouraged people to embrace a career strategy that was on par with spending all their money on the lottery each day in hopes of striking it rich.

It's okay to hope that you'll meet an influential stranger who can forever change your life. However, if hoping is all you do, you're screwed. It is the height of folly to sit back and do nothing, taking a passive approach to your career while waiting for the good fairy to show up and tap you on the head with a magic wand. On second thought, maybe a tap on the head is just what the doctor ordered. It might just knock some sense into you.

Am I a mean person for attempting to shatter your hopes and dreams? Absolutely not. If you believe in this path to success, I'm merely doing my best to watch your back for you, since you're not doing much of it yourself. It's a tough universe out there. Nobody's going to hand you fame and fortune on a silver platter. If you want the goodies, you're going to have to work for them. That may not be a popular thing to say, but truth is often an unwelcome guest until it works in your favor.

As I mentioned, there's nothing wrong with hoping you catch a break. I've certainly experienced good luck on occasion, and I'm a big fan of it. However, you have to manage your life, and your career, with the assumption that you won't encounter any magical transformations.

If you adopt my recommended line of reasoning, you'll get out there and do all the hard work of creating your own opportunities and good things will continually come your way as a result of your efforts. Should someone step out of a black limousine and change your life, that's a nice bonus. However, if it never happens, you can still eat on a regular basis. I'm also a big fan of eating.

In other words, rather than taking a high-risk all-or-nothing approach to success, you're better off hedging your bets. The everyday work you put into moving your career forward will continually yield benefits. You'll also do the work of making sure the limo knows where to find you. That's the hidden part of the Cinderella story that no one ever hears about.

For musicians, the holy grail has always been to land a record contract. I have an older cousin in Chicago who's a much better guitarist than I am. He spent a lot of years making a living playing in bars. In addition to being talented, he also happens to be a good guy. People just like hanging out with him. He kept playing bar gigs but also continually expanded his network of people who at one time or another had a good experience working with him.

Have Fun, Get Paid

One day, he heard from a singer he'd worked with in the past. She'd landed a record deal and wasn't interested in auditioning guitarists. The gig was his if he wanted it. He went on to make records with her. He hadn't sat on his tail waiting for the good fairy to show up. He had kept working, meeting more people, and building a reputation both as a musician and, even more importantly, as someone who was a good guy to hang out with. Even if he hadn't caught a break, he would have kept working and paying the bills. This was not a passive career strategy. He worked hard at it.

In the world of writing, many dream of landing a book deal. As with music, there's often the hope that they'll be discovered, and it's an equally bad bet. The fact that I've written books has some good luck attached to it, but that good fortune was enabled by commonsense and focusing my efforts on the right things.

In the beginning, I knew I was no one from nowhere. As an author, I had no resume to speak of. I'd written a column for a new age publication, but that wasn't the sort of thing that was going to get me career and business book deals. Consequently, I wrote a column for a popular tech Web site, which not only raised my visibility but also made me some money and a few more contacts.

The chances of you being "discovered" and living thereafter as a rock star—no matter how great your talent—are about the same as buying a winning lottery ticket. You're better off using the money you'd spend on tickets to buy a cheeseburger. Work to create your own opportunities.

From there, I made it known to my friends that I wanted to start writing books. One of them introduced me to a friend of his, who in turn introduced me to my publisher. My first book was career advice to programmers. One of the industry rock stars, who I got to know because he was writing a column for the same Web site as I was, ended up penning the foreword to the book.

In my case as well as my cousin's, there were no spontaneous limousines. We considered what actions we could take to move our respective careers forward, did the work, and to a large degree created our own luck. There are a lot of guys out there who play guitar better than he does, and there are certainly writers who are more eloquent than I. We didn't get these gigs because we're superstars. We got them because we put one foot in front of the other, while many with superstar talent chose instead to sit on the porch looking for long black automobiles. Dream big, and dream often. Then get off your tail and do the work.

Venues

Having dispensed with the quick and easy path to riches, let's turn our attention to the less glamorous but far more exciting topic of paying the bills by doing what you love. If you're a performing artist, much of your work will be related to venues. If you're an actor, the theater itself may not pay you. Instead, your paycheck may come from a production company or some other such entity that happens to rent the theater. If you're a dancer, you may be paid by the company that you work for, which, once again, interacts with the venue itself.

However, this is not a constant. Dinner theater is closer to its seedy cousin from the wrong side of the tracks, the nightclub. Both may pay the performers directly. In fact, this relationship is common to bands, who only start dealing with intermediaries such as promoters when they've escaped the bars and have moved up to the concert level. Much like musicians, a stand-up comic will probably be working the local comedy clubs, dealing with the aspects of larger theaters and halls only when she hits the big time.

In its simplest form, a venue is merely a place where people congregate in order to see your work. If you read poetry or play acoustic guitar, you may also find opportunities far from the glamour of the lighted stage, setting up shop in the corner of your local coffeehouse. Like bars and dinner theaters, you'll typically be paid by the establishment itself. However, you may also work for tips.

Whether you're working an upscale nightclub or Joe's Cup o' Joe (no relation to the Bar and Grille), the venue may also have a cover charge that patrons pay upon arrival. How this money gets split up between the owner and the entertainment varies greatly. Sometimes, it's the only money you'll see, a practice known as playing for the door. Other times, you'll get a fixed amount for the night's work as well as a percentage of the door. Unless you have a very dependable following, working for the door is pretty much a crapshoot.

"Playing for the door" means you get a percentage of the cover charge the venue collects from patrons. If you have a solid base of fans, this can be lucrative. Otherwise, it's a bad gamble.

Up to this point, we've been focusing on four walls and a ceiling. However, many venues are a bit more gypsy in nature. You might find work at an annual outdoor festival, whose performance area will run the gamut from a professionally built and well-lit stage to a couple of flatbed trailers parked together. The money can come directly from the festival or through intermediaries such as promoters.

Conferences are similar in nature, albeit with a conspicuous lack of flatbed trailers. They're more akin to theaters and concert halls in that the event will rent the location, and the producers of the event therefore contract with the entertainment.

Agents and Unions

So far in this chapter, we've been considering scenarios where the money comes from the paying entity and goes directly to you. There is yet another middleman who often appears in these opportunities and has a part in the transaction. They go by different names depending on your art, but you'll recognize them as talent agencies, booking agents, management companies, and other such intermediaries. These are great people to have in your corner because they exist to find you work. The reputable ones only make money when you do, typically as a percentage or agreed-upon flat fee per gig.

When you get a job through an agency, it's common for the agent to negotiate the payment for the gig and also to collect it. After removing the appropriate fee for their services, they then pay you.

There are tradeoffs with this arrangement. It's great to have someone hunt down the work for you, and personally I never have a problem with paying them for their efforts. They earn their money. However, because you're not dealing directly with the venue, there can be an additional delay involved in getting paid. First, the venue has to mail the check to the agent, after which the agency gets the money to you. Depending on how each agency runs their business, this can be fast or slow.

Anytime you put someone between you and the money, there's also a chance for you to get screwed. This happens so often in the creative world that no one is even surprised when they hear yet another tale of an artist being ripped off. To a certain degree, if you have an intermediary involved in the transaction, and there are a lot of good reasons to do just that, you're at risk.

The best thing you can do is to perform due diligence before taking the gig or entering into an arrangement. Do the research and see if there are complaints of others being cheated or their money being delayed. If so, no matter how shiny the opportunities seem, walk away. It's your only defense.

For those who think that a lawyer will get you out of such a jam, you'll find that attorneys are the only people who ever really win in such disputes. The law is a very tricky thing, and even winning the case doesn't guarantee payment. Your lawyer, however, gets paid either way. Do your homework up-front, and if the deal seems shady, avoid it. That's your best protection.

Another way of covering your posterior is actually mandatory in some cases. Unions exist for actors, musicians, and many other creative arts. In cities where there are major creative industries like New York and Los Angeles, you'll find many gigs that hire only union members. That doesn't mean you can't get work as a nonunion creative, but before you spend time and effort chasing the work, know what the requirements are.

Is being in a union worth it? That's a question that simply doesn't have an absolute answer. The benefits vary depending on how many gigs you will or won't get in your area as well as the going rate for such work. In general, union rates are much higher than nonunion, but that's not always the case. If your services are in demand and you know how to negotiate, or have hired someone who does, the money you can earn is limited only by what the market will bear.

Unions also offer benefits that creatives don't always have access to, such as health and equipment insurance. In return for what they offer, you'll be paying dues for your membership. The cost-benefit analysis once again varies greatly by industry and region. One of the things you're supposed to get by being a union worker is protection. If a venue tries to screw you out of your money, they don't have just you to contend with but your union as well. These can be powerful entities.

Even so, there are no guarantees. A friend of mine was a union musician all his life. One day he got screwed out of two weeks' pay from a venue that just figured they could get away with it. He reported it to the union who did little more than stare at their shoes. Nothing was ever done about it, my friend wasn't compensated by the union in any way, and the venue got away with it.

You'll hear strong claims from people on both sides of the union issue. Take them both with a grain of salt, as you would when listening to anyone who has an agenda to promote. Instead, take your time, do your homework, and then make the best decision for your particular situation. Sometimes, there's just no substitute for doing a little research and using your brain.

Merchants and Merchandising

Another class of revenue can be lumped under the general heading of merchants. As with all the opportunities we're considering, merchandising manifests in a number of ways and also varies with the art form.

We've been concentrating on the performing arts thus far, but there are of course many who create physical objects as their form of creative expression. Drawings and paintings can be put into a frame and hung on a wall. Sculptures can sit on a coffee table, assuming they're smaller than an elephant. In fact, once you open the door to what we think of as arts and crafts, there are an endless number of things that can be created and sold. Who does the selling, and how they do it, is the primary consideration when it's time to think about your bank account.

We don't want to leave our performing friends behind, however. Selling merchandise before, during, or after a gig is a time-honored way of supplementing the performing artist's income. It can occasionally pay better than the gig itself.

There's yet another kind of product we can sell as well, providing we don't require it to be physical in nature. Software developers and even graphic artists often produce creations that are virtual in nature. If this is your field, you might offer apps for cell phones or a set of fancy graphics for PC backgrounds.

Alternatively, if you're of the camera-wielding variety, you could market your work to film production companies that need stock footage, either in the form of stills or video, since they often don't have time to do the shooting themselves. Audio falls in this category as well. While the purchase might take the physical form of a CD, it's common these days to sell it as a download.

As you can see, from paintings, to T-shirts, and all the way into the virtual world of the bits and bytes, there are many ways to make money selling merchandise. As for the transaction itself, there can be a lot of players, but they tend to fall into a few basic categories.

The first form of merchant is exactly what you would think, someone who runs a store. They'll typically buy your products wholesale, mark them up to turn a profit, and then sell them to the consumer. Sometimes this takes place in a physical building, where customers walk in and pay in person. However, the model works just as well on the Internet. Stock audio and video companies often do a lot of business on the Web. It's also not uncommon for the artist to sell directly to the consumer through her own Web site.

Selling merchandise at gigs is typically done by the artist himself, or the people who work for the group, at least at the bar and small-venue level. Once you're a rock star or can fill a theater for your performances, it's often more profitable in terms of time and effort to outsource sales to a middleman who buys wholesale and handles sales at their own booths at your show. You make less this way, but it's much easier money since you don't have to handle the transactions or manage the people.

Another grassroots method of moving merchandise can be found at flea markets and other special-interest gatherings across the country. This follows a split model, with artists running their own booths next to retailers who buy and sell products rather than creating them personally.

If you're a performing artist, what you sell should be more than just a rendition of your what you do live. Musicians can sell CDs of their music and dancers can sell DVDs of their performance, but those only scratch the surface. If you've built up an enthusiastic fan base, much of what you can sell is more along the lines of souvenirs, mementos that allow the audience to remember the event or just show their passion for your work. The forms these can take are almost limitless, from the time-honored T-shirt to coffee mugs, beer coolers, posters, and pretty much anything else you can slap your branding on.

Sell more than just the music or art you create—think in terms of creating a souvenir for your fans. That opens up the possibilities to T-shirts, mugs, calendars, and any other related product that displays your brand.

There is a risk associated with selling your own merchandise. If you buy a thousand T-shirts to get the best price, you have thousands of dollars tied up in inventory. If they're not selling quickly, that money can be unavailable to you for a long time.

One solution to this is to work with print-on-demand services that create and ship products one at a time as they're ordered. You don't make as much money per unit, but you have no risk since you're not gambling on how much you can sell, as you must when you buy inventory. This model works well online.

If you're not interested in e-commerce and shipping orders, opting instead to sell merchandise in person at shows or flea markets, you can take a similar approach. Rather than focusing on getting the lowest price, you buy only the quantities you're confident you can sell. You'll make less money per sale but once again have less risk.

Advertising

If producing film or video is any part of your work, monetization is no simple matter. The traditional path for films has been to get your work into a festival and hope you snag a distribution deal. However, more and more people are finding that even if they succeed in accomplishing this, and your odds of doing so are only slightly better than seeing a black limousine parked outside of your house, they don't make enough off the distribution to offset the costs of creating the movie, let alone turn a profit. Sometimes this is due to treachery on the part of the distributors, but more often it's just the result of an audience who is less and less inclined to pay for the media it consumes.

The next most common source of revenue for film and video is the advertising that appears alongside them when they are shown on the Internet. This is far less profitable than what a successful film makes in a theater run. On the Web there are really just two business models that have proven consistently profitable. One is the virtual mail-order catalog, best illustrated by companies like Amazon that sell and ship physical products. The other is selling advertising.

You Tube is a very recognizable example. You post your work, attach ads, and get paid based on the number of times the ad is viewed. You're not working with millions of dollars in this world. Transactions are often spelled out in fractions of cents. In this scenario, YouTube is a middleman, since it sells the ads to businesses looking to get in front of more eyeballs.

Due to a combination of the huge volume of ads on the Web and the low return on investment that the advertiser receives compared to what they were used to back in the days of print media, the rates paid by advertisers are very low and the payoff to creatives lower still.

Alternatively, you could sell your own ads. Trust me, this is not something you want to do. I spent many years teaching professionals how to sell a variety of products and services, and I was good at it. In all that time, the single most difficult thing to sell was advertising. The reason for this is simple. If you're a business and you buy a box of pencils, it's very easy to see the value you received for the money spent. Not so with ads.

Trying to sell your own ads on the Internet is a losing proposition. Even if you have years of sales training, you'll bust your tail for hardly any revenue. Hire a professional. The percentage you pay them for their efforts is worth it.

The purpose of advertising is to generate more business. The problem is that it's notoriously difficult to know which ads directly result in the sale. You might encounter ads for a soft drink on TV, in magazines, on the radio, and on billboards, as well as on the Web. One day, you walk into a store and buy a bottle. Which ad, and therefore what advertising expense, was responsible for this sale? The joke in the business world is that half of the ads they pay for don't work. They just don't know which half.

Selling a T-shirt is easy. Selling ads is not something you want to attempt. If you're going to use advertising as a stream of revenue, use a third-party provider like YouTube and don't count on huge profits.

There is another form of advertising available to all creatives that's a bit of a long shot but pays off better than YouTube. Much like what you see on a day at the stock-car races, you can find a sponsor or two and integrate their branding into the presentation of your work. From an artistic point of view, this might be seen as diluting the purity of your creativity. On the other hand, it can improve the effectiveness of your bank account. There are no set rules for such sponsorship. If you're good with negotiating, it's only limited by what the market will bear.

Coming back to the world of film, TV, and video, a related form of sponsorship is known as product placement. In this scenario, you charge the client for prominently displaying its product and branding in your show. This doesn't have to be cheesy. If a character in your movie is sipping a soft drink, it will look very natural if you insert a can of your client's product. It's what the real world looks like. Placement can also be handled in a clumsy or heavy-handed manner that looks bad, but that's an artistic issue more than a business consideration. Bear in mind that product placement is still a form of advertising and thus not an easy sale.

The last form of advertising revenue is not the kind you sell but the kind you create for others. It is perhaps the most profitable and least offensive to artistic sensibilities. You can produce the actual ads that your clients then display in other places. If you're into film and video, you can create commercials for network TV and cable. Audio skills translate nicely to the production of radio ads. Graphic artists will be adept at creating what are known as display ads, those colorful boxes of propaganda that we see on Web sites, in magazines, and even on billboards. You can do this freelance, or, as we'll cover momentarily, you can get a corporate gig with ad agencies and other such media-oriented businesses.

Teaching

Another way to make full-time or supplemental income is by teaching those who are interested in learning your particular art form. A college degree certainly has no influence on booking a nightclub job. However, depending on where you're trying to get work, a degree in the arts can be quite valuable in terms of landing a teaching gig. If you're looking for work teaching in a university or grade school, you'll absolutely need a degree. Corporations who hire trainers will also respect a good sheepskin.

On the other hand, for many of the teaching opportunities you encounter, a degree will be irrelevant or, at best, of marginal influence. A good example of this is the person who gives music lessons. She could teach piano by visiting the homes of her students. Alternatively, she could enter into an arrangement with a music store and hold her classes there. In this case, whether or not the store gets a cut of the lesson fee is a matter of negotiation. Often, the store benefits by selling the sheet music that the teacher requires for the lesson, so it's a mutually profitable relationship.

Depending on your experience and credentials, be they from a university or the body of work you've done over your career, you can also teach seminars or do speaking gigs.

Seminars offer two types of opportunities. National seminar companies often hire independent contractors to teach for them. This approach offers a simpler life in return for more structure and oversight. Alternatively, you can fly solo, creating and marketing your own seminars.

If you go the entrepreneurial route, you'll be expected to create a structured course, including the appropriate handouts and other educational materials. Additionally, like a concert promoter, you'll be selling your own tickets and speculating on the chances of making a profit. The expense of the venue, typically a meeting room at a hotel, is something you'll have to pay no matter how many tickets you sell. The cost of refreshments is also on your nickel, as is the cost of any advertising you do to sell the tickets.

This can be a very profitable experience but it comes with significant risk. If you're on the hook for thousands in expenses and sell only three tickets, you just lost a lot of money. On the other hand, if you price the seminars with a healthy margin and pack the house, you could make a lot of money on each event.

The other side of this coin is straight-up public speaking. You'll find opportunities at conferences specific to your art and often at corporate meetings and other such gatherings where they're looking for an after-dinner speaker. I personally prefer this to the world of creating and promoting seminars, as I enjoy speaking and have spent most of my life talking to people from the stage. After playing rowdy biker bars, there's nothing even remotely scary about a conference or corporate gigs. I don't even need chicken wire.

There's another opportunity for the people who want to pass along what they've learned, but it's only for those who are capable of running a business. Instead of selling lessons as a solo endeavor, you can open a school. Dance schools are everywhere, and there are opportunities for most of the other arts as well. For most people, your best source of income is teaching children. You can make a good living running a school for the arts, but you'd better be 100 percent businessperson or it's a disaster in the making. Do it properly or not at all.

Opening a school is not for the faint of heart, but it can be a great way to make a living in the art you love. You'll need solid business skills and the ability to sell, persuade, and influence, but these are things that you can learn if you're willing to put in the effort.

Corporate Opportunities

We touched on this briefly when considering advertising. Depending on your art, there can be a wealth of opportunity in the corporate world. You can work as a software developer and make pretty decent money, with stability of income thrown in for good measure. Graphic artists and videographers can find a great deal of work with advertising agencies, as can writers.

These same skills are also in demand by many corporations. One of my friends, for example, worked at an investment company that had a large sales force. He was constantly shooting video and mixing audio for the educational and motivational materials they used to train the sales force.

If you like bringing your art to life in both a physical and functional manner, you might enjoy the world of architecture. We think first of artists who draft pictures of buildings, but I once knew a guy who made a steady living building models for such firms. It's far more effective to pitch a client with a high quality three-dimensional representation of the new business park you're proposing than by merely showing her a picture.

All mid- to large-sized companies also have a corporate communications department, which is a great place for writers and artists to find work. From marketing materials to internal company newsletters, a business needs to speak eloquently and present a visually appealing image. If you have the talent to contribute to this, they'll pay you well for it.

We won't spend a lot of time in the business world because frankly, to most creative people, this feels more like a day job than an artistic endeavor. Whether or not you enjoy this sort of work and the perks it brings is a highly individual affair. Nonetheless, if you want to get paid for your creativity, these companies pay well.

Business Considerations

We've covered quite the hodgepodge of opportunities, so while you should see a great many possibilities for income in your future, it's quite a varied collection. Even so, there are some common considerations that cross most boundaries. It's worth stepping back to get the big picture when considering your options, as it will make you much more effective no matter which you choose.

Much as you would when running any business—and it's important to remember that you are in fact your own cottage industry—you need to ask yourself fundamental questions about the nature of your enterprise. Among the things you should consider are the basics for any business. What are the products and services that you're offering, and what is the cost of making and fulfilling a sale? That expense can be merchandise cost as well as advertising, shipping, fixed overhead such as rent and utilities, and anything else that costs money in the process of delivering the goods to your customer.

You should also consider how wide a range of products you'll have as well as how easy it is to create new offerings. Time to market, that period between when the idea is created and when it's ready for sale, will also be a factor in your decisions. If you're selling merchandise, you need to know your supply sources, their dependability, and what kind of up-front investment you'll have to make in order to work with them.

Turning your gaze outward, you need to consider who your primary market is as well as to investigate the secondary or less obvious markets. In all cases, you need to know who the authorized buyer is as well as how much and how often he can afford to pay you. Who performs the transaction is another important piece of the puzzle. It can vary from your soundman selling CDs from behind the mixing board to hiring firms that manage sales for you. Before you can make that choice, you must first decide if you're selling retail or wholesale.

As you might imagine, depending on what you're selling, this can involve a lot of effort and no small amount of paperwork. Done properly, however, it can be a very profitable endeavor. There's no feeling like making your living with your creativity.

Embrace business skills. There's no better feeling than having someone hand over cash for a ticket to your show, your CD or video, a commissioned work of art, or any other product of your creativity. It also comes in handy when it's time to pay the rent.

Mix and Match

Just as there is no single approach that's best for everyone, so too are you free to choose the buffet rather than ordering off the menu. It's important to remember that everything looks good on paper. Because of this, it's easy to get excited about a particular approach to making money, only to find that it's not as successful as you'd hoped.

The safest and most profitable bet is to mix and match, using every approach that you're comfortable with to create multiple streams of revenue. If you have five things going and one of them doesn't pan out, you're still making money with the other four.

You're also free to change the rules as you go. Your art, and your life, will change as the years go by. The world won't stand still, either. Pick the options that work for you today and put your best effort into making them a success. Additionally, make it a habit to review what you're doing a few times a year. Based on market conditions, the direction in which your art is headed, and the success or failure of your various ventures, you can always make corrections in the course you're taking.

It's never been easy making a living as a creative creature. This is due in part to supply and demand. When there are a lot of people creating, you're working in a very crowded room. However, many people have difficulty paying the bills not because it can't be done but simply because they never took the business of their art seriously. When you do, you'll see a world of opportunity. You'll also find that once you weed out the people who aren't willing to approach the business side of art, the room isn't nearly as crowded as you were expecting it to be.

CHAPTER 11

Taking Care of Business

No matter how you make your money, certain realities apply. There are taxes to be paid, books to be kept, and occasionally even lawyers to be retained. Depending on your type of income, you may need to create a business entity such as an subchapter S corporation or limited liability company (LLC). There will also be a bit of red tape to navigate, such as business licenses and other governmental adventures.

Addressing the day-to-day details of running a business can be tedious for anyone. It's especially difficult for those of the artistic mindset, who would prefer to be daydreaming about their latest creations. However, make no mistake: the effort you put into keeping your affairs in order will pay for itself many times over when you find yourself living an uncomplicated, well-managed, and relatively stress-free life.

The mark of a true professional is someone who takes care of business and keeps his house in order. You probably already know that the business world views creative people as flaky, irresponsible, and undependable. When your affairs are orderly and well managed, you get more than the peace of mind that comes from having your life under control. You're seen by the industry as a serious player, someone who's both talented and worth doing business with.

When you're making a living with your art, having a solid reputation will get you work. In a very real sense, it's currency you can spend.

Protect Your Future

One of the most annoying habits that tomorrow has is its tendency to become today. No matter how hard you try to wish it away, the future will not simply vanish over the horizon, never to be seen again. Instead, it will knock impatiently on your door, wondering why you're not ready.

Doing paperwork, paying taxes, and managing all those other tedious details that come with running a business is not even remotely enjoyable. Because of this, creatives have the practice of aversion down to a science. The philosophy is quite simple. If it's not fun, ignore it. Maybe it will go away. Unfortunately, unpleasant details are a lot like food. Sure, you can push that half-empty box of pizza into the corner because you don't feel like cleaning the living room. In fact, you can ignore it for weeks. That is, if you can stand the smell.

Left to its own devices, over time a half-eaten pizza at room temperature will transform into something very unpleasant. As it turns out, that's exactly what happens with all those business matters you've been avoiding. It's easy to come up with an excuse to avoid doing the things that you don't enjoy. However, there are no actions without consequences, even when the action is doing nothing at all.

If you don't balance your checking account, you'll find out that you made an accounting error the hard way. That discovery usually shows up in the form of bounced checks or a declined purchase with your ATM card. By some perverse universal law, these things will always happen at the most inconvenient moment possible.

An even better example is everyone's personal favorite, the Internal Revenue Service. All year long, you made money and you never put a penny into savings for your taxes. When tax time rolls around and you discover you owe the government $10,000, you have nothing to offer but excuses. Government officials aren't particularly receptive to such things. They also don't care that the dog ate your tax return. In fact, they'll probably consider the dog an undeclared asset and tax you for it.

If you've never become entangled with the IRS, ask around. It's likely that someone you know has. Regardless of the specifics, what you'll generally hear are details of a most unpleasant situation. In a way, this could be a very productive conversation, as it will give you the ability to compare a couple of bad experiences.

On one side, you have all that tedious paperwork to do, those expenses to track, and the receipts to organize. There's also the irritation of putting half the money you make each week into savings instead of being able to spend it. Thanks to your less fortunate friends, you now have the opposite extreme to compare it with. This can include garnishment of wages and a host of other less-than-appealing scenarios.

Do you really need a pocket calculator to do the math? You can deal with some mildly tedious things today and keep yourself straight, or you can pretend the situation doesn't exist and have financial and perhaps even legal hassles for years to come. Which would you prefer?

If you want to be treated like a professional, it's important to act like one. That means being responsible, getting paperwork filed on time, and doing anything else you need to do in order to keep your business in order.

Set aside the time now to take care of business matters such as bookkeeping, taxes, and the like. Staying on the straight and narrow can keep you out of serious trouble, which sometimes takes years to untangle. That sort of thing will most certainly interfere with your ability to create good art. The stress it can cause is also none too good for your health, both mental and physical.

You'll also get another bonus. Once you bite the bullet and train yourself to take care of legal and financial matters as quickly as possible, you'll most likely realize that there used to be a small knot in your stomach, which is now gone. It was caused by a constant low-level stress. You knew that you were ignoring things that would come back to bite you, whether you consciously acknowledged it or not. Once you get in the habit of good housekeeping, that tension will disappear, making one less thing to worry about in the often uncertain life of a creative creature.

A dancer stretches every day, even when it's uncomfortable. A guitarist endures muscle pain in the hands from hours of playing. Neither of them give it a second thought. It's just something they have to deal with in order to do what they love. Taking care of business is no different.

Boring Business Stuff

Because you are in fact your own business, certain rules apply. One of the first things to consider is the type of business entity you require. As you may know, if you do business as an individual and anything goes wrong, all your personal assets are at risk. You could lose your car, your house, and anything else of value. They might even take the dog.

This is why people form companies that limit liability. You can think of a business entity as a kind of virtual person or group that's separate from you and your personal belongings. It's a paper creation that can buy and sell things, deposit checks, and even own other companies. If something goes wrong and lawyers go after your company, they can take what the company owns if they win. They can't, however, take what you personally own because they're not suing you, the individual. They're attacking a stack of paper.

Sure, if you had money in your company account and had even bought a few pieces of equipment with it, the loss would suck. However, it wouldn't be nearly as bad as someone coming to the front door of your house and for all intents and purposes stripping you bare. Having a company puts a layer of protection between you and bad things.

There are a number of different types of companies, some common across the country and some that vary state by state. Generally speaking, the simplest form is a sole proprietorship, often referred to as a d/b/a, or doing business as. It's a lot like you personally doing things but just using another name (e.g., "Joe Smith d/b/a Joe's Bar and Grille.") It lets you cash checks made out to that name but doesn't really put much distance between you and the business. It affords you very little protection.

It's safer to employ one of several forms of incorporation. A corporation is in fact the virtual entity I referred to earlier and does create something separate from you, the individual.

There are different types of corporations, reflecting increasing levels of complexities. The C corporation is a full-on corporation and is the type that the real estate company or manufacturing facility down the road might use. It has shareholders but is otherwise not related to an individual. A simpler form is the S corporation. Like a C corp, this type of corporation still has to file its own tax returns, but its bottom line profit or loss is then entered on a single line on the individual's personal tax return. It gives you protection with less complexity. An even simpler form is the LLC, or limited liability corporation, which is also designed to protect your personal assets while minimizing the paperwork.

These are very crude summaries of the various entities that you might create to represent the business of you, the creative creature. I am not a lawyer, accountant, or MBA, so my purpose is merely to make you aware of the types of options you have at your disposal. Which one should you choose? That brings us to our next consideration.

If you play in a band, you probably didn't think twice about spending a few thousand dollars on instruments and amplifiers. You can't play a gig without the gear, so it's just the cost of doing business. However, most musicians resist spending even a hundred dollars for a consultation with an accountant or lawyer, even though it's an even more critical consideration than the brand of guitar you play.

You pay hundreds, if not thousands, of dollars a year in supplies and equipment to ply your craft or art. Be smart and spend another couple hundred on a good accountant or lawyer to set up your company. You'll sleep much easier as a result.

Should you set up your own company to make it easier to manage your business and protect your personal assets? Absolutely. Which form? Don't ask me. Ask a professional. That's what I do when I need advice on these matters. You need to build a solid, long-term relationship with an accountant, and this is a great place to start.

Some will charge a fee while others might even offer a free initial consultation, and they're who you want to discuss your incorporation options with. They'll ask you about the type of work you do, your expenses, and other relevant questions and then make recommendations on the type of business that makes most sense for you.

An accountant will also do the paperwork of setting up your company for you. The cost will go up or down a few hundred bucks depending on the type and where you live. It's not as much fun spending money on starting one as it is spending it on a new dance outfit, but it's very much worth it in the long run. The pain of an unexciting expenditure fades quickly. The peace of mind it buys lives on, year after year.

Once you've formed your business, your accountant will also let you know what sort of records you should keep. You should have frank and honest conversations with her about what is and isn't a legitimate business expense, how much money you should put into savings for taxes, and other such practical, day-to-day matters.

Speaking of expenses, that's another thing this boring paperwork will buy you. Depending on the specifics of your art, there will be things you purchase that you can legitimately deduct from your taxes. This can include supplies, equipment, and other such things. If you have space in your house that's dedicated to nothing but business use, you may also be able to write off a percentage of your rent and utility bills. These are just a couple of examples. Your accountant will let you know what is and is not acceptable.

I urge you to get recommendations from friends when choosing a lawyer and an accountant. These professionals will advise you and you should follow their instructions. Consequently, you need to make sure that they're respected by others so that you can be sure the advice is solid.

I wouldn't trade my accountant for a pot of gold. He knows what's important to me and advises me accordingly. While I like saving money on taxes as much as the next guy, my highest priority is to keep things on the straight and narrow. Therefore, he never points me in the direction of questionable deductions or grey areas of the tax code. When in doubt, I pay the extra taxes. That's the way I want it, and he makes sure that we color within the lines.

As an illustration of what you have to watch out for, let me tell you about my previous accountant. I hired him to set up a corporation for me. He showed up with a book that he wanted me to have. The title was something to the effect of sneaky secrets that the IRS didn't want you to know. That told me everything I needed to know about how he would advise me and manage my affairs. I paid him for the consultation, thanked him for his time, and never called him again.

You don't play games with the federal government. That's just trouble waiting to happen. When you go shopping for professional services, you want someone who's going to help you manage your business in an honest and legitimate manner. Sometimes you'll pay a little more in taxes, fees, and the like. Other times you'll save money. When you do, you can sleep well at night, knowing that you're playing it straight and aren't generating unpleasant consequences by cheating the government. All in all, it makes for a much more stress-free existence. By the way, lack of stress is also good for your art.

Your Home Office

Now that your business is set up and you're officially You, Inc., it's time to create an environment that makes it easy for you to keep up with the details. The first thing you should do is schedule time on a regular basis to perform any administrative duties. I usually do this once a month unless something comes up that demands my immediate attention. However, that's what works for me. You'll need to consider the amount of details you have to keep up with, what your daily reality is like, and where your free time lies and come up with a schedule that works for you.

If you're a photographer who goes out on shoots and bills clients for the work, you'll probably want to plan for a shorter cycle than every month. Your clients aren't going to pay your invoice until they receive it, so if you screw around for a month after the job before you finally send it, you're delaying your payment unnecessarily.

In this case, it would be worthwhile to sit down once a week at the very least and send out the invoices for the work you did. Of course, there will also be incoming checks to deposit, receipts to file, and other such chores. Because you stay on top of them, they won't stack up on you.

Set aside time each day, week, or month—whatever makes sense given your business—to take care of paperwork, invoice customers, pay estimated taxes, make entries in your bookkeeping software, and so forth. If you attend to such things haphazardly, your business will suffer, sputter, and die.

If you've opened a dance school that holds classes five days a week, sells clothing, and other supplies and charges students monthly, you'll probably want to sit down at the end of each day and catch up on paperwork so that it doesn't swamp you. If you expand the school to the point where you have people working for you, give some of this paperwork to your employees.

As you can see, there's a wide variety in the amount of administrative duties as well as scheduling that might be needed by your company. It's not important what kind of schedule you keep, only that it's regular and it works for you. If you haven't already discovered this, plans and schedules that run counter to your nature or exceed your capacity for self-discipline quickly fall by the wayside, so be realistic in your self-assessment.

If you're not running a storefront operation but are instead just a girl who sings in a local band, your schedule and office needs will be simple and straightforward. If you're more than the singer and in fact run the band, along with a healthy merchandising operation, you can still run the business out of a home office, but your schedule will have greater requirements.

In my case, I have a fairly decent variety of creative activities, but I keep my operation simple. I have a bedroom in my house that I use as an office. It's dedicated exclusively to this purpose and not just for the sake of taxes—talk to your accountant about the home-office deduction—but for the ability to walk out of it at the end of the day, close the door behind me, and be done with it. Regardless of your creative pursuits, it's important that you develop the ability to walk away and leave your business at the office while you go out and spend time with friends and family. It will keep you sane.

Since my office doesn't have to serve multiple purposes, it's filled with predictable furniture and equipment, such as a desk, filing cabinets, a copy machine, a printer, phone, computer, and all the other things you'd expect a business office to contain. In terms of software, I have the standard office tools like a word processor, spreadsheet, and e-mail. I also have accounting software that's powerful enough to capture the information my accountant says I need to track but simple enough to use easily. I have no desire to become a CPA.

There are bulletin and whiteboards on the walls, various trays to keep track of paperwork, and a shredder for the inevitable credit card offers and other mail that comes in with my personal information preprinted on it. In other words, nothing fancy, just the things I need in order to take care of business.

When setting up your office, if at all possible, carve out a dedicated space for it, even if it's just a desk in the corner of a room. It will help you keep everything in one location and also allow you to click in and out of business mode. Need to take care of paperwork? Go to your office space and be a businessperson for an hour. All done? Walk away. You're now a creative creature again.

Having dedicated office space offers you psychological distance: it allows you to put on your business hat for an hour or two, then leave, shut the proverbial door, and become the carefree artist you want to be for the rest of the day.

Being able to mentally partition these things makes it easier for you to keep your office in its own little space, away from your creative self. It also allows you to enter that space to work efficiently without tripping over a lot of clutter, be it physical or mental, meaning you get in and out in the shortest amount of time possible. You keep your affairs in order with the minimum impact on the hours in your day.

Trust No One

There's another aspect of running your business that might be unpleasant to consider, but it's too important to leave unsaid. At the end of the day, the only person responsible for your money and legal obligations is you. If things don't get handled properly because someone else didn't take care of business, tough. It's still you who takes the heat. This means you need to accept that responsibility and adopt an attitude of accountability as well as an unwillingness to pass the buck.

The single most common cause of arguments in a marriage is money. People have different spending habits or money-management philosophies. One person wants to buy something and the other has done something that prevents that from happening. Bang, instant argument. It doesn't matter if the cause of the occurrence was unintentional, you had no responsibility for it, or the it was the result of a comet crashing in your bedroom and breaking the piggy bank. You now have a conflict.

There are plenty of couples who never fight and have no quarrels over how the finances are managed, and that's great. However, it doesn't change the fact that money is a flashpoint. Now consider this: If money can cause problems between two people who are in love, how much of a mess do you think it can create in your creative business?

When money is involved, people get weird. The larger the amount, the greater the capacity for bad behavior. The stories are common in the arts. Your booking agent was supposed to be depositing all the checks but was instead skimming off the top and reporting bogus figures. The accountant was supposed to send in the check for your taxes but bought a new boat and sailed to the Bahamas instead. The IRS doesn't go after him. They come after you, since you're the one who owes the taxes. You've had a great year and made a ton of money. You come home from the road only to find your bank account empty and your manager long gone. The scenarios are endless.

The list doesn't end with professional relationships. Fathers and mothers, sisters and brothers, all show up in the tabloid accounts of those who decided to take the money and run. While there's no justification for such treachery, it's not that difficult to understand.

Like electricity, money is simply a form of raw power. If you have a circuit board operating at low voltage, you may never detect a flaw that exists. Crank a large amount of juice through it, however, and suddenly that flaw is going to light up like a fireworks display.

The same thing happens with people. We all have our weaknesses and character flaws. Most of them are never a problem because we're never put to the test in those areas. Crank a large amount of money through our lives, however, and what used to be a minor weakness may become huge and dangerous as a result. In other words, bad things happen with people who were once our friends.

Sad but true: Place blind trust in no one but yourself when dealing with money. Partners, spouses, professional advisors, best friends—they can all siphon money from your accounts and sometimes feel no guilt or shame about doing it. Keep a close eye on your money and double check all financial advice offered. That doesn't make you a bad person. It makes you a smart one.

If people get weird, you risk losing money. If you get weird about their behavior, you risk losing relationships. The way to avoid losing either is simple. Become self-sufficient wherever possible. That part's easy. Also, trust no one. That's pretty harsh, and deserves an explanation.

Life would be unbearable without friends and family to count on. We need people we can confide in and whom we can trust to take care of things when there's more to do than we can personally handle. And yet, that very trust, the handing over of your responsibilities to someone else, is a powder keg waiting to go off. If it does, you lose money or friends, maybe both. The culprit in this case is not trust. It's blind trust. There's a big difference between the two.

I mentioned having an accountant that I value greatly. In fact, over the years I've come to consider him a friend, and I trust both his work and his advice. Nonetheless, I live by the motto of "Trust, but verify." I look over his work carefully, and his recommendations get equal scrutiny. If anything were to smell even a little fishy, I would dig very deep in short order. If it turned out there was something bad going on, I'd drop him in a heartbeat. If it was illegal, I'd prosecute without hesitation.

At first glance, that probably sounds ruthless. However, there's another side to the story. I trust no one. Not blind trust, anyway. In all the years I've known him, and it's been over a decade, everything he's done has consistently demonstrated to me that he's got my back. I recommend him to others every chance I get, and as I mentioned earlier, I wouldn't trade him for a pot of gold. If I didn't sleep with one eye open, I wouldn't be so confident in what he does for me. Eternal vigilance doesn't just protect you from bad things. It also shows you who the good guys are.

I don't believe in blind trust. I am, however, a big fan of trust that's earned. If he fell and hit his head, waking up the next day as a radically changed person who was out to screw me, he'd get a little of my money. However, because I keep an eye on things, he wouldn't get a lot. That's not just a matter of watching the other guy. It's also about knowing who's ultimately responsible for my fortunes, and that's me.

Bad things happen to creatives all the time, and the cause is more than just the power of money. It's far too common for an artist to let someone else take care of all that boring business stuff because she really doesn't want to deal with it. When you give away your responsibilities like that, you're leaving yourself wide open and you have no one but yourself to blame for whatever happens next.

The alternative is to stay active and involved in your business affairs, even the ones you farm out to others. Keep your finger on the pulse of what's happening, review paperwork and figures frequently, and make sure you understand what's going on. If you don't, ask questions. If you don't feel comfortable with the answers, immediately transfer that power to someone else, even if you're taking it away from someone who you consider a friend. Especially if it's a friend. Better to have a week of awkwardness than to leave someone in a position that will ultimately result in you losing him forever.

It's your business. It's your responsibility. Take it seriously and your risk of things going south on you will diminish significantly. You'll also enjoy the feeling of being well informed and in control of your own life.

Get Educated

As with our earlier considerations of marketing, my intent here is not to give you a complete mastery of business matters but rather to get you thinking about the various pieces of the puzzle. Once you know the areas that need attention, there are a wealth of resources you can find that will help you take it to the next level.

Of course, the Internet will be of use to you in many of these areas. However, when it comes to law, accounting, and similar areas of critical importance, remember that there's a great deal of bad advice on the Web, no matter how loudly it's offered. When you need legal advice, talk to a real lawyer. When you have questions about accounting and money management, hire an accountant. Sure, they cost money. However, there are times when it's crucial to get advice you can count on.

In addition to professional services, there's another set of resources that I highly recommend. Find people in your field who clearly have their act together and buy them lunch. Not only will you get referrals for the professional services you need; you'll get a lot of practical, down-to-earth advice from people who have lived to tell the tale. You'll benefit just as much from the horror stories they tell as from the organizational tips and tricks that they pass along.

Taking care of business is something that many people avoid because it sounds tedious and unpleasant. I'll let you in on a little secret. In the beginning, sometimes it is. However, like anything else in life, we enjoy the things that we're good at. As you continually learn and grow as a businessperson, you're going to gain skill and insights. Eventually, these things will become second nature to you. When that happens, you'll no longer dread running your business. Instead, it will be a source of immense satisfaction. There's really no substitute for being the master of your ship.

CHAPTER 12

Your Personal Style

We've covered a lot of topics that will help you build a solid and stable career as a creative person. It would be great if I could give you a simple numbered list, like those articles you see all the time on the Web, telling you exactly what to do in order to achieve stardom, or at least be able to pay the bills with ease. Unfortunately, such a list does not exist.

Each person is different, a complex combination of aspirations and fears, talents and turmoil, that simply cannot be stuffed into a single, one-size-fits-all box. We could just as well be snowflakes, although that might be a bit inconvenient when standing beneath a bank of blistering stage lights.

The specifics that apply to you won't work for the guy standing next to you. He has a unique personality and his own strengths and weaknesses, and he possesses a collection of skills and talents that vary either a little or a lot from your own. An approach that's successful for you might be an absolute disaster for him.

What we're left with, then, are proven concepts rather than explicit, step-by-step instructions. In other words, having considered the examples and done your best to grasp all the things we've covered, you still have one more task to complete. You have to become a translator, mapping the concepts and techniques into a specific plan of action that's realistic for your life, your personality, and your career. What, you thought there wouldn't be any homework?

Tell Them What They Want to Hear

There's a common practice in writing that you'll see in TV commercials, books, articles, and all points in between. It's consistently effective even though it's not terribly ethical, but those looking to get rich quick are rarely concerned with the latter. Among this crowd, the approach is simple—tell the people what they want to hear. It doesn't matter if it's true or not. If you follow this rule, you'll always have an audience.

People filled with hopes and dreams aren't necessarily rational in their outlook. Many are also lazy. It's not difficult to see how this plays out. Every form of media on the planet will have a little corner where unrealistic but appealing scenarios are offered. Want to lose weight fast but not interested in changing your diet or exercise habits? No problem. Here's how to lose thirty pounds in one week eating nothing but cheese pizza!

You may scoff and feel that you're too smart to fall for something that stupid, but it keeps showing up because it works. It's also rarely that blatant. Read the blogs and Web sites of your art long enough and you'll see plenty of variations. They'll be more subtle, but you'll click the link and read the article because you hope it's really that easy. They win, because the page view was all they were after.

Truth is rarely a welcome guest. We love to hold onto our unrealistic dreams because on the off chance that they actually come true, we get something for nothing: Weight loss without lifestyle change. Fame and fortune without hard work. When you tell people that the real world doesn't work this way, they'll usually ignore you and go read another numbered-list article on how to get what they want without putting forth any effort.

When I first got the idea for this book, I had mixed emotions about it. The title conveys exactly what I wanted to say. However, down in the basement, my inner demons gleefully poured another batch of martinis when I realized that I was also telling people exactly what they wanted to hear. Have Fun. Get Paid. Make a living with your creativity. Yep, that's exactly the sort of thing that tends to be followed by a numbered list of empty promises.

Fortunately, I have a fire hose, and I'm not afraid to use it. There's an extra ingredient in all that I've said and it's powerful enough to knock those martini-swilling troublemakers right off their padded barstools. You can absolutely have fun and make a living doing the things that you love. I've been doing it all my life, and I've known countless others who have done the same. However, you have to work at it, and you have to work hard.

That one little addendum is what separates the success stories from the wannabes: hard work. It's the differentiating factor that matters far more than raw talent or good looks. If I leave out the part about the effort required on your part, I'm just cheating you, offering no more than empty platitudes that tell you what you want to hear. I could do that, and maybe I'd have an even larger audience if I did, but it's just not how I'm wired. I want to see my friends succeed. There are few things as rewarding to me as hearing from someone who learned a couple of things from me and achieved great results with them.

I can't accomplish that by pandering to the something-for-nothing crowd. I know how to con them if I want to. It's really not that hard to do. I also know that they'll walk away empty-handed. This sort of reader will never succeed no matter how many get rich quick articles she consumes because she's unwilling to employ the magic ingredient of hard work. The fact that you've made it this far is solid proof that you live outside this circle of wishful thinkers. That gives you a tremendous advantage not just in your field but in all aspects of your life.

If you've made it this far in the book and are willing to put forth the effort, you're among the rare few who really will get paid for doing what they love. You know by now that it takes hard work to succeed, and that there are no shortcuts. However, there's always luck, which, as ever, favors the prepared. That's you.

I've been honest and straightforward at every turn about the fact that elbow grease is required in order for you to achieve the results you're looking for, whether it's part time or full time work you desire. You've hung in there, so you're obviously up for the adventure. What remains, then, is one last round of tweaking so that you have a plan of action that will stand the test of time.

It's common knowledge that people make ambitious resolutions on New Year's Eve only to discard their effort by March. It says a lot about them that they wanted to improve their lives in the first place, since so much of the human race prefers to sit on its collective hands and whine. Unfortunately, by the Ides of March, the resolve of January has vanished along with the potential for positive change. The problem wasn't making a resolution. It was laying out a plan of action that wasn't in harmony with their true nature.

You've just read pages and pages of things that you can do to improve your career. However, if you make bold resolutions that require you to change who you are in order to succeed, you'll find yourself an honored guest at the annual Ides of March party, wondering what happened to your ambition and plans.

Fortunately, it doesn't have to go this way. Don't worry; there are plenty of other parties you can still attend, but they'll be full of people who achieved their goals and moved that much closer to their dreams. All you have to do to keep yourself on track is to create a plan that's realistic for your personal nature. It's really that simple.

Level Management

Entire books have been written on self-discovery, and it might be worth the trip to your local bookstore to browse a few. However, since we don't have that kind of time, let's focus on the aspects of your personality that have an effect on your career efforts.

To get the greatest benefit, take the time to make another pass through this book, skimming rather than reading word for word. By now you already know the concepts and techniques that caught your attention in each chapter. As you flip back through the pages, make a list of the things that you felt would be helpful when you first read them.

Some of them will have resonated with you, leaving you with the feeling that they're great ideas. You are excited about diving into them. That will be level one. There will be a second level of things, which are those that you very much want to do but know they are going to take self-discipline to accomplish. These are both groups of things that will come easily to you.

The third level will be things you feel that you should do. Even though you're not excited about them, they make sense to you logically and so you feel obligated to pursue them. The fourth level will be things that don't really apply to your specific art form. For example, if you're working as a software developer, the paragraph about booking a gig at Joe's Bar and Grille probably didn't have a direct application to you, so you passed it by.

Of the four, it's the level-three issues that most often trip us up. Feeling like we should do something has very little motivational value. It's an intellectual consideration that may well be valid, but the intellect doesn't drive us to act. Emotions and passion do. Even so, we often clutter our to-do lists with these well-intentioned tasks even though they do little more than take up space on the page.

For example, anyone who can read knows that smoking cigarettes is bad for you. That knowledge has very little impact on a smoker's behavior. I smoked for many years, even though I was perfectly capable of reading the little label that said it wasn't something my body was terribly fond of. Many of us who smoked knew that we should make a change, but we didn't. That's because the desire to quit smoking was a level-three goal, something we felt like we were obligated to do. That kind of motivation never works.

No one ever quits smoking because they think they should. They try but start back up a week or a month later. Don't ask me how I know. People only succeed in quitting when they *want* to. That seems like a subtle distinction, but it moves the action from level three to level one, and that makes all the difference in the world.

In my twenties, I suffered a minor collapsed lung. Not once. Three times. Bizarre though it may seem, I kept smoking. I never said I was the brightest bulb in the box. However, it was not only an unpleasant experience; it was interfering with my ability to sing. The third time it happened, I got fed up and said screw it. I pulled half a carton of smokes off the top of the refrigerator, gave them to a friend, and I was done with it.

There were no nicotine withdrawal devices available then or any other such nonsense that people want to sell you products for. However, despite the fact that I'd been smoking three packs a day, it wasn't at all difficult to do. I knew I was used to having a cigarette in my mouth and playing with it between my fingers, so I did something about it. I bought boxes of wooden matchsticks and toothpicks and kept them in my pocket for a couple of weeks. I chewed on them and twirled them between my fingers instead of reaching for a smoke.

I never succeeded in quitting when I thought it was something that I should do. I quit in a heartbeat when it was something I wanted to do. If you attempt to accomplish your list only out of a sense of obligation, it's very likely that you won't accomplish the goals in level three because you'll have no fire in the belly (unless you swallow the cigarette, of course). Sure, you can force yourself to try for a few weeks, but eventually your true nature will prevail and you'll quit.

When you change the "should dos" to "want to dos," your professional life as an artist will change dramatically. You'll start attending to the parts of the your career that lead to new and better opportunities.

That doesn't mean there's nothing you can do with your level-three goals. It merely indicates that you have to know your nature and approach them accordingly. When I wanted to quit smoking, it moved from level three to level one, but that alone wasn't enough. I knew my nature. By buying matchsticks and toothpicks, I took the appropriate steps to preempt trouble before it happened. This is what you'll need to do if you're to move a goal up a couple of levels.

Chapter 12 | Your Personal Style

I'll offer an embarrassing little story of my own as an example of how this can work. I made a joke in an earlier chapter about having had a hard time keeping the living room vacuumed before robots came along. It wasn't a joke. Living in Atlanta, allergies are a reality for a lot of people, and I'm not immune to such little inconveniences. One of the basic things you should do, of course, is dust and vacuum on a regular basis so that there's less stuff floating around in the air to annoy you.

I'm a single guy living alone, and while I keep the place clean in general, housekeeping isn't something I'm highly motivated to do. This means the floors don't get vacuumed with clockwork precision. From a level-three point of view, it's something I know I'm supposed to do consistently. As someone who spends a fair amount of time in self-examination, I also know that since it's a tedious and time-consuming task, I'm always going to find an excuse to procrastinate in favor of doing more interesting things.

The way I moved vacuuming from level three to level one was to buy a Roomba, one of those little round robots that vacuum a room automatically without any need for supervision. This solution was in harmony with my nature in a couple of ways. To start with, I'm not just a creative creature; I'm also a geek. Robots are fun. Additionally, they require very little time and effort, so they destroy the procrastination barrier. The floors now get vacuumed with stunning regularity. I'm still looking for a droid that can handle the dusting.

This particular example involved spending money, but that isn't the point and will rarely be the case. What it illustrates is that I understood my weaknesses and looked at the problem from different angles until I found a solution that I wouldn't abandon. Sure, I could have just said this is something I need to do and expected self-discipline to get me to the finish line. Were that the case, you'd see me having drinks at the Ides of March party.

I've advocated self-discipline at several points along the way, and yet at this point I'm quickly throwing it out the window. That will seem like a bit of a mixed message and thus deserves clarification.

I'm not wild about paying my bills. I have the money in the bank, so there's no financial stress involved. It's just a tedious and time-consuming chore that I don't particularly enjoy. You know, like running a vacuum cleaner.

Nonetheless, every month I sit down, fire up the checking software, go through all the bills, make the payments, and clean up all the empty envelopes when I'm done. It's a task I don't want to do, but I'm able to employ self-discipline to accomplish the goal anyway. Why is this different?

The secret lies in consequences, which can be a powerful motivation. If I don't vacuum the floor for a few weeks, it's not a crisis, so I can get away with procrastination. If I don't pay my electricity bill, they turn off my power. That's not a consequence I'm willing to live with, so I show a little backbone and get the bills paid. Understand your nature, be honest with yourself about what you want to do versus those level-three obligations, and review the consequences. Combined, these things will help you either move something to level one or realize that it's okay to leave it where it is and spend your time on other tasks.

We don't want the fourth level to feel completely left out, so let's give it a quick look. While the items on this list aren't high priority for you today, some of them may have value to you in a future effort. When you have the important stuff under control and your career is rocking along, you might make another sweep through the chapters to find ways to take your career up a notch.

If you're a software developer, you're probably not going to get a gig at Joe's Bar and Grille where you sit on stage with your laptop and ignore the crowd while you write a program. On the other hand, Joe is always looking for ways to take his business to the next level too, and most of his crowd shows up with a cell phone in their pockets. Is there an app you could write for Joe that would make the experience better for his customers and in turn make him more money? That's how you get some mileage out of a level-four goal. Look at it sideways and see what reflects off the paint job.

As you go back through the book skimming the chapters for things to do, you'll learn a lot about yourself by examining your gut reaction to each task. By being honest with yourself and placing each activity at the right level, you'll be able to build a plan of action that is realistic for your personality. That means you can skip the Ides of March party. You'll be too busy accomplishing your goals to attend it.

Track It

In the world of million-dollar Madison Avenue marketing campaigns, they don't just kick out a couple of ads and hope they do the client some good. There's an entire industry built on tracking and measuring the response to an advertising campaign. Ad agencies create campaigns based in part on the data they've gathered and analyzed from previous attempts. They track what works and what doesn't, and apply what they learn to create ever more effective ads for their customers.

As an example, if you live anywhere near the software business, you'll hear people kicking around phrases like "A/B testing." This type of test might be something as simple as deploying two Web pages that have identical content but different design elements, such as varying color combinations, the use of buttons rather than links, and so on. The analysts will then track which page performs best in terms of the action they want the visitor to take.

While you probably have little desire to become a professional data analyst, there's a lesson to be learned here. If you embark on a new initiative to improve your career, how are you going to know which aspects of your plan worked and which underperformed?

Without that knowledge, you can easily waste a lot of time on something that's not going to give you an adequate return on your investment. You'll have some vague notions of things improving or staying the same, but you won't know why. Without information, it will be difficult for you to make corrections in our course to improve the situation. However, if you're well informed, you'll be able to isolate a part of your plan that isn't delivering the way you'd like and tweak it until it either works or can be written off as not worth the trouble.

Test and analyze your efforts. When you find something that works (advertising, business development, a promotional event, etc.), stomp your foot on the gas pedal. You've just discovered something important. Likewise, lay off efforts—as soon as possible—that result in meager gains. The point is to look for the things that will move your career as an artist to the next level, and to document the steps you took to achieve that particular success so that you can reproduce it in the future.

We've been talking about staying true to your nature, and there is another area where it is important to keep this in mind. If you buy a bunch of software to track and analyze data along with making ambitious plans to log each and every event that happens in mind-numbing detail, your efforts will only succeed if you're really into that sort of thing. If balancing your checkbook is tedious beyond belief, there's no way you're going to use all that fancy software. It'll just sit and gather dust. If it helps, I know where you can get a really cool robot, but you'll have to put the CDs on the floor.

Fortunately, there's more than one way to keep track of your career. At a high level, all you're really looking to accomplish is maintaining a record of how your efforts go so that you can refer to them later. With that in mind, you have a lot of options.

I use a surprisingly low-tech method to keep up with the events of my life and career. I keep a journal, which sounds far more formal than it really is. Tucked away in the corner of my reading room is a stack of cheap spiral notebooks, the kind you can buy for a couple of bucks in the school-supplies section of your local grocery store. I invested another few dollars in a clipboard.

That's it. That's my journal. All I need is a pen. I don't have to worry about rebooting it, or a hard drive becoming corrupted. It works in bright sunlight or a candlelit room. Just as important for my own preferences, I don't have to worry about it becoming obsolete. I have notebooks going back to the early 1980s. They still work.

For the most part, I merge all my creative endeavors and life's little lessons together in these books. I often sit down with a pen and legal pad to scribble out notes for some project I'm working on, but if it's something I want to remember thirty years from now, I make note of it in the journal.

Anyone who knows me will attest to the fact that I'm not averse to technology. I've paid the bills writing software; I have state-of-the-art audio and video production facilities; and there are computers, pads, and cell phones littering my house. I even have maintenance droids to vacuum and mop my floors. Even so, there are times when it's just more comfortable for me to sit down with a legal pad on a clipboard and scribble things with a pen. There's also the longevity factor that paper offers. So, this is what works for me.

You may find pen and paper clumsy and prefer a completely different scenario. There are a lot of good ones to choose from. Some prefer to use a camera, whether in their laptop, pad, or cell phone, and record events vlogger style (that's slang for video logging for those not up on such things). It's simple and easy to do. Press Record, talk, and press Stop when you're done. If you like, you can employ a similar approach using a microphone, doing an audio-only version.

You can also use your computer and write documents with your favorite word processor or text editor. Maybe you print them for posterity, maybe you don't. Your notes can be a series of paragraphs or a highly structured outline. All that matters is that it be a method of communication that feels natural to you and is easy to comprehend when you come back later to ponder your musings.

You'll find a lot of Web-based services as well. Today, it's trendy to refer to this as "Putting things in the cloud." Five years from now, there will be a different buzzword. The only caution I would offer regarding this approach is that the service you're using is probably free or very cheap. There's no guarantee the company will be around five years from now and if they die, they'll take your notes with them.

If the cloud works for you, it's what you should use. Just make sure you have backups so you don't lose anything. We keep notes because we don't have a clear recollection of what we did on the 2nd of August ten years ago. You won't be able to reconstruct your notes from memory if you lose them.

This is not an exhaustive list of your options, but it should give you a good idea of what's available. The next question is simple: what should you record in your notes?

Track What?

There are several benefits that you can derive from this practice, so that's what should drive your actions. The first one we've already touched on. If you're taking steps to improve your career, you'll want to make note of what you did, when you did it, and how.

There's nothing more frustrating than doing something, seeing positive results, and then coming back in the future to do it again but not remembering all the steps you took. In today's increasingly technological society, things can be complex. There's no shame in having a cheat sheet to walk your future self through the steps.

Timing is often important as well. If you did a promotion to help sell your band's CDs and it was a huge success, you'll want to repeat that plan when you record something new. However, to your dismay, you find that this time around, it doesn't bring you the same results. How could this be? Does your music suddenly suck?

While audiences are notoriously fickle and the creative output of a band is far from constant, in this case you did your first promotion in October, just in time for the holiday shopping season. The second promotion was done in April, right before tax time. Far from being in a shopping mood, your fans were more concerned about paying the IRS. You lose.

With this information, you might try again when the holidays roll around and enjoy the same success as your previous release. The timing might have escaped your attention and you might have simply given up on your latest CD. Instead, it becomes yet another big seller.

In addition to tracking efforts to help with making necessary changes, there's another benefit to keeping notes. As you put more and more effort into building your business, you'll be doing things that are hard work and occasionally outside of your comfort zone. When it comes time to doing yet another difficult thing, motivation is important.

Keeping careful notes on what you did and how things turned out is important for another reason: The practice is hard at first, but the results show you that yes, indeed, it is possible to leave your comfort zone. They also remind you that good things happen when you do. That's motivation that will carry your career forward.

As you sit there staring at that item on your to-do list and trying to gear up for the effort, sometimes it helps to look back at your previous efforts, particularly the ones that were difficult. If you're keeping track of things in an organized manner—in other words in the organizational style that works for you—you'll be able to review that time period when you were doing the hard work and then check your notes further down the road to see the kinds of results you got. When I'm making entries about things going well, I make it a point to mention the effort that was responsible so that I can easily relate cause and effect.

Armed with this information, you can see that you did some hard work. However, with the results logged in addition to the effort, it reminds you that it was all very much worth it. Nothing fires us up like getting results. That makes it easier to get up off the couch and do that next batch of hard work.

When *Apollo 13* had a blowout in the middle of nowhere, NASA got the crippled spaceship home again with all the astronauts alive. They referred to the mission as a successful failure. Yes, the mission had to be aborted and thus was a failure. On the other hand, they succeeded in coping with the crisis and saving the crew. It could very easily have gone the other way. From that perspective, the failure was a success.

Sometimes you'll put heart, body, and soul into a plan and it simply won't pan out. In the simplest terms, the effort was a failure. When this happens, and it will, you'll want to analyze what went wrong. The insights you gain on why your plan didn't work may very well show you how to do it right the next time, as in our previous example of timing and holiday shopping. In short, you want all your failures to be successful failures. Keeping track of things allows you to do exactly that.

Your notes don't have to be all about you, by the way. There are a lot of people out there engaged in the same form of creativity as you. Some are rock stars, but a lot are working at your level. They are your peers, and they're just as interested in moving their careers forward as you are with your own. If you pay attention to how they do things, you can learn a lot.

Sometimes they'll give a performance that's absolutely brilliant and their audience will respond in kind. They might have similar success with an approach to booking gigs or selling merchandise. Whatever it is, you can learn from it. Obviously there are boundaries regarding emulation, particularly in the expression of the art itself. That said, you can always learn from others, and it's a pretty good bet that your expression will be your own so there's little risk of being a copycat.

Your peers will also show you where the potholes are so that you don't have to break an ankle finding out about them the hard way. If a local band ends the show by firing a bunch of confetti cannons into the audience at the end of the show, the crowd may love it. It might therefore surprise you that management will not book them back into that venue anymore.

When the show's over and the crowd goes home, the people who work in the bar have to clean up the mess. If they get tired of all the extra work the band is causing, they may complain enough to get the band bounced off of the booking list. As you hear the tale from a waitress friend who works there, you make a mental note. Confetti cannons, bad. Very bad. Check.

Ebb and Flow

There is nothing normal about being a creative creature, including the flow of our lives. Just like regular people, we have ups and downs in our relationships, our health, and every other aspect of life. Careers will be a roller coaster as well. Sometimes the best thing you can do is just wave your hands in the air and go with it.

It's common when embracing a particular area of self-improvement to have a period of inspiration and go great guns for a while, giving it everything you've got. This is inevitably followed by the effort coming to a complete halt, possibly forever. Naturally, in a life that may well last a hundred years, this doesn't get you very far in pursuit of your dreams.

True success comes from long-term, steady effort, not short bursts of effort followed by prolonged periods of inactivity. It's actually easier to put out a high-intensity effort for a brief period than it is to sustain a lower-level effort for a long time. That's because the bright flash of activity is typically triggered by something that excites us, and the energy we feel from it is what powers our Herculean push. Of course, it doesn't last, but it's fun while it does. Putting one foot after another, day after day, often doesn't feel like high-voltage electricity coursing through our veins. It feels like work.

Regardless of the sensation, the math is easy enough to do. If you spend nights and weekends putting in 40 hours of effort every week, you might be able to stick with it for a couple of months before you burn out. Then you never attempt it again. Eight weeks of this gives you a grand total of 320 hours of effort.

Now let's look at a different level of effort, where you spend only 10 hours a week. Because it's not so overwhelming, you have no trouble keeping it up. At the end of one year, you'll have put in 520 hours. In five years, you've racked up 2,600 hours. You're going to wake up five years from now one way or the other. Would you rather have a couple thousand hours of effort behind you or a few hundred? That's the power of a sustained initiative.

Even if you go the slow-and-steady route, there will be times when you get knocked off track. Count on it. Other things will happen in your life to distract you. When you return to your art, you'll realize that you haven't done anything for weeks. It's not uncommon for people to never get back on track at this point, letting their efforts fall by the wayside.

Anyone who's spent a little time trying to meditate will be familiar with this cycle, which happens in a much shorter time frame when you sit to clear your mind. You're trying to think of nothing, and that ain't easy to begin with. You managed to clear your head for the briefest of moments and the next thing you know, you're thinking about the fact that you need to do the laundry.

In the classic tale of the tortoise and the hare, the turtle won the race by consistently putting one foot in front of the other. The rabbit used up all his energy early on and had to take a nap. Unless you're running the hundred-meter dash, slow and steady wins the race.

Frustrated that you can't stay focused, you now have two problems. Not only is your mind not clear; now you're thinking about the fact that you're frustrated, at which point you become impatient with yourself for your frustration, which feeds back on itself in an endless loop. Naturally, your mind isn't getting any clearer.

I heard a story about a guy who used to meditate in his backyard. Every now and then, a jet would pass noisily above him. At first, this was a distraction. Eventually, however, he just started meditating on the airplane. When the airplane was out of earshot, he'd transition back to where he was before.

A little too cosmic for you? The moral of our little diversion into the land of lotus blossoms isn't difficult to grasp. Life will knock you off track. When it does, instead of indulging in self-recrimination for your inconsistencies, just let it go. Getting angry with yourself doesn't move you forward. Dive right back in, and before you know it you'll be happily immersed in productivity again.

And what of those times when you're on track but life tugs insistently at your sleeve? Meditate on the airplane. If life needs your attention, it's not going to give up. Instead of fighting it, just roll with it. Deal with life, do what you gotta do, and after the airplane passes return to what you were doing. It's actually not hard at all.

One thing that will help you return to your regularly scheduled efforts when you get bounced off track a bit is to have a few baby steps that you can take. If you're trying to put together a promotion plan, part of the work might be something simple and mindless like searching the Web to build a list of bloggers you want to contact. That's something that you can always use, and it's easier than the other things on your list.

If you wake up and it's been a few weeks since you were following your plan, don't try to dive back in with all four paws if that seems overwhelming. Instead, let yourself do some light work for a few days, like building your list. Doing so will get your head back into the game, and before you know it, you'll return to full power.

You're in this for the long haul, so you're going to experience high tides as well as low over the course of your life. Instead of fighting the current, learn how to go with the flow. You'll get wet either way, but at least your arms won't be as tired.

You Can Do It

Creatives are empowered today as never before. We don't have to spend hundreds of thousands of dollars to gain access to professional audio or video resources. We can take our art directly to the people via the Internet. The management tools on the average home computer offer the kind of power once reserved for major international corporations. It's a great time to be alive.

It's never been easy to succeed in the arts, but today most of the roadblocks are gone. While you do have to possess talent, that used to be just a small part of the equation. In the past, there were many other qualifications that were beyond the reach of the average artist, who had to make it past gatekeepers or come up with a huge budget in order to create. Today, all that's required to make a decent living is consistent effort and a bit of commonsense.

Even though the possibilities are now opening up to us more with each passing day, most of the creative people you know won't succeed. Some may be more talented than you, and their audience may love them. However, without that secret ingredient of hard work, it just doesn't matter. There is no quick and easy path to fame and fortune, and there is certainly no reward without effort. Nonetheless, if you're willing to roll up your sleeves and put your back into it, you'll be amazed at what you can accomplish.

As you're advancing your career, don't forget how important it is to build sincere and lasting relationships. It's the glue that will hold your life together, and you have a long life ahead of you. Don't wait for friendship to show up on a silver platter. No matter how little you think you know, you're a few steps ahead of someone else. Seek those people out and be a mentor. If you can't be a mentor, be a helper in some area of their own plan where their skills are weak.

While there's value in building a good reputation, there's another reason that's just as valid. Helping others feels good. As it turns out, we do some of our best work when we're happy.

In fact, that's why I write books. Unless you have a Harry Potter on your hands, this sort of thing doesn't really make you fabulously wealthy. I do it because for me, helping people is fun. It's one of the reasons I exist. Well, that and the tequila.

If you had a good time and picked up a few ideas that will help your career, I'd be grateful if you'd tell your friends about this book, along with posting a review to tell others what it can do for them. Like any creative creature, I want to reach as many people as possible with what I do. To me, the only recommendations that really matter are the ones that come from people like you who have read my work.

I'd also love to hear your success stories. Getting to know people and hearing about the brilliant things they do with their careers is the high point of my day. You can always find me at www.ChristopherDuncan.com.

You wouldn't start out as a weight lifter by trying to bench press a dump truck. Chances are good you'd strain a muscle. You might even ding the paint job on the truck when you dropped it.

In a similar fashion, some of the things we've talked about will take some practice. Don't try to get there overnight. Start out slow, find the things that are in harmony with who you are, and work your way into a consistent routine. You'll get better with each passing month, and your career will most certainly improve the longer you do it. If you keep it up, not only will you have fun, you'll get paid.

Thanks for spending some time with me. See you out there!

Index

A

Advertising, 35
   display ads, 172
   product placement, 172
   virtual mail-order catalog, 171
   YouTube, 171–172
Agents and unions, 167
Amazon, 104
Artist & repertoire (A&R) people, 33
Artistic idealism
   appealing to masses, 13
   marketing, 14
Assistants
   power, 151
   virtual authority, 151

B

Benevolence
   anonymous interaction, 146
   good karma, 147
   long-term approach, career building, 145
   networking activities, 146
   number of contacts, 146
   positive attitude, 145
   relationships, 146
   reputation, 147–148
   social media, 146
Brand awareness, 17
Business
   advertising, 35
   being discovered, 33

booking agent, 24
boring stuff
   accountant, 181
   corporation, 180
   expenses, 181
   lack of stress, 182
   lawyer, 181
   personal assets, 179, 181
   sole proprietorship, 180
corporate gigs, 36
death and taxes
   discipline, 27
   entrepreneurial adventure, 26
   financial disasters, 26
   interest and penalties, 25
   savings account, 26
   self-employed artist, 26
education, 187
future
   Internal Revenue Service, 178
   paperwork, paying taxes and management, 178
   professional treatment, 179
   stress, 179
   tax returns, 178
getting paid, 21
help other people, 22
home office, 182
limited liability company (LLC), 177
marketing mischief
   active on social media, 29
   dependable person, 29
   sales, 27
merchants and merchandising, 34
opportunities, 33

Business (cont.)
   people skills, 30
   promoters, agents and distributors, 23
   quality, art, 22
   speaking, 38
   teaching, 37
   trust
      accountant, 186
      control, 186
      money, marriage, 184, 185
      responsibility, 184
   venues, 33
Business plans, 89

C

Corporate gigs, 36
Corporate world
   grips, 158
   interactions, 157
   pyramid effect, 150
   R-E-S-P-E-C-T, 154
   virtual power, 151
   worker bees, 152
Creative arts
   age, 141
   age-related considerations, 136
   audience, 139
   benefit of experience, 140
   career curve, 141
   Lee, Stan, 142
   younger people, 140
Creative mindset
   acceptance, audience, 6
   artistic idealism. see Artistic idealism
   artistic urges, 2
   audience, 5
   charting a course, 19
   emotional art, 6
   fun
      business/marketing, 11
      competition, 13
      lack of motivation, 11
      responsibilities, 12
      sheer terror, 11
   intellectual approach, 6
   modern technology
      album creation, 8
      competition, 9
      composer, 7
      computers, 8
      dancer, 7
      digital content creation, 8
      distribution side, 9
      gatekeepers, 9
      record contract, 10
   passion and inspiration, 2
   patron saints, 16
   performing arts, 3
   personal experiences, 6
   rules in art, 6
   starving artist, 4
   technology, 4
Cult of ego, 101
Customers, marketing, 129

D

Desire
   belief, 81
   capacity, enduring rejection, 78
   children, 80
   comfort zone, 81
   discomforts and sacrifices, 79
   hard work, 81
   job security, 79
   monetary requirements
      dream to life, 74
      full/part time work, 73
      living standard, 72
      real-world example, 74
      time and attention, people, 73
      working-class musician, 72
   need for validation
      audience, 68–69
      gatekeepers, 69
      inner dialogue, 69
      male culture, 69
      public speaking, 70
      recognition, 69
   perfect gig
      commercial enterprise, 75
      cultural tides,
         young adults, 76
      finding work, 74
      gratification, 75
      wide-angle lens, 77
      writing books, 77

Index

plan of action, 78
relationships, 79
success, 65
working for living, 71
Doing business as (d/b/a), 180

E

Emotional art, 6
Entertainment business
  being discovered
    hard work, 164–165
    influential stranger, 164
    writing world, 165
Expectations management, 52

F

Freelancing
  client base, 92
  marketing options, 93
  petty office politics, 92
  referral generation, 93
  savings account, 94
  security, 92
  simple business entity, 94

G

Gatekeepers, 150
Grips, 158

H

Home office
  ability to walk away, 183
  administrative duties, 183
  invoices, 182
  space, 184
  time schedule, 182

I, J

Image building
  being yourself
    clothing, 106–107
    creative outlets, 107
    "get the gig", 108
    positive self-image, 105
    vision outward, 105
  cult of ego, 101
  fake it 'til you make it, 116
  first hurdle
    criticism, 101
    insecurity, 100
    positive and professional self-image, 101
    quality of work, 99
    secret fears, 101
    self-doubt, 100
  language, 108
  rejection
    Amazon reviews, 104
    Internet, 103
    reviews, 104
    validation, audience, 103
  success emulation, 113
  touch points, 111

K

Know thyself, 59

L

Lee, Stan, 136, 142
Limited liability company (LLC), 177, 180
LLC See Limited liability company (LLC)

M, N, O

Marketing
  age, 141
  attention business, 120
  avoiding displacement, 141
  benevolence. see Benevolence
  Buddy system, 132
  business model, 124
  customers, 129
  helping others
    accounting, 138
    areas of weakness, 137
    image enhancement, 135
    reputation building, 139
    timing, 138
  in-depth understanding, products, 124
  internet
    "social media" and "search engine optimization" (SEO), 121
    web site, 121

Index

Marketing (cont.)
    intimate understanding, products, 122
    know yourself
        brand, 127
        colorful packaging, product sales, 126
        quality, art, 127
        unique selling proposition, 128
    Lee, Stan, 136
    people power, 143
    radio song, 122
    reputation building, 137
    services, income potential, 123
    writing books, 123
Merchants and merchandising, 34

P, Q

Paying bills
    advertising, 170
    agents and unions, 167
    being discovered, 163
    business, 174
    corporate opportunities, 174
    merchants and merchandising, 168
    mix and match, 175
    multiple streams, revenue, 163
    teaching, 172
    venues, 166
People power, 143
Personal style
    "A/B testing", 195
    ambitious resolutions, 191
    bold resolutions, 191
    doing things you love, 190
    ebb and flow, 200
    hard work, 190–191, 202
    keeping notes, 198
    level management
        emotions and passion, 192
        goal accomplishment, 193
        ideas, 192
        procrastination, 194
        robots, vacuuming, 194
        self-discipline, 192, 194
        smoking behavior, 192
    level-three goals, 193
    Madison Avenue marketing campaigns, 195
    maintaining record, 196
    reputation building, 203
    "should dos" to "want to dos", 193
    sincere and lasting relationships, 202
    successful failure, 199
    test and analyze, efforts, 191, 196
    timing, 198
    truth, 190
    unrealistic appealing scenarios, 190
    web-based services, 197
"Prison with pay", 92
Public speaking, 38
Pyramid effect, corporate world, 150

R

Reality check, 49
Rejection
    audience, 103
    creative person, 105
    critics, 104
    internet, 103
    reviews, 104
R-E-S-P-E-C-T, 154

S

Search engine optimization (SEO), 121
Self-sufficiency
    discomfort
        contracts, 43
        dishonesty and fraud, 44
        laziness, 42
        manager, 44
        noncreative stuff, 46
        regular job, 43
        sales jobs, 45
        successful artists, 42
        trustworthiness, 44
        uncomfortable experiences, 42
    expectations, 52
    getting smart, 62
    hiring expert
        established expert, 46
        personal career bodyguard, 48–49
        yourself, 47
    know thyself, 59
    long-term strategy, 57
    reality check, 49

SEO. *See* Search engine optimization (SEO)
Small business
    advertising industry, 97
    teaching, 96
    youth oriented art forms, 95
Software development, 4
Sole proprietorship, 180
Start-up company
    art and business, 84
    business plans, 89
    construction tools, 84
    creative hobby, 83
    help, 91
    hired guns, 92
    imagination, 84
    inspiration, 85
    mindset, 97
    product
        audience approval, 86
        egos and arrogance, 85
        emotional connection, 85
        promotion, art, 86
    small business. *see* Small business
    tech start-ups. *see* Tech start-ups
Starving artist, 4
Success
    clear and unambiguous goals, 67
    goals list, 67
    heart's desire, 67
    living as dancer, 66
    street address/GPS coordinates, 66
    timeline, 68

T

Teaching, 37, 96
    degree, 172
    profitable relationship, 173
    public speaking, 173

Tech start-ups
    dot-com crash, 88
    experience, 89
    Internet, 88
    launch, 89
    software development, 87
    successful entrepreneur, 87–88
    tax returns, 87
    venture capitalist, 88
    Web site creation, 87
The Buddy System, 132

U

Unique selling proposition (USP), 128
USP. *See* Unique selling proposition (USP)

V

Venture capitalist, 88

W, X

Web design, 4
Worker bees, corporate world, 152
Working for living, 71

Y, Z

Youth oriented art forms
    actors, 95
    dance, 95
YouTube, 171

Get the eBook for only $10!

Now you can take the weightless companion with you anywhere, anytime. Your purchase of this book entitles you to 3 electronic versions for only $10.

This Apress title will prove so indispensible that you'll want to carry it with you everywhere, which is why we are offering the eBook in 3 formats for only $10 if you have already purchased the print book.

Convenient and fully searchable, the PDF version enables you to easily find and copy code—or perform examples by quickly toggling between instructions and applications. The MOBI format is ideal for your Kindle, while the ePUB can be utilized on a variety of mobile devices.

Go to www.apress.com/promo/tendollars to purchase your companion eBook.

All Apress eBooks are subject to copyright. All rights are reserved by the Publisher, whether the whole or part of the material is concerned, specifically the rights of translation, reprinting, reuse of illustrations, recitation, broadcasting, reproduction on microfilms or in any other physical way, and transmission or information storage and retrieval, electronic adaptation, computer software, or by similar or dissimilar methodology now known or hereafter developed. Exempted from this legal reservation are brief excerpts in connection with reviews or scholarly analysis or material supplied specifically for the purpose of being entered and executed on a computer system, for exclusive use by the purchaser of the work. Duplication of this publication or parts thereof is permitted only under the provisions of the Copyright Law of the Publisher's location, in its current version, and permission for use must always be obtained from Springer. Permissions for use may be obtained through RightsLink at the Copyright Clearance Center. Violations are liable to prosecution under the respective Copyright Law.

Other Apress Business Titles You Will Find Useful

**Unite the Tribes,
2nd Edition**
Duncan
978-1-4302-5872-8

**Control Your
Retirement Destiny**
Anspach
978-1-4302-5022-7

Common Sense
Tanner
978-1-4302-4152-2

**Design Thinking for
Entrepreneurs and Small
Businesses**
Ingle
978-1-4302-6181-0

Business Journalism
Hayes
978-1-4302-6349-4

**Healthcare, Insurance,
and You**
Zamosky
978-1-4302-4953-5

Plan Your Own Estate
Wheatley-Liss
978-1-4302-4494-3

Underwater
Lauer
978-1-4302-4470-7

**Managing Humans,
2nd Edition**
Lopp
978-1-4302-4314-4

Available at www.apress.com

GPSR Compliance

The European Union's (EU) General Product Safety Regulation (GPSR) is a set of rules that requires consumer products to be safe and our obligations to ensure this.

If you have any concerns about our products, you can contact us on

ProductSafety@springernature.com

In case Publisher is established outside the EU, the EU authorized representative is:

Springer Nature Customer Service Center GmbH
Europaplatz 3
69115 Heidelberg, Germany

www.ingramcontent.com/pod-product-compliance
Lightning Source LLC
LaVergne TN
LVHW040736250326
834688LV00031B/329